WOMEN IN REPUBLICAN CHINA

——— ASIA AND THE PACIFIC ———

series editor: Mark Selden

This new series explores the most dynamic and contested region of the world, including contributions on political, economic, cultural, and social change in modern and contemporary Asia and the Pacific.

ASIA'S ENVIRONMENTAL MOVEMENTS
Comparative Perspectives
edited by Yok-shiu F. Lee and Alvin Y. so

CENSORING HISTORY
Perspectives on Nationalism and War in the Twentieth Century
edited by Laura Hein and Mark Selden

CHINA'S WORKERS UNDER ASSAULT
Anita Chan

THE CONTENTIOUS CHINESE
Elizabeth J. Perry

THE POLITICAL ECONOMY OF UNEVEN DEVELOPMENT
The Case of China
Shaoguang Wang and Angang Hu

THEATER AND SOCIETY
An Anthology of Contemporary Chinese Drama
edited by Haiping Yan

WOMEN IN REPUBLICAN CHINA
A Sourcebook
edited by Hua R. Lan and Vanessa Fong

Asia
and
the
Pacific

WOMEN IN REPUBLICAN CHINA

A Sourcebook

HUA R. LAN
AND
VANESSA L. FONG
EDITORS

INTRODUCTION BY
CHRISTINA KELLEY GILMARTIN

AN EAST GATE BOOK

M.E. Sharpe
Armonk, New York
London, England

An East Gate Book

Copyright © 1999 by M.E. Sharpe, Inc.

All rights reserved. No part of this book may be reproduced in any form
without written permission from the publisher, M. E. Sharpe, Inc.,
80 Business Park Drive, Armonk, New York 10504.

Library of Congress Cataloging-in-Publication Data

Women in Republican China : a sourcebook / edited by Hua R. Lan and
Vanessa L. Fong.
p. cm.—(Asia and the Pacific)
"An East gate book."
Includes bibliographical references and index.
ISBN 0-7656-0342-X (hc : alk. paper).—
ISBN 0-7656-0343-8 (pbk. : alk. paper)
1. Women—China—History—20th century. 2. Women—China—Social conditions.
3. China—History—May Fourth movement, 1919.
I. Lan, Hua R., 1945–   . II. Fong, Vanessa L., 1974–
III. Series : Asia and the Pacific (Armonk, N.Y.)
HQ1737.W67 1999
305.42′0951—dc21   99-10680
CIP

Printed in the United States of America

The paper used in this publication meets the minimum requirements of
American National Standard for Information Sciences—
Permanence of Paper for Printed Library Materials,
ANSI Z 39.48-1984.

BM (c) 10   9   8   7   6   5   4   3   2   1
BM (p) 10   9   8   7   6   5   4   3   2

Contents

Introduction: May Fourth and Women's Emancipation

Christina Kelley Gilmartin

During the World War I era, while American women suffragettes were launching a full-scale effort to secure their right to vote and Russian Bolsheviks were proclaiming that their "proletarian" revolution would bring about complete gender equality, Chinese cultural iconoclasts and social activists championed the cause of women's emancipation with compelling conviction. This era, which later came to be called the May Fourth era (1915–1924), witnessed both the production of a voluminous literature on the topic of women's emancipation and the growth of female social activism in various public arenas, as young women joined anti-Imperialist marches, boycotted Japanese goods, became visible as writers on the issue, called student strikes to denounce the poor quality of women's secondary education, promoted women's suffrage, and joined the women's and student's sections of the Nationalist and Communist parties, which formed an alliance in 1923 to remove the various warlord realms and establish a modern nation-state.

To be sure, women's emancipation was not the only significant issue of the May Fourth era, which commenced in 1915 as an iconoclastic critique of Chinese culture and soon was broadened into a wide-ranging discussion of such issues as social Darwinism, democracy, pragmatism, the outmoded ideas of Confucianism, the need to replace Chinese classical writing forms with the vernacular, and the value of Western aesthetics, social sciences, scientific training, medical knowledge, and technological power. At the time, writers referred to their intellectual endeavor as a "thought revolution," "new culture movement," or "enlightenment." It was only after the outbreak of student demonstrations in Beijing on May 4, 1919, protesting the unfair terms of the postwar peace treaty drawn up in Versailles that the two somewhat disparate manifestations of the period—the iconoclastic thrust to create a new culture and the anti-Imperialist mass social mobilization—came to be called the May Fourth Movement.[1]

The prominence of women's emancipatory issues in the May Fourth era was recognized by Chinese scholars as early as the 1920s, but it was not until Roxane Witke completed her doctoral dissertation on the subject in 1970 that Western scholars began to show a similar appreciation.[2] To date, however, no monograph has been published on the subject, and most of the existing scholarship is scattered in a variety of books and essays.[3] Similarly, translations of these May Fourth seminal writings are in short supply. Thus, the publication of this volume is significant for two reasons: It provides English-language readers with access to a sizable quantity of original essays on the subject for the first time, and it offers some reflections on the main issues and questions that scholars have raised about this literature. Exploring the origins, nature, and outcomes of the May Fourth discourse and practice on women's issues are the chief concerns of this introduction. To this end, several important questions are considered: What roots did May Fourth formulations on women's emancipation have in China's historical experiences? Why did the issue of women's emancipation achieve such popularity in the late 1910s? Why were so many men writing about this issue? Were there any discernable differences between essays crafted by men and women on this subject? Can May Fourth expostulations on this subject be considered feminist? What, if any, impact did these May Fourth articulations have on the contemporary women's movement, government policies about women's issues, or women's roles in the public and private spheres?

Historical Connections

The May Fourth discourse on women's issues was embedded in a vocabulary and intellectual framework that valued "modernity" and spurned "traditional" modes of thought and behavior. This rhetoric of rupture condemned ideals and practices that were viewed as Confucian, meaning archaic, and embraced all that was new. For many people, however, this orientation readily translated into a complete rejection of anything Chinese and uncritical approval of Western values, ideas, and practices. The call for a nationwide cultural awakening was located in a modernizing discourse that showed great disdain for the past and placed much significance on newness (xin), as reflected in the names of journals of the period: *New Youth, New Tide, New Century, New Education, The New Voice of Society,* and *The New Woman.*

The sense of newness that pervaded this modernizing discourse on women's issues, however, was somewhat misleading: many formulations and issues on women's emancipation articulated in the mid-1910s can be traced back to earlier times. May Fourth perspectives on female chastity codes, women's education, and the inhumanity of arranged marriages echoed concerns that had been voiced in scholarly and literary writings since the sixteenth century.[4] Indeed, as many recent studies have shown, male and female writers of late Imperial China produced a considerable body of literature that Ellen Widmer has labeled "proto-feminist."[5]

However, May Fourth modernizers were very selective in their uses of these historical precedents, choosing to ignore much of this "proto-feminist" literature because they considered it tainted by certain despicable traditional customs (e.g., polygyny, concubinage, and footbinding) practiced by its creators. As a result, these May Fourth iconoclasts shunned poetry that eulogized accomplished women who challenged prevailing gender norms and were willing to become "warriors." In their eyes, even the previously celebrated Qiu Jin, a dedicated anti-Manchu feminist revolutionary who had taken up arms against the Qing dynasty and was executed in 1907 for her rebellious actions, seemed unworthy of special commendation.

At the same time, these advocates of women's emancipation in the May Fourth era invented a usable historical past to legitimate their totalistic condemnations of "tradition." To this end, certain radical condemnations of gender practices contained in writings such as the satiric novel *Jinghua yuan* [Flowers in the Mirror], by Li Ruzhen, were retrieved from obscurity and showcased in various publications. Hu Shi, a recently returned student from the United States who rediscovered this 1810 novel and republished it with his introductory essay to the publication, became one of the leading figures in this astute May Fourth effort to manipulate the past to serve the present.

While much remains to be known about the precise links between May Fourth cultural rebels and the "proto-feminist" writings of late Imperial China, it is evident that the blossoming of feminist thinking in the 1910s owes much of its immediate origins to the emergence of a nationalist agenda in the late nineteenth century. China's confrontation with Western and Japanese imperialism in the 1890s motivated constitutional reformers and political revolutionaries to consider the creation of a modern nation-state, a project that included a close examination of the roles that women might play to facilitate this endeavor. In their view, the cause of women's emancipation was potentially beneficial to this quest for modernity because it would facilitate the emergence of a modern-minded citizenry in place of docile subjects. Liang Qichao, one of the foremost reformers of the period, articulated this link between nationalism and women's emancipation when he argued that China would not be able to meet the Western challenge unless its parasitic women, symbolized by their hopelessly dysfunctional bound feet, became independent and productive citizens.[6]

What is significant about this late nineteenth-century discourse on women's issues is that it was informed by Western ideals. Unlike their Indian counterparts, who spurned much of Western feminism as a tool of imperialism, China's modernizing elites freely held up European and American gender practices for emulation even though their imperial state was seriously threatened by the prospect of Western colonization.[7] A leading Chinese reformer, Kang Youwei, echoed not only Western condemnations of footbinding and arranged marriages, but also Western calls for women to acquire full civil rights, hold public offices, and mingle freely with men in public spaces.[8] While more research is needed to fully explicate the reasons for this contrast between Chinese and Indian attitudes toward Western feminism in the first decades of the twentieth century, one crucial factor may well have been the difference between the perceived threat of a formal as opposed to an informal Western colonial empire.

May Fourth Perspective on Women's Issues

May Fourth viewpoints on gender practices were not merely adopted wholesale from the modernist discourse of such political theorists as Kang Youwei and Liang Qichao at the turn of the century, but were also profoundly shaped by the manifest failure of the 1911 Revolution to establish Republican institutions. The political impotence of the Chinese Republican state propelled a group of modern-minded intellectuals to undertake a totalistic cultural transformation as a prerequisite for political transformation. In so doing, they gave the issue of women's emancipation greater centrality in their modernizing discourse than had the case for the earlier generation of reformers.

Chen Duxiu, one of the preeminent champions of this new culture movement, played the pivotal role in rendering the issue of women's emancipation into a central concern of May Fourth writings.[9] In 1916, when Chen launched his verbal assault on the sway of traditional cultural practices in the widely read journal *Xin qingnian* (New Youth), he devoted much of his critique to the multiple forms of gender subordination that were commonly associated with the ancient sage's teachings. In his influential essay "The Way of Confucius and Modern Life," Chen lambasted Confucian familial norms for relegating women to spiritually and physically demeaning lives in their homes, barring them from discussing public issues, and inculcating them with the value of submission to patriarchal authority. As a result of such subordination, he contended women were robbed of a sense of personhood (*ren'ge*). Most objectionable, in his view, was the Confucian injunction that a wife should always comply with her father or husband's directives and, to prove his point, he quoted the instructions verbatim from the *Liji* (Book of Rites; IX:24): "To be a woman means to submit."[10] In his view, these enshrined principles of proper social conduct for women were incompatible with a modern way of life, which rests on the concepts of equality and independence.

By 1918, the May Fourth critique of the oppressive nature of the Confucian family system produced vigorous discussion of women and gender issues in a host of publications. Most popular among the wide range of topics discussed were the condemnation of arranged marriages and the rejection of the ideal of female chastity. Indeed, the double standard in sexual mores for men and women that the chastity ideal represented inspired some of the best writers of the era, including Lu Xun, Hu Shi, and Liu Bannong, to publish on the topic. In compelling fashion, they berated the social codes that condoned men's frequent visits to brothels, taking of concubines, and ease of remarriage while instructing women to uphold the highest of standards of chastity, barring them from remarrying under any conditions after the death of their husbands and enjoining them to commit suicide should they be raped. Other traditional standards that came under attack at this time were the notions that the ideal woman should strive to be an excellent wife and virtuous mother (*xianqi liangmu*) and that a daughter should exhibit boundless filial piety toward her parents (*xiaonü*) and, after remarriage, to the parents of her husband.

Another distinct feature of the May Fourth perspective on women's emancipation was its inclusion of themes of sexuality in public discourse. The rapid expansion of the periodical press in the late 1910s and early 1920s was the main vehicle for this new current, as indicated by its numerous articles on such diverse topics as human reproductive anatomy, birth control, venereal disease, prostitution, and sexual desire and practice.[11]

Yet another distinguishing characteristic of this broad-ranging literature on women's issues was that it was largely a male discourse. Through the torrent of words that poured from their pens, May Fourth male intellectuals set the terms of the radical discussion on women's issues and also assumed the right to speak on behalf of women. The fierce passion displayed in much of their writings revealed the great personal significance they attached to this issue. As Vera Schwarcz has suggested, at least some of these men may have been attracted to its symbolic value; that is, they likened the plight of women to their own feelings of powerlessness in the face of an all-embracing family system that entrapped them in subordinate roles and demanded their total obedience to authority figures.[12] Whatever their motivations, however, most of the male writers failed to consider women subjectively in their writings. Rather, they generally represented the oppression of women as an abstraction.

A distinct concern that emerged in these male essays was the manner in which women were victimized by China's inhumane social system. This preoccupation bore some resemblance to the female martyr (*lienü*) literature of late Imperial times. In both eras Chinese elite men found it useful to invest a female construct to honor as a type of sacrificial lamb. *Lienü* were extolled in Ming and Qing dynasty county gazetteers for sacrificing their lives in order to protect their virtue, whereas their May Fourth counterparts were portrayed not as defenders of traditional morality but as victims of an inhumane Confucian family system. As the selections in this volume reveal, this body of literature aimed to evoke much sympathy for the dilemmas of women through harrowing accounts of their victimization. Powerful essays in this volume, for instance, by Hu Shi and Cai Yuanpei reveal how a young woman named Li Chao sacrificed her health and perished while trying to pursue her studies rather than acquiesce to family demands to enter into an arranged marriage.

The account of Mao Zedong about Zhao Wuzhen's suicide, republished in this volume, is similarly compelling, but research into the circumstances of this suicide suggests that May Fourth male writers may have overlooked evidence of female empowerment when they wrote about women martyrs. In a series of ten essays Mao published in November 1919 on Zhao's suicide, he portrayed her successful attempt as an act of despair against an evil system. In doing so, he transformed her into a revolutionary martyr who struck a blow for the cause of woman's emancipation.[13] Of the several female suicides that occurred that autumn, Mao selected Zhao's because of its spectacular and very public nature. She slit her throat with a razor, which had been concealed in her foot bindings, while she was being carried in the bridal sedan to the bridegroom's house. Mao's interpretation of this suicide touched off a major discussion on the significance of the event in the pages of a Changsha newspaper, *Dagong bao* (Public Interest), where most of his articles on this issue appeared, with the result that Zhao's case gained national exposure.

Among the flurry of articles that were published on this case were some that contained a different interpretation from that of Mao Zedong.[14] They revealed that the Zhao whom Mao portrayed as a despairing victim of the hegemonic Confucian system looked upon suicide as a weapon of female empowerment.[15] A strong believer in the eight immortals and a vegetarian on religious grounds, Zhao believed that her ghost would have greater power to seek revenge both upon her parents and upon the Wu family if she ended her life while en route to her future in-laws' house rather than while still residing in her parents' home. Indeed, Zhao succeeded in her purpose: Her suicide brought about the financial ruin of both families. Both the prosperous Wu family and her parents paid a high price for her funeral and sold their houses at a great loss.[16] If Mao sought to use his writings about women martyrs to enhance popular disdain toward traditional social practices, other May Fourth intellectuals sought to use their writings to "awaken women," give them a sense of personhood (*ren'ge*) and break the feudal bonds shackling them to traditional roles. At least one May Fourth iconoclast, however, doubted whether men who had "bullied and oppressed women" for thousands of years could actually emancipate women. Zhang Shenfu, in his 1919 essay "The Great Inappropriateness of Women's Emancipation," charged that the male discourse on this subject showed "insincere sentimentality and seemed interested in using talk to gain prestige and superiority." At the same time, however, Zhang Shenfu held a low estimate of women's contemporary social status. He saw women as "bound and enslaved," not yet ready to seek their own independence "through their own efforts."

Some women, however, in many ways were showing that they were ready to seek their own independence during the May Fourth era. First, they sought to inject women's voices into the male-dominated periodical literature. An important contribution to this volume is the inclusion of writings by ten women authors. Their writings suggest that a sizable group of Chinese women participated in shaping May Fourth formulations about women. To be sure, not all pieces crafted by women presented a distinct female voice. For example, Tao Yi's essay about Zhao echoes many of Mao Zedong's views on this May Fourth martyr. But many essays written by women invoke female experiences and insights that are lacking in the writings of males. Most important in this regard are the writings of Yang Zhihua, which reveal a creative and lively approach to women's problems. Her two essays on love and social interactions present very real dilemmas that young women who dared to socialize with members of the opposite sex were likely to encounter and reveal the feelings aroused by destructive misunderstandings. Through her writings on this subject and divorce, she effectively conveys the problematic experiences of women who put their ideals into action and in so doing become pioneers in the effort to change Chinese culture.

Female Agency

Women did not restrict their activities to writing culture. The May Fourth patriotic demonstrations of 1919, protesting the terms of the Versailles peace treaty, energized a new wave of female activism in schools, in political organizations and even among women factory workers. Many female students who participated in local May Fourth demonstrations and boycotts of Japanese goods began to rebel against school rules that enforced traditional values of female decorum. Yang Zilie and five other students at the Hubei Provincial Girls' Normal School in Wuchang bobbed their hair to signal their emancipation from traditional bondage.[17] Wang Yizhi and her schoolmates at the No. 2 Hunan Provincial Girls' Normal School mobilized the student body to abolish the moral ethics course (*xiushen ke*), which extolled the Confucian virtues of female chastity and subservience to male authority in the wake of the May Fourth incident.[18]

Such instances of female students' protests increased during the 1920s. The press often carried reports of students striking to protest against repressive rules or outdated dress codes, or principals such as Yan Shiji at the Baoding Girls' Normal School, who responded to any instance of female activism with harsh tactics, prompting critics to charge that Yan sought to produce "submissive" and "fearful" women graduates.[19]

The May Fourth era also brought waves of woman's rights mobilization: They occurred in the immediate wake of the 1919 patriotic demonstrations, again in the wake of the call for a constitutional conference of 1922, and once again in the fall of 1924, when Sun Yat-sen agreed to go to Beijing to discuss the establishment of the national assembly with the political regime of Duan Qiru. In the wake of the May Fourth mass protest, independent women's organizations bearing the name Federation of Women's Circles (Nüjie lianhehui) sprang up in Shanghai, Guangdong, Zhejiang, and Hunan. Invigorated by nationalist, anti-Imperialist politics, they quickly widened their scope of operation to include issues of women's civil rights. Both their achievements and their internal difficulties were widely reported in the press. Much national attention, for instance, was focused on the conflict that erupted in the Guangdong Federation of Women's Circles over the issue of admitting concubines, with one-third of the membership, including the chairperson, voting against their inclusion.[20] Equally newsworthy was the tremendous coup of the Hunan Federation of Women's Circles, which stunned the nation by engineering the election of several women to the provincial assembly.[21]

Similarly, when Wu Peifu's warlord regime in Beijing announced in 1922 that it would resuscitate the effort to create a constitution, women again formed organizations to press for women's citizen rights. The Women's Suffrage Association (Nüzi canzheng xiejinhui), which was established for this purpose, promoted the goal of women's suffrage, women's inheritance rights, and the elimination of the traditional curriculum from girl's schools. While this group spread from Beijing to many cities in China, a rival organization named the Women's Rights League (Nüquan yundong tongmenghui) attracted a greater following because of its broader articulation of goals. In addition to calling for women's suffrage and inheritance rights, it also advocated legal equity in marriage: prohibition of prostitution, concubinage, girl slavery, and foot binding; and the enactment of legislation protecting female laborers from wage discrimination, granting paid maternity leave for female factory workers, and providing legal guarantees for women's access to equal educational institutions.[22] Together these organizations succeeded in activating many women intellectuals, professionals, and students thereby significantly expanding the women's networks that had been constructed since the 1911 Revolution.

When government leaders in Beijing once again raised the prospect of formulating a national constitution in 1924, women activists immediately responded by founding organizations in many cities that demanded women's rights be included. In February 1925 this campaign was energized when a National Assembly planning session called by Duan Qirui, the chief executive of the warlord government in Beijing, adopted a draft regulation that specified in Article 14 that only men would be enfranchised. Through these actions, this body of male politicians essentially construed women as passive subjects rather than as mature citizens in the proposed new state structures. Ultimately the calls for honoring women's civil rights fell on deaf ears. Duan's government refused to bow to the public pressure, but in the process many hundreds if not thousands of women gained valuable political knowledge and skills.

In surveying these various forms of female activism, as well as the points of view expressed in women's writings of the period, the question arises as to whether it is appropriate to consider them feminist. It is useful to recognize that many of these women activists identified with groups that used the terms *nüquan yundong* and *nüquan zhuyi*, which translate into English as "feminist movement" and "feminism," respectively. It is significant that the controversial connotations associated with these words in China since 1949 did not exist in the 1920s. Even Chinese Communists of the early 1920s did not reject the terms and were willing to participate in the establishment of nationwide organizations that included the words *nüquan yundong* in their names.[23] To Communists of that era, an appealing feature of the *nüquan yundong* groups was that they saw women's issues from a nationalist perspective.

Nonetheless, some aspects of the May Fourth agenda on women's emancipation, particularly its strong connections with nationalist priorities, do not seem to fit Western definitions of feminism. Indeed most studies of the May Fourth women's question refrain from applying such terminology. Recently, however, some scholars have questioned whether Western criteria should serve as the sole yardstick for determining whether social change movements in the third world have a feminist character. In contesting the very meaning of the term "feminism," these scholars draw attention to the fact that women's movements in non-Western localities have felt compelled by their localities to address the intersection of gender oppression with imperialist, racial, and class oppression.[24] Perhaps the most articulate spokesperson for this approach to third world feminism has been Chandra Talpade Mohanty, who has noted:

> Unlike the history of Western (white, middle-class) feminisms, which has been explored in great detail over the last few decades, histories of third world women's engagement with feminism are in short supply. . . . In fact, the challenge of third world feminisms to white Western feminisms has been precisely this inescapable link between feminist and political liberation movements. In fact, black, white and other third world women have very different histories with respect to the particular inheritance of post-fifteenth-century Euro-American hegemony; the inheritance of slavery, enforced migration, plantation, and indentured labor, colonialism, imperial conquest, and genocide.[25]

In other words, modern feminist movements in the third world have been compelled by the realities of Western hegemony to broaden their agendas by connecting their effort to end gender oppression with struggles for national liberation. Thus, in this context, it does seem appropriate to consider the May Fourth discourse and social mobilization on women's issues feminist.

The Impact of the May Fourth Feminism on Political Parties

The strong articulation of women's emancipatory ideals in the May Fourth era had a profound impact on the political programs of the two most important Chinese political parties of this century, the Communist and Nationalist parties. Feminist goals were accorded an unusual prominence and respect in the mass propaganda and social mobilization programs of the nascent Chinese Communist Party, largely because its founding coincided with a period of extraordinary political and social ferment in China, including the burgeoning of feminism.

This feminist orientation was first reflected in the writings of the party's founders, who were overwhelmingly male. Deeply influenced by the feminism of the May Fourth era, they shared a set of expectations about the importance of women's equality in developing a new political and social order. Indeed, the cluster of men in the party who were dedicated to the prospect of women's emancipation constituted a special breed in the world of international communism, and these men helped create a greater compatibility between Marxism and feminism in the Chinese Communist Party during its first phase (1920–1927) than generally existed elsewhere in the international socialist movement.

To be sure, some Chinese Communists were attentive to the tensions between Marxism and feminism that were articulated in Western communist and socialist parties. Most notably, the famous writer Mao Dun stood out among Shanghai's male feminists as a sharp critic of certain contemporary feminist positions and practices. Yet, at the same time, he was also known as a tough critic of traditional "feudal" gender practices, often delivering searing attacks in his writings against the old morality, which he branded an evil poison. Like many others of his generation, he strove to forge a new modern morality that based marriage on love. Perhaps because Mao Dun and those of his persuasion were such dedicated advocates of the cause of women's emancipation, their skepticism about the merits of the suffrage issue and about their party's association with women's rights organizations did not seriously impair the development of a feminist-oriented Communist woman's program. Their attack on liaisons with independent women's groups was also effectively countered by other male feminists in the party, particularly party cofounders Chen Duxiu and Li Dazhao.

Chen Duxiu represented those Chinese Communists for whom May Fourth anti-family issues were integrated into an overall socialist feminist stance. He believed that the "woman question" would be solved with the advent of socialism, yet he did not allow this stance to become a justification for ignoring the issue of woman's emancipation during the revolutionary process or for simply reducing it to a form of class exploitation. He not only continued to discuss women's issues in his writings but also provided the political leadership for Communist efforts to forge links with the independent women's movement. Li Dazhao clearly articulated the logic of nationalist anti-Imperialism in his rationale for supporting women's rights initiatives. At a time when China was beleaguered by marauding warlords and truculent Imperialist forces, he argued that the independent women's movement was essentially revolutionary because it agitated for full civil rights for women, and he believed that they should be brought into the political realm in the name of national interest. Thus, unlike the nationalisms in many Western countries of the late nineteenth and early twentieth centuries, which served to confine women to the private sphere and exclude them from citizenship, Chinese nationalism in the early 1920s constructed women's relationship to the state in much more egalitarian terms.

Similarly the Nationalist Party after its reorganization in 1923 revealed the distinct influence of the May Fourth ideals about women. It established a women's department under He Xiangning that articulated a feminist action program. The male leaders in her party were willing to signal a radical break with tradition in the cultural sphere by extolling at least symbolically the ideal of women's emancipation in many of the festivals, publications, and theatrical productions in the new revolutionary order.

The coalition that formed between these two parties in the mid-1920s in order to end warlordism and unite the country provided the political context for a large-scale mobilization of women that often involved May Fourth ideas about women's emancipation. In areas where revolutionary forces were able to gain political control, such as in Guangdong, Guangxi, Hunan, and Hubei, activists often were able to establish grass-roots women's associations that vigorously challenged patriarchal power. It was in Guangdong, where the revolutionary forces held power for the longest period of time (1924–1927), that woman's associations were able to undertake the most sustained effort to alter traditional and highly hierarchical gender arrangements. The launching of the Northern Expedition in mid-1926 and the establishment of a revolutionary government in Wuhan temporarily expanded the terrain for feminist mobilization.

The unraveling of the coalition between these two political parties brought a halt to the May Fourth feminist-oriented women's mass mobilization campaign. In the changed political climate ushered in by the civil war between the Nationalists and the Communists, both parties imposed constraints on women's active agency, particularly through the instruments of mass movements dedicated to radically changing the gender system. After 1927, May Fourth feminist programs lost their political backing as both parties became increasingly wary of repeating the full-scale assault on patriarchal social controls over women that had occurred earlier.[26]

Despite this turn of events, the May Fourth perspective on women's issues did not disappear with the demise of the movement. From time to time, in every decade since the 1920s, men and women whose identities and views were profoundly shaped by May Fourth ideals on women's emancipation have given voice to this orientation. As the writings of Lu Xun, Xiao Hong, Ding Ling, Shi Congwen, Zhou Zuoren, and Ye Shengtao (including his 1930 essay on his marriage, included in this volume) indicate, May Fourth formulations on women's emancipation have provided an enduring legacy and challenge to subsequent generations of Chinese people.

Notes

Many thanks to Mark Selden and Ye Weili for their critical reading and suggestions on earlier versions of this introduction. I would also like to express my appreciation to Hua Lan and Vanessa Fong for providing me with the opportunity to work with them on the publication of this book.

1. As some of the translated essays in this volume show, in the immediate aftermath of the May Fourth incident it was common to use the term "May Fourth Movement" merely to refer to the political demonstrations and boycotts of 1919, as distinguished from the iconoclastic writings that preceded it. Gradually the entire period of intellectual ferment and social activism were lumped together under the May Fourth rubric. However, no consensus emerged among scholars as to the precise dates of this era. Chou Tse-tsung in his pioneering work *The May Fourth Movement: Intellectual Revolution in Modern China* (Cambridge, MA: Harvard University Press, 1960) selected the years 1917 to 1921. But when he published his *Research Guide to the May Fourth Movement: Intellectual Revolution in Modern China, 1915–1924*, (Cambridge, MA: Harvard University Press, 1963) he reconsidered the issue. Subsequently most scholars have come to agree that the movement began in 1915 with the founding of *Xin qingnian* (New Youth) magazine, but they have yet to agree on the ending date, often settling on either 1921, with the founding of the Chinese Communist Party, or 1923, with the reorganization of the Nationalist Party. In terms of the discourse on women's issues, the dates 1915 to 1924 seem most appropriate, although articles on the subject written from a May Fourth perspective continued to be published for many years thereafter.

2. It should be noted that Chou Tse-tsung did devote a few pages of his lengthy book on the May Fourth Movement to the issue of women's emancipation. Roxane Witke's "Transformation of Attitudes Towards Women During the May Fourth Era of Modern China" (Ph.D. dissertation, University of California, 1970) was never published as a monograph.

Perhaps the most noted of the early Chinese texts on the topic was produced by

Chen Dongyuan (*Zhongguo funü shenghuo shi* [A History of the Life of Chinese Women] [Shanghai, 1928; repr. Taibei: Taiwan shangwu yingshuguan, 1975]). Jonathan Lipman is currently working on a translation of Chen Dongyuan's book.

Since 1979 new scholarly attention has been focused on this issue in China. At first, publications consisted mainly of collections of essays on women's emancipation from the May Fourth era and memoirs of women activists. Representative publications of this type of literature included Wang Yizhi, "Wusi shidai de yige nüzhong" [A Women's School in the May Fourth era]," in *Wusi yundong huiyilu* [Memoirs of the May Fourth Movement] (Beijing: Zhongguo shehui kexue chubanshe, 1979); and *Wusi shiqi funü wenti wenxuan* [Selections on the Woman Question from the May Fourth era], ed. Zhonghua quanguo funü lianhehui funü yundong lishi yanjiushi [All-China Women's Federation, Research Department on the History of the Women's Movement] (Beijing: Sanlian shudian, 1981). The latter volume inspired Hua Lan and Vanessa Fong to embark on the translation project that resulted in this book. Somewhat later scholarly analyses began to appear as well, such as those included in general histories like Liu Jucai, *Zhongguo jindai funü yundong shi* [A History of the Modern Chinese Women's Movement] (Liaoning: Zhongguo funü chubanshe, 1989); and Feng Yuan ,"Yi nüzi lichang kan 'wusi' yichan [Adopting a Woman's Standpoint To View the Heritage of 'May Fourth'], *Funü yanjiu luncong* [Collected essays on women's research], no. 1 (1999): 33–38. I am grateful to Zhu Hong for recommending Feng Yuan's article.

3. This situation will soon be remedied with the publication of Wang Zheng's *Women in the Chinese Enlightenment: Oral and Textual Histories* (Berkeley: University of California Press, 1999).

Monographs and edited volumes containing some discussion of women's issues in the May Fourth era include Elisabeth Croll, *Feminism and Socialism in China* (London: Routledge and Kegan Paul, 1978); Christina Kelley Gilmartin, *Engendering the Chinese Revolution: Radical Women, Communist Politics, and Mass Movements in the 1920s* (Berkeley; University of California Press, 1995); Merle Goldman, ed., *Modern Chinese Literature in the May Fourth Era* (Cambridge: Harvard University Press, 1977); Kay Ann Johnson, *Women, the Family and Peasant Revolution in China* (Chicago: University of Chicago Press, 1983); Leo Ou-fan Lee, *The Romantic Generation of Chinese Writers* (Cambridge: Harvard University Press, 1973); Kenneth Lieberthal et al., eds., *Perspectives on Modern China: Four Anniversaries* (Armonk, NY: M.E. Sharpe, 1991); Kazuko Ono, *Chinese Women in a Century of Revolution*, ed. Joshua A. Fogel (Stanford: Stanford University Press, 1989); Vera Schwarcz, *The Chinese Enlightenment: Intellectuals and the Legacy of the May Fourth Movement of 1919* (Berkeley: University of California Press, 1986); and Weili Ye, *Becoming Modern: The Experiences of Chinese Students in the United States, 1900–1927* (Stanford: Stanford University Press, forthcoming 2000).

4. Ming dynasty playwright Tang Xianzu, for instance, lamented the inhumanity of arranged marriages in his famous play *Mudan ting* (Peony Pavilion), trans. Cyril Birch (Bloomington: Indiana University Press, 1981). For a discussion of the concern of Ming scholars about women's education, see Joanna F. Handlin, "Lü K'un's New Audience: The Influence of Women's Literacy on Sixteenth-Century Thought," in *Women in Chinese Society*, ed. Margery Wolfe and Roxane Witke (Stanford: Stanford University Press, 1975). A discussion of Ming dynasty elite concerns about problem-

atic chastity codes are found in Hsiung Ping-chen, "The Relationship Between Women and Children in Early Modern China" (paper presented at the annual convention of the National Women's Studies Association, Seattle, June 19–23, 1985).

5. Ellen Widmer, "Traditional Women Writers in Twentieth-Century China" (1999), p. 7. I am grateful to the author for sharing this unpublished paper with me.

For some examples of recent studies on women in late Imperial China that challenge the prevailing views of weak docile women, see Susan Mann, *Precious Records: Women in China's Long Eighteenth Century* (Stanford: Stanford University Press, 1997); and Dorothy Ko, *Teachers of the Inner Chambers: Women and Culture in Seventeenth-Century China* (Stanford: Stanford University Press, 1994).

6. For a discussion of Liang Qichao's ideas on women's emancipation, see Leslie Collins, "The New Women: A Psychohistorical Study of the Chinese Feminist Movement from 1900 to the Present" (Ph.D. dissertation, Yale University, 1976), pp. 239–42.

7. For a discussion of Indian reactions to Western feminist ideas, see Antoinette Burton, *Burdens of History: British Feminists, Indian Women, and Imperial Culture, 1865–1915* (Chapel Hill: University of North Carolina Press, 1994); and Mrinalini Sinha, Colonial Masculinity: The 'Manly Englishman' and the 'Effeminate Bangali' in the Late Nineteenth Century (Manchester: Manchester University Press, 1995).

8. Witke, "Transformation of Attitudes Towards Women," pp. 34–36.

9. Chen Dongyuan, *Zhongguo funü shenghuo shi*, p. 365.

10. Chen Duxiu, "Kongzi zhi dao yu xiandai shenghuo" [The Confucian Doctrine and Modern Life], *Xin qingnian* [New Youth] 2, no. 4 (December 1, 1916).

11. For a discussion of the sexual revolution in Republican China, see Frank Dikötter, *Sex, Culture and Modernity in China: Medical Science and the Construction of Sexual Identities in the Early Republican Period* (Honolulu: University of Hawaii Press, 1995).

12. Vera Schwarcz, *The Chinese Enlightenment: Intellectuals and the Legacy of the May Fourth Movement of 1919* (Berkeley: University of California Press, 1986), pp. 114–116.

13. Roxane Witke, "Mao Tse-tung, Women and Suicide," in *Women in China: Studies in Social Change and Feminism,* ed. Marilyn B. Young (Ann Arbor: Center for Chinese Studies, University of Michigan, 1973), pp. 7–31.

14. See, for instance, Mai Jun, "Wo duiyu Zhao nüshi zisha de ganxiang" [My Feelings on Miss Zhao's Suicide], *Dagong Bao*, November 21, 1919.

15. Research on Miss Zhao's suicide was conducted by an innovative college student in Changsha and presented in Eric Rosenblum, "The Last *Lie nü*, the First Feminist: Miss Zhao's Use as an Icon During the May Fourth Period: An Analysis of the Nature of Female Suicide in China" (senior thesis, Department of East Asian Studies, Harvard College, 1992).

16. Ibid., pp. 69–70.

17. Yang Zilie, *Zhang Guotao furen huiyilu* [Memoirs of Mrs. Zhang Guotao] (Hong Kong: Zhongguo wenti yanjiu zhongxin, 1970), p. 86.

18. Wang Yizhi, "Wusi shidai de yige nüzhong," p. 518.

19. Xiang Jingyu, "Zhili di'er nüshi xuechao zai nüzi jiaoyu gexin yundong shang de jiazhi" [The value of the Student Education Reform Movement in the Student Unrest of Zhili's Second Provincial Girls' Normal School], *Funü zhoubao*, no. 33 (April 9, 1924), pp. 2–3.

20. Wu Zhimei achieved national prominence for her role in developing the

Guangdong Federation of Women's Circles. She encountered much hostility not only for voting against the addition of concubines as members, but also for her controversial decision to engage the group in suffrage activism. Despite these stressful moments, which were widely covered in the national press, this organization grew into the largest and most influential woman's association in China during the early 1920s (*Shanghai minguo ribao*, January 1, 1920).

21. For a discussion of these groups' leadership and activities, see Tan Sheying, Zhongguo funü yundong shi [A History of the Chinese Women's Movement] (Shanghai, 1936); and Liang Zhanmei, Zhongguo funü douzheng shihua. [Discussions of the History of the Chinese Women's Movement] (Chongqing: Jianzhong Chubanshe, 1943).

22. Two good sources on these developments are Liang Zhanmei, *Zhongguo funü douzheng shihua*, pp. 85–86; and Gao Shan, "Zhongguo de nüquan yundong " [The Chinese Women's Rights Movement] *Funü yundong* [The Women's Movement] (1923) 2:110.

23. For more information on this issue, see Gilmartin, *Engendering the Chinese Revolution*, pp. 6–7, 81–84, and 128–129.

24. For further discussion of this point, see Chandra Talpade Mohanty, Ann Russo, and Lourdes Torres, eds., *Third World Women and the Politics of Feminism* (Bloomington: Indiana University Press, 1991); Bell Hooks, *Feminist Theory from Margin to Center* (Boston: South End Press, 1984); Kumari Jayawardena, *Feminism and Nationalism in the Third World* (London: Zed Books, 1986); and Deniz Kandiyoti, "Identity and Its Discontents: Women and the Nation," *Millennium: Journal of International Studies* 20, no. 3 (1991).

25. Chandra Talpade Mohanty, "Cartographies of Struggle: Third World Women and the Politics of Feminism," in Mohanty, Russo, and Torres, ed., *Third World Women and the Politics of Feminism*, pp. 3–4 and 10.

26. This is not to say that the women's policies pursued by these two parties were exactly the same. There were in fact important and significant differences, which are beyond the scope of this essay. It is also important to note that mass women's groups and even certain women's leaders in both parties exerted pressure on these parties to develop more feminist policies from time to time, most notably by Ding Ling in Yanan in the early 1940s and by feminists in the Nationalist Party in Chongqing during World War II.

Editors' Preface

This collection includes forty-three essays about women's issues in China by thirty-one leading activists of China's May Fourth Movement. To provide a synchronic snapshot of discussions of the woman question at the height of the May Fourth Movement, we have chosen mostly essays published between 1919 and 1922, a short but critical moment in twentieth-century Chinese history. Our goal is to provide a sample of the wide range of theoretical and practical issues relating to the "woman question" that were discussed by May Fourth activists. To this end, we include a number of additional essays spanning the years 1916 to 1930.

Most of the essays in this collection were originally published as articles in the newspapers and journals that flourished during the May Fourth Movement. We selected these essays as a representative sample of the issues, perspectives, and people that were most influential in the May Fourth Movement's discourse on women's issues. Many of the writers represented here eventually became prominent politicians, eminent scholars, acclaimed writers, and influential activists. The writers in this collection range from Communist Party founders Mao Zedong, Li Dazhao, and Chen Duxiu, to liberals like Hu Shi and Zhang Weici, some of whom later became identified with Nationalist anti-Communism, to Japan sympathizers Wang Jingwei and Zhou Zuoren, to top women leaders of the early Communist movement like Xiang Jingyu, Yang Zhihua, and Wang Huiwu, to the Chinese Christian doctor Ida Kahn, to leading writers and intellectuals like Lu Xun, Cai Yuanpei, Bing Xin, and Lu Yin. Thirteen of the essays were written by women and the others by men. The essays in this book were written before sharp lines were drawn between the Communist and Nationalist camps. For this and other reasons, the writings of those who later became identified with the Communist Party and the writings of those who later became identified with the Nationalist Party share many themes in common, such as the view of women's subjugation as a sign of national disgrace and backwardness and the vision of women's emancipation as a means to promote social change and national salvation.

The written language of May Fourth Movement activists reflects the
vitality as well as the chaos of their era. To further their project of
dismantling tradition and making writing more accessible to the
masses, most of these activists chose to write in a vernacular or semi-
vernacular style, rather than in the classical style used in late Imperial
China. Because the vernacular writing style had not yet been standard-
ized, they had to experiment, and this often resulted in awkward com-
binations of vernacular and classical language. On top of that, they
were working with a plethora of new concepts, many of which were
translations of foreign ideas. Thus, many of the original Chinese texts
we have translated are linguistically inconsistent and stylistically awkward. In the process of translation, we have tried to smooth over lin-
guistic rough edges whenever that could be done without seriously
distorting the original meaning. For the sake of readability, fluency,
and logic, we often had to use several different words in English for
the same word in Chinese. Several particularly problematic translation
issues should be noted. One has to do with the term *ren'ge*, a prominent term in May Fourth Movement discourse on women, which can
be translated as "character," "personality," "personhood," "human dignity," "individuality," "human worth," or "moral quality." For the sake
of consistency, we translate *ren'ge* as "character" whenever possible,
but we also use the other translations when necessary. Another issue
has to do with the difference between Chinese pronouns, which are
often ungendered or omitted altogether, and English subject pronouns
(e.g., he/she), which tend to be ubiquitous and gendered. Because gender is of central significance to the discussions in this collection, we
have been especially careful about using gendered pronouns in our
English translations only when the gender of the subject is clearly
specified in the Chinese original. Finally, we have consistently translated *jiefang* as "emancipation," instead of "liberation," because
"emancipation" was the term used by English-speaking contemporar-
ies and predecessors of the May Fourth activists represented here.

We hope that this book will be useful to readers interested in the
work of China's leading May Fourth Movement intellectuals and in the
history of China's May Fourth Movement. Essays like the ones in this
collection shaped not only the sociopolitical discourse of that period
but that of subsequent decades as well. These essays reveal much
about the worldview of intellectuals, the interplay and clash of ideas,
and the flavor of political debate during a seminal time in twentieth-

century Chinese history. The political discussions that flourished during the May Fourth period were conducted by iconoclastic intellectuals who had been freed from Imperial orthodoxy but were not yet constrained by Nationalist or Communist orthodoxies. They drew from an eclectic, often contradictory mix of elements from late Imperial Chinese traditions, Western thought, and their own revolutionary subculture. Reading their idealistic, often utopian arguments, one can almost hear their bold voices, vibrant with the spirit of an exciting and significant moment in twentieth-century Chinese history.

The essays in this collection shed light on women's issues, as well as on intellectual and social changes in twentieth-century China. They are significant both because they address concerns shared by many feminists worldwide and because they are products of a women's emancipation movement with characteristics quite distinct from those of the West. The "woman questions" asked by May Fourth Movement activists remain relevant to women worldwide. What are the necessary conditions for women's emancipation? What form should a women's movement take? What roles should women play in the family, and what is the significance of these roles? How should women balance their public and domestic obligations? How should women acquire and maintain their personal independence? How can the complex relationship between class and gender be assessed? The similarities between the "woman questions" asked by May Fourth Movement activists and those asked by many contemporary feminists suggest that these questions are far from resolved, in China or elsewhere.

Unlike most Western feminist movements led by women positioned at some distance from dominant and male-dominated discourses and institutions, the women's movement that emerged from China's May Fourth Movement was part of a broader agenda of national salvation that was created largely by male intellectuals and revolutionaries. Male leaders of the May Fourth Movement expressed great enthusiasm for women's emancipation. Nevertheless, the male and female voices of the May Fourth women's movement differ in certain respects. Many of the female voices suggest a greater sense of personal urgency concerning the issues at stake. Unlike the male activists, female activists were speaking for themselves as well as for others when they wrote about women's suffering and women's aspirations. Yet the May Fourth Movement men and women who advocated women's emancipation also had much in common. Most were young activists with a powerful sense of mission. They were deeply troubled by China's political and military humiliations and strongly influenced by Western Enlightenment thought, liberalism, anarchism, Marxism, and the 1917 October Revolution in Russia. Their vision of women's emancipation was inextricably linked to a vision of total social transformation. The essays in this collection exemplify the possibilities as well as the limitations of such a movement. We hope that this collection will contribute to a greater understanding of modern China and its women's emancipation movement, as well as to a more pluralistic and multivocal feminist discourse.

Last but not least, we are deeply grateful to Amherst College for its research grants and its superb library service, and to the University of Hawaii Press, Oxford University Press, Columbia University Press, and the John King Fairbank Center for East Asian Research at Harvard University for permission to include their copyrighted materials in this book. We would like to extend our sincere thanks to Ms. Wang Simei of the Women Studies Institute of All-China Women's Federation in Beijing for her gracious support of our project. We take great pleasure in acknowledging some special people for their unfailing support throughout our efforts. Our deepest gratitude goes to Professors Mark Selden and Christina K. Gilmartin, whose expertise, dedication, and most valuable advice have made the book possible. We are also immensely thankful to our colleagues and friends: Xiaolan Bao, Amrita Basu, Jerry Dennerline, Deborah Gewertz, Miriam Goheen, Roselyn LeVay, Tong Shen, and Wako Tawa for their constant inspiration, timely encouragement, and eternal patience during the past decade.

Biographical Notes on the Authors

BING XIN (1902–1999) is well known for her poetry, short stories, novels, and essays. Bing Xin, which means "ice heart" in Chinese, is the pen name of Xie Wanying, the daughter of a Qing Imperial Navy officer. She spent most of her childhood in Fujian and Shandong. She attended an American high school in Beijing, converted to Christianity, and came of age during the May Fourth Movement, when she started to write short stories and poetry. She received a B.A. from Yanjing University and an M.A. from Wellesley College. After studying at Wellesley, she returned to China and continued to write and work in the area of cultural affairs. She was forced to stop writing during the Cultural Revolution (1966–1976), yet has remained active both as a writer and as a social-literary critic since the end of that period.

CAI YUANPEI (1868–1940), also known as Cai Jiemin, was one of the leading intellectuals of the May Fourth Movement. He started out as a Confucian scholar-official, winning the national jinshi degree— the highest degree available in the Imperial civil service examination system—when he was only twenty-two. He was a member of the prestigious Hanlin Academy. He helped found the Chinese Education Society, an anti-Qing revolutionary group, in 1902. He served briefly as the minister of education under Sun Yat-sen and Yuan Shikai in 1912. He served as president of Beijing University from 1917 to 1926 and was part of the group of Beijing University scholars responsible for much of the theoretical grounding for the May Fourth Movement. The other scholars in this group included Yan Fu, Chen Duxiu, and Hu Shi.

CHEN DUXIU (1879–1942) was a pioneer of both May Fourth Movement thought and Chinese Marxist thought. Born to a wealthy Anhui official family, he received a classical Confucian education but failed the Imperial examination at the provincial level in 1897. He went on to study in Japan. In 1915, he joined Beijing University's faculty and became the founder and editor of *New Youth*, the influential revolutionary journal often credited with ushering in the May Fourth Movement. Along with his Beijing University colleagues Yan Fu, Cai Yuanpei, and Hu Shi, Chen Duxiu helped lay the theoretical foundations behind the May Fourth Movement. Chen helped found the Chinese Communist Party in 1920 and became the party's first secretary-general in 1921. He kept this position until 1927, when he was blamed for promoting the United Front policy and forced to step down. Chen Duxiu delivered the speech "The Woman Question and Socialism" (essay 42 in this collection, part five) while serving as education minister in the government of Chen Jiongming, a progressive Guangdong warlord affiliated with Sun Yat-sen. Guangzhou had a strong reputation for women's activism, dating back to the 1911 Revolution. At the time, the Guangdong Federation of Women's Circles was the largest and most influential independent women's group in China. This speech was also published in *Awakening*, a special supplement to the *Republican Daily*. During his brief tenure (November 1920 to August 1921) in Guangdong, Chen tried to reform the schools in accordance with May Fourth ideals, appointed a radical principal who made the First Middle School coeducational, established a Communist cell, and helped found the journal *Labor and Women*, the first Communist journal specifically dedicated to exploring the relationship between gender and class. Fiercely critical of Confucian doctrines, Chen Duxiu often wrote about the relationship between women's emancipation and national salvation.

CHEN WANGDAO (1891–1977) was a founding member of the Shanghai cell of the Chinese Communist Party in 1920. He became politically active at the First Normal School in Hangzhou and published the first complete Chinese translation of Karl Marx's *Communist Manifesto* in April 1920. He established the Communist publications *Labor World* and *Communist Party* and edited several other periodicals, including *New Youth, Awakening,* and *Women's Critic.* Though interested in feminist issues, Chen often criticized the women's movement for neglecting class issues. In the People's Republic of China, he served as minister of culture, president of Fudan University, and vicedirector of the Chinese Democratic League.

CHU, T.C. (dates unknown) was a member of the Methodist Episcopal Church at the time she wrote the essay in this volume. She held a bachelor's degree and did considerable literary and social work. She was a member of the Christian Literature Council and chair of the National Committee of the YWCA of China (*Chinese Recorder* 1919, "Notes on Contributors").

DENG CHUNLAN (1898–1982) was a leading activist in the May Fourth Movement women's movement. The year after she wrote the essay in this collection, Deng Chunlan was accepted into Beijing University's first coeducational class and thus became one of the first women to attend a previously all-male university in China. She was born in Gansu and attended a women's normal school that her father helped run in Lanzhou, Gansu's capital city. While in Lanzhou, she opened a primary school along with her sisters and helped found *New Gansu*, the province's first progressive youth magazine. She held several academic and administrative positions in Gansu after 1949.

DENG ENMING (1901–1931) helped found the Communist cell in Jinan and served as one of the Jinan Communist cell's two representatives at the First Congress of the Chinese Communist Party in 1921. A native of Guizhou and a member of the Shui minority, Deng Enming was active in the May Fourth Movement and helped found a study society called Promote the New, which began publishing a semimonthly magazine of the same name in November 1919. He held leadership positions in the Communist cells of Shandong and Qingdao before he was arrested in 1928 and killed in 1931. He was also known by the names Enming and Huang Paiyun.

HU SHI (1891–1962) was a leading member of the influential group of Beijing University scholars (including Yan Fu, Cai Yuanpei, and Chen Duxiu) responsible for much of the formative thinking behind the May Fourth Movement. Born in Shanghai, Hu was schooled in the classics by his family but attended Western-style secondary schools in China, went to the United States and earned a B.A. from Cornell University, did graduate work at Columbia University (where he studied with the philosopher John Dewey), and became a philosophy professor at Beijing University in 1917, where he helped his revolutionary colleagues edit the influential magazines *New Youth* and *Weekly Review*. He was a leading proponent of the New Culture Movement and the vernacularization of Chinese language and literature. Hu advocated gradual reform through mass education rather than revolution along Marxist lines. He helped found the reformist magazines *Endeavor*, *New Month*, and *Independence Review*. Hu served as the Nationalist government's ambassador to the United States from 1938 to 1942. He served as Nationalist China's representative to the United Nations in 1957, and in 1958 he went to Taiwan to assume the presidency of the Academia Sinica, Nationalist China's leading scholarly organization. He remained in this post until his death in 1962. Hu Shi was also known as Hu Shizhi.

IDA KAHN (dates unknown) was a Chinese mission school graduate who went to the United States in 1892 to earn her medical degree at the University of Michigan, and returned to China in 1896 to open her own practice. She had been adopted while a child by Miss G. Howe. At the time she wrote the essay in this collection, she was a member of the Methodist Episcopal Church and in charge of the Methodist Episcopal Hospital of Nanchang (*Chinese Recorder* 1919, "Notes on Contributors").

LEE, B.E. (dates unknown). At the time he wrote the essay in this collection, he was an editor in the English Editorial Department of the Commercial Press in Shanghai (*Chinese Recorder* 1919, "Notes on Contributors").

LI DAZHAO (1889–1927) was one of the earliest and most influential Chinese Marxists. Born to a peasant family, he received a Western-style education in China and went on to study political economy in Japan. He was appointed head librarian of Beijing University in 1918 and soon stood at the vanguard of Chinese Marxist studies. Inspired by the October 1917 Bolshevik Revolution in Russia, he established the Marxist Research Society in 1918, published widely on Marxism and its relevance to China, and was a cofounder of the Chinese Communist Party in 1920. From that time onward, he taught social science courses at Beijing University and courses on sociology and women's suffrage at the Women's Normal College in Beijing. Mao Zedong was one of the students in his Marxist study group, along with Qu Qiubai and Zhang Guotao. Li Dazhao headed Beijing's Communist cell and was executed by the anti-Communist warlord Zhang Zuolin in 1927.

LU QIUXIN (biography unknown).

LU YIN (1899–1934), born Huang Lu-yin, was one of the best-known women writers in China during the 1920s. Her father was an educated Qing dynasty bureaucrat, but she was neglected and despised by her illiterate mother, whose own mother had died on the day Lu Yin was born. She attended a Protestant missionary school outside Beijing. She enrolled in Beijing Women's Normal College in 1919. She was known for her radical and flamboyant lifestyle. She married Guo Mengliang, who died two years after their marriage, leaving her with a child. In 1930, she married the poet Li Weijian, who was nine years her junior, and the couple published their love letters in a newspaper in 1931. She died in childbirth in 1934.

LU XUN (1881–1936), a native of Shaoxing, Zhejiang, is widely recognized as the foremost essayist and short story writer of twentieth-century China. Lu Xun is the pen name of Zhou Shuren, who was born to an impoverished but scholarly family. He received a solid education in the Confucian classics before he studied in the Nanjing Naval Academy, the Jiangnan Army Academy, and the Medical College in Sendai, Japan. Between 1909 and 1927, he wrote, edited magazines, and taught at various high schools and universities, including Beijing University. After 1927, he devoted all his time to writing, editing, and political activism. Many of his writings mocked Confucianism and extolled revolutionary causes.

MAO ZEDONG (1898–1976), alias Mao Runzhi. Born into a peasant family in Xiangtan, Hunan, Mao was one of the founding members of the Chinese Communist Party (CCP). He rose to party leadership by the 1930s, led the CCP on the Long March (1934–1935), and founded the People's Republic of China in 1949. He launched the Cultural Revolution in 1966, which ended when he died in 1976. For more than three decades, he was the supreme leader of the CCP and the People's Republic of China and the theorist of Chinese Communism. He was also known for his accomplishments as a poet.

MING HUI (biography unknown).

SHAO LIZI (1882–1967) wrote many articles on women's issues, served as vice-president of Shanghai University, and became a director of the political department of Whampoa Academy in Guangzhou. He joined the Revolutionary Alliance in 1908 and participated in the 1911 Revolution. He established *Democracy* in 1912. In 1919, he joined the Nationalist Party and became chief editor of *Awakening*. He was also a member of the Communist Party for a short time in the mid-1920s, but resigned his Communist membership in 1924 or 1925 while retaining his Nationalist affiliation.

SHEN YANBING (1896–1981) was a leading Chinese left-wing writer. His pen name was Mao Dun. A native of Zhejiang, he studied literature at Beijing University but had to drop out in 1916 when he ran out of money. He worked as an editor, writer, translator, and teacher and founded the Literary Research Society in 1920. He edited several journals, including *Short Story Monthly* and *Women's Weekly*. He joined Shanghai's Communist cell in 1921 and served on the faculties of the Common People's Girls' School and Shanghai University. He is known as a pioneer of socialist realism in Chinese fiction, and his trilogy *Eclipse* (published in 1930) and his novel *Midnight* (published in 1933) won him international acclaim. Left-wing critics attacked *Eclipse* for focusing too much on bourgeois psychology, but Shen Yanbing argued that writing about the middle class was not necessarily evidence that the author shared their values. His later writings, however, were more in line with Communist Party doctrine. His best-known pen name, Mao Dun, is a homonym for "contradiction." He held several important posts in the People's Republic of China, including head of the Writers' Association, minister of culture, and chief editor of *People's Literature*.

TANG JICANG (dates unknown) was from Wuxing County (renamed Huzhou City in 1981) in Zhejiang Province. In 1911, Tang wrote an introduction for *Chinese Women's Newspaper,* a publication that appeared every ten days. Tang also contributed essays on the woman question to *The New Woman*.

TAO YI (1896–1923), born Tao Siyong, was a May Fourth activist from Hunan. She was a member of Mao Zedong's New People's Study Society and a close associate of Xiang Jingyu. An active participant in the May Fourth Movement in 1919, Tao Yi helped organize the Federation of Hunan Women's Circles in 1921. She died of illness in 1923.

WANG HUIWU (1898–1990?) was a leading Communist who helped found and ran the Shanghai Common People's Girls' School and *Women's Voice,* the first Communist-sponsored journal written and edited primarily by women. Born in Jiaxing, Zhejiang, Wang was educated at the Jiaxing Women's Normal School and the Hujun Academy for Girls. In Shanghai, she rented a room in Chen Duxiu's house. There she met Li Da, another leading intellectual and Communist, whom she married and later divorced. After 1949, she worked for the Legal Committee of the Central Government.

WANG JIANHONG (1902–1924) was an activist in the May Fourth Movement women's section. Born in Sichuan, Wang graduated from the Number 2 Hunan Provincial Girls' School in Taoyuan and then went to Shanghai with her lifelong friend Ding Ling. In Shanghai, Wang studied at the Communist-run Shanghai Common People's Girls' School. An anarchist who refused to join the Communist Party, Wang adopted a Marxist perspective on many issues and engaged in a consensual union with Qu Qiubai, a leading Communist in Shanghai. She died of tuberculosis in 1924. Wang's life served as a model for many of the "modern girl" characters in Ding Ling's stories.

WANG JINGWEI (1883–1944), alias Wang Zhaoming, was born in Fanyu, Guangdong, and was an early associate of Dr. Sun Yat-sen and a member of the Tongmeng Society in Japan. He held several positions in the Nationalist government during the Communist and Nationalist alliance (1923–1927) and in Chiang Kai-shek's Nanjing government (1927–1938). He openly collaborated with the invading Japanese forces in 1938 and formed the puppet government in Nanjing in 1940. He died in Japan in 1944.

YANG ZHIHUA (1900–1973). Born in Xiaoshan, Zhejiang, she entered Hangzhou No. 1 Female Normal School in 1919 and was later expelled as a result editing a progressive student journal. In 1922, she joined the Chinese Socialist Youth League. She went to Shanghai University in 1923, majoring in sociology, and became a Communist member in 1924. She participated in the May Thirtieth Movement and the third armed uprising of workers in Shanghai in the 1930s. She was one of the four women accorded official delegate status at the Communist Party's Fifth Congress of 1927, where she was confirmed as director of the Women's Bureau and elected as the only woman on the Central Committee. In 1928, she attended the Sixth Congress of the CCP and remained to study in Moscow's Sun Yat-Sen University. In 1941, she was arrested by Sheng Shicai in Xinjiang on her way back from the USSR and was not released until after World War II. After the founding of the PRC, she held important positions in the All-China Women's Federation, and All-China Worker's Union. Imprisoned for many years during the Cultural Revolution, she was persecuted to death. She married Qu Qiubai, who was the head of the Chinese Communist Party from 1927 to 1928 and was later arrested and executed by Nationalist forces in 1935. Yang and Qu are survived by their only daughter, Qu Duyi; brought up in the USSR, she returned to China after 1949 and worked for the Xinhua News Agency as an editor and translator. She now lives in Beijing in retirement.

YE SHENGTAO (1894–1988), alias Ye Shaojun, was a native of Suzhou, Jiangsu. A strong advocate of May Fourth New Literature, one of the founders of the Literary Association (*wenxue jianjiu hui*) and a close associate of Lu Xun, Shen Yanbing, and other left-wing writers; he held positions in the Chinese Communist government after 1949, including vice-minister of education. His achievements as an educator, essayist, poet, and critic are highly esteemed in China and internationally acclaimed as well.

YUN DAIYING (1895–1931) was a leading member of the early Chinese Communist Party. Born to a Jiangsu scholar-official family living in Hubei, he became politically active while a student at Zhonghua University in Hubei. Together with Lin Biao and Chang Hao, Yun Daiying cofounded the Social Welfare Society and the Social Benefit Bookstore in 1919. At the time he wrote the essay that appears in this collection, he was already well known as an essayist and as the translator of Karl Kautsky's *Class Struggle* and selections from Friedrich Engels's *The Origin of the Family, Private Property, and the State* (a book that greatly influenced May Fourth and Chinese Communist views of gender and the family). He vocally condemned arranged marriages and was highly critical of the Chinese family. An anarchist at the time he wrote this essay, he joined the Chinese Communist Party in 1922 and edited the Communist-run journal *China's Youth* from 1925 to 1927. He was one of many Communists invited to join the staff of the Nationalist Central Women's Department's Party Training Class for Women in Wuhan in 1927. In 1931, he was executed by the Nationalist government for his Communist activities.

XIANG JINGYU (1895–1928) was the leading female Communist leader of her day. A native of Hunan, she graduated from Zhounan Girls' School in 1915 and then founded the Shupu Girls' School. She began organizing fellow students at Zhounan Girls' School and spoke out against Prime Minister Yuan Shikai for his tolerance of Japanese demands and his attempts to make himself emperor of China. She was a member of Mao Zedong's New People's Study Society and studied in France between 1919 and 1921 with a radical work-study group. In 1922, she became the first woman member of the Central Committee of the Chinese Communist Party. She served as head of the party's Women's Department from 1922 to 1925, when she went to meet with the Comintern and study for a year. After she returned to China, she continued working in the women's movement and the labor movement until she was executed in 1928.

ZHANG RUOMING (1901–1958) was a Tianjin activist during the May Fourth Movement. She joined the Chinese Communist Party in France during the early 1920s but resigned from the party in 1924. She became one of the first Chinese women to obtain a doctorate in France. She returned to China in the 1930s and held faculty posts in Beijing and Yunnan until her death in 1958. She participated in the Chinese Democratic Alliance in the last decade of her life.

ZHANG SHENFU (1893–1986), alias Zhang Songnian, was a European-educated scholar and one of the founders of the Chinese Communist Party. He actively participated in the major events in post-Imperial China. In 1925, he left the Communist Party. He later became professor of Western philosophy and mathematical logic at Qinghua (Tsinghua) University. Zhang was politically disgraced and labeled a Rightist in 1957 and was rehabilitated in 1981. His lifelong personal friendship with Zhou Enlai started in their student days in France and Germany. His common-law wife for three decades, from the 1920s to the late 1940s, was Liu Qingyang, one of the May Fourth intellectual leaders, a seasoned feminist and early Communist member in Europe.

ZHANG WEICI (1893–?), also known as Zhang Zixun and Tsu H. Chang, was one of the more moderate Beijing University professors who supported the May Fourth Movement. Born in Jiangsu, Zhang studied at Fudan University in Shanghai and then went to the United States, where he received an M.A. in political science from Princeton University and a B.A. and Ph.D. in political science from the State University of Iowa. Well versed in Western theories of liberalism and democracy, he served as professor of political science at Beijing University from 1917 to 1927. Though he associated with Marxist colleagues such as Chen Duxiu and Li Dazhao and worked on the radical magazine *New Youth* before it became a Communist organ, Zhang was a liberal; like Hu Shi, Zhang emphasized cultural rather than political change (though the two were often difficult to distinguish). He later served the Nationalist government as secretary of the Ministry of Railways and commercial attaché of the Chinese Embassy in Washington, D.C.

ZHOU ZUOREN (1885–1967), a native of Shaoxing, Zhejiang, and brother of Lu Xun (real name Zhou Shuren), essayist and translator, went to study in Japan in 1906. He was an active advocate of May Fourth New Literature, cofounder of the Literary Association, editor of *The New Tide*. He collaborated with the invading Japanese forces during the war and was compelled to publish under pseudonyms after the war. In his late years, he wrote memoirs about himself and Lu Xun and translated a large amount of foreign literature, including Greek mythology. He died in humiliation during the Cultural Revolution in Beijing.

Part One

Love, Marriage, and
the Family

Editor's Introduction

May Fourth intellectuals attacked traditional regulations on love, marriage, and the family, and demanded changes. But they disagreed over what kind of changes they wanted. The flaws in the traditional system are described in Lu Xun's "My Views on Chastity" and "The New Year's Sacrifice," Ye Shengtao's "Is This Also a Human Being?" B.E. Lee's "How Can We Honor Women?" and Chen Duxiu's "The Way of Confucius and Modern Life." There was much more disagreement over what kind of system should replace the existing family.

Chen Duxiu's "The Way of Confucius and Modern Life" and Lu Xun's "My Views on Chastity" attack the traditional family system and the classical prescriptions supporting it. Chen Duxiu cites passages from the classics and denounces them as hopelessly outdated. Lu Xun devastatingly mocks the traditional cult of female chastity by examining glaring inconsistencies and absurdities in its logical underpinnings.

Even more powerful are Ye Shengtao's "Is This Also a Human Being?" and Lu Xun's "New Year's Sacrifice," stories about women who are victims of the traditional family system. These two stories bear many similarities in theme and plot.[1] Both depict the tragic fate of poor peasant women in an oppressive family system. These women are tormented, coerced, sold, and, as Ye Shengtao emphasizes, treated like

animals. In both stories, work—even the hard, menial work of a servant—is seen as a means of escape from that system. However, neither
author presents this kind of work as a solution; indeed, in both stories
the position of maidservant is ultimately too low, dependent, and vulnerable to protect the protagonist from further exploitation. These two
stories do not present solutions; they merely expose the horrific abuses
of the traditional family system.

It was hard to find a perfect solution to the problem of the oppressive family system. The controversy surrounding suggestions about the
kind of system that should replace the old one is apparent in the defen-
sive tone of the essays by Lu Qiuxin, Yang Zhihua, and Yun Daiying.
Yun Daiying argues that individual families should be completely replaced by a system of communal childcare and dining facilities. Yang
Zhihua was less radical, and her essays on social contact between men
and women emphasized the superiority of marriage over casual sex
and free love. Yang's essays also demonstrate the difficulty of getting
those who advocate gender integration in theory to provide an environment supportive of such integration in practice. She lambasts these
hypocrites as "older than the old and dirtier than dirt." Her essay "The
Debate over 'Love and Open Socializing between Men and Women'"
rebukes a man who criticized her earlier essay because she had rejected his advances. The dispute between Yang Zhihua and this failed
suitor suggests that gender relations between iconoclastic activists themselves were not by any means problem-free. Yang Zhihua recognizes
this in her essay on divorce, arguing that even marriages that start out
as free-choice love matches should be allowed to dissolve if love
fades. She focuses on the importance of true love as the basis of
marriage, arguing that the option of divorce should always be available
in the absence of true love—a factor that she admits is unpredictable
and likely to atrophy. Lu Qiuxin cleverly points out the dissonance
between male activists' liberal views on the political system and their
more conservative views on marriage. She argues that completely free
marriage is the natural counterpart of democracy and compares the
consensual arranged marriage advocated by some liberal male activists
to constitutional monarchy, an arrangement those same activists would
despise. Yet, as Ye Shengtao's essay on his own marriage demonstrates, not all traditionally arranged marriages were unhappy.

Though May Fourth activists strongly supported the incorporation
of women into the male-dominated public sphere, they were more

ambivalent when it came to challenging the assumption that women would always be responsible for childrearing and domestic work. The essays by Tang Jicang, Yun Daiying, and Zhang Weici deal with how women's domestic work and childrearing might be handled after women are emancipated. They all look to the socialization of domestic work for an answer, but they differ in the extent to which they are willing to let public institutions usurp the role of the family. Yun Daiying takes the most radical perspective, arguing that the institution of the family is not necessary to a healthy modern society and proposing that public institutions take over all the work of childrearing except possibly the nursing of infants, even if it means doing away with the family entirely. In presenting his detailed proposal about how public dining halls and childcare facilities might work, Tang Jicang also imagines a large role for public facilities, though he does not attack the family directly. Zhang Weici presents a more conservative vision of the "transformed" family, in which women remain responsible for and defined by domestic work, with the difference being that each woman would specialize in a specific kind of domestic work, get paid for doing it, and presumably benefit from the public interaction that would result from such an arrangement.

Activists such as Daiying, Tang Jicang, and Zhang Weici believed that the emancipation of Chinese women from the Confucian family was essential to the project of "modernizing" China. Zhang Weici's discussion of how "women's narrow-mindedness is a big obstruction to social evolution" reflects the common May Fourth belief that China could not compete with Western nations because the Confucian family produced petty-minded drones inferior to the patriotic citizens of the idealized West. Chinese men and women could become modern, patriotic citizens only if they were freed from the fetters of Confucianism. Yet, as the arguments of Yun's opponent Yang Xiaochun suggest, many feared the social disorder that might result if women abandoned their domestic roles.

Though public childcare and public dining halls did not replace the family, as Yun Daiying hoped and Yang Xiaochun feared, such services did indeed become available in urban areas of the People's Republic of China. Yet, with the possible exception of short-lived experiments implemented during the disastrous Great Leap Forward, the socialization of domestic work never became as comprehensive or ubiquitous as Tang Jicang and Yun Daiying hoped. Of the essays in this section, Zhang Weici's comes closest to predicting what the transformation of the family and women's roles would look like in the New China.

Note

1. While the former is largely unknown to readers in present-day China, the latter has enjoyed enormous popularity, both in China and abroad, and has been adapted into many versions of opera, ballet, and film in China. Ye Shengtao's story was originally published in February 1919, while Lu Xun's story was originally published in February 1924. It is not possible to tell whether the similarities between their stories result from one's influence on the other or from both men's independent observation of a ubiquitous phenomenon and subject of public discourse.

1

The Way of Confucius and Modern Life

Chen Duxiu (December 1916) (*Excerpts*)

Originally published in *New Youth,* vol. 2, no. 4 (December 1916): 3–5. This translation was previously published in *Sources of Chinese Tradition*, ed. William Theodore De Bary, Wing-tsit Chan, and Burton Watson, New York: Columbia University Press, 1964, pp. 815–818. It is reprinted with permission from Columbia University Press. The Wade-Giles romanizations have been converted to pinyin for consistency with the rest of our collection.

The pulse of modern life is economic and the fundamental principle of economic production is individual independence. Its effect has penetrated ethics. Consequently, the independence of the individual in the ethical field and the independence of property in the economic field bear witness to each other, thus reaffirming the theory [of such interaction]. Because of this [interaction], social mores and material culture have taken a great step forward.

In China, the Confucianists have based their teachings on their ethical norm. Sons and wives possess neither personal individuality nor personal property. Fathers and elder brothers bring up their sons and younger brothers and are in turn supported by them. It is said in chapter 30 of the *Book of Rites* that "while parents are living, the son dares not regard his person or property as his own" [27:I4]. This is absolutely not the way to personal independence. . . .

In all modern constitutional states, whether monarchies or republics, there are political parties. Those who engage in party activities all express their spirit of independent conviction. They go their own way and need not agree with their fathers or husbands. When people are bound by the Confucian teachings of filial piety and obedience to the point of the son's not deviating from the father's way even three years after his death[1] and the woman's obeying not only her father and husband but also her son,[2] how can they form their own political party and make their own choice? The movement of women's participation in politics is also an aspect of women's life in modern civilization. When they are bound by the Confucian teaching that "to be a woman means to submit,"[3] that "the wife's words should not travel beyond her own apartment," and that "a woman does not discuss affairs outside the home,"[4] would it not be unusual if they participated in politics?

In the West some widows choose to remain single because they are strongly attached to their late husbands and sometimes because they prefer a single life; they have nothing to do with what is called the chastity of widowhood. Widows who remarry are not despised by society at all. On the other hand, in the Chinese teaching of decorum, there is the doctrine of "no remarriage after the husband's death."[5] It is considered to be extremely shameful and unchaste for a woman to serve two husbands or a man to serve two rulers. The *Book of Rites* also prohibits widows from wailing at night [XXVII:2I] and people from being friends with sons of widows [IX:2I]. For the sake of their family reputation, people have forced their daughters-in-law to remain widows. These women have had no freedom and have endured a most miserable life. Year after year these many promising young women have lived a physically and spiritually abnormal life. All this is the result of Confucian teachings of decorum [or rites].

In today's civilized society, social intercourse between men and women is a common practice. Some even say that because women have a tender nature and can temper the crudeness of man, they are necessary in public or private gatherings. It is not considered improper even for strangers to sit or dance together once they have been introduced by the host. In the way of Confucian teaching, however, "Men and women do not sit on the same mat," "brothers- and sisters-in-law do not exchange inquiries about each other," "Married sisters do not sit on the same mat with brothers or eat from the same dish," "Men and women do not know each other's name except through a matchmaker and should have no social relations or show affection until after marriage presents have been exchanged,"[6] "Women must cover their faces when they go out,"[7] "Boys and girls seven years or older do not sit or eat together," "Men and women have no social relations except through a matchmaker and do not meet until after marriage presents have been exchanged,"[8] and "Except in religious sacrifices, men and women do not exchange wine cups."[9] Such rules of decorum are not only inconsistent with the mode of life in Western society; they cannot even be observed in today's China.

Western women make their own living in various professions, such as that of lawyer, physician, and store employee. But in the Confucian way, "In giving or receiving anything, a man or woman should not touch the other's hand,"[10] "A man does not talk about affairs inside [the household] and a woman does not talk about affairs outside [the household]," and "They do not exchange cups except in sacrificial rites and funerals."[11] "A married woman is to obey," and the husband is the standard of the wife.[12] Thus the wife is naturally supported by the husband and needs no independent livelihood.

A married woman is at first a stranger to her parents-in-law. She has only affection but no obligation toward them. In the West, parents and children usually do not live together, and daughters-in-law, particularly, have no obligation to serve parents-in-law. But in the way of Confucius, a woman is to "revere and respect them and never to disobey day or night,"[13] "A woman obeys, that is, obeys her parents-in-law,"[14] "A woman serves her parents-in-law as she serves her own parents,"[15] she "never should disobey or be lazy in carrying out the orders of parents and parents in-law." "If a man is very fond of his wife, but his parents do not like her, she should be divorced."[16] (In ancient times there were many such cases, like that of Lu Yu [1125–1210].) "Unless told to retire to her own apartment, a woman does not do so, and if she has an errand to do, she must get permission from her parents-in-law."[17] This is the reason why the tragedy of cruelty to daughters-in-law has never ceased in Chinese society.

According to Western customs, fathers do not discipline grown-up sons but leave them to the law of the country and the control of society. But in the way of Confucius, "When one's parents are angry and not pleased and beat him until he bleeds, he does not complain but instead arouses in himself the feelings of reverence and filial piety."[18] This is the reason why in China there is the saying, "One has to die if his father wants him to, and the minister has to perish if his ruler wants him to." . . .

Confucius lived in a feudal age. The ethics he promoted is the ethics of the feudal age. The social mores he taught and even his own mode of living were teachings and modes of a feudal age. The political institutions he advocated were those of a feudal age. The objectives, ethics, social norms, mode of living, and political institutions did not go beyond the privilege and prestige of a few rulers and aristocrats and had nothing to do with the happiness of the great masses. How can this be shown? In the teachings of Confucius, the most important element in social ethics and social life is the rules of decorum and the most serious thing in government is punishment. In chapter 1 of the *Book of*

Rites, it is said that "the rules of decorum do not go down to the common people and the penal statutes do not go up to great officers" [1:35]. Is this not solid proof of the truer spirit of the way of Confucius and the spirit of the feudal age?

Notes

1. Referring to *Analects*, I:ll.
2. *Book of Rites*, IX:24.
3. *Book of Rites*, IX:24.
4. *Book of Rites*, I:24.
5. *Book of Rites*, IX:24.
6. *Book of Rites*, 1:24.
7. *Book of Rites*, X:12.
8. *Book of Rites*, X:51.
9. *Book of Rites*, XXVII:17.
10. *Book of Rites*, XXVII:20.
11. *Book of Rites*, X:12.
12. *Book of Rites*, X:24.
13. *I-li* ch. 2; Steele, Vol. 1, p. 39.
14. *Book of Rites*, XLI:6.
15. *Book of Rites*, X:3.
16. *Book of Rites*, X:12.
17. *Book of Rites*, X:13.
18. *Book of Rites*, X:12.

2
My Views on Chastity

Lu Xun (August 15, 1918)

This translation was published in *Silent China: Selected Writings of Lu Xun*, ed. and trans. Gladys Yang, published by Oxford University Press, 1973, pp. 148–154. It is reprinted with permission from Oxford University Press.

"The world is going to the dogs. Men are growing more degenerate every day. The country is faced with ruin!"—such laments have been heard in China since time immemorial. But "degeneracy" varies from age to age. It used to mean one thing, now it means another. Except in memorials to the throne and the like, in which no one dares make wild statements, this is the tone of all written and spoken pronouncements. For not only is such carping good for people; it removes the speaker from the ranks of the degenerate. That gentlemen sigh when they meet is only natural. But now even murderers, incendiaries, libertines, swindlers, and other scoundrels shake their heads in the intervals between their crimes and mutter: "Men are growing more degenerate every day!"

As far as morality goes, inciters to evil are not the only degenerates. So are those who simply condone it, delight in it, or deplore it. That is why some men this year have actually not contented themselves with empty talk, but after expressing their horror have looked around for a remedy. The first was Kang Youwei.[1] Stamping and sawing the air, he declared "constitutional monarchy" the panacea. He was refuted by Chen Duxiu,[2] who was followed by the spiritualists who somehow or other hit on the weird idea of inviting the ghost of Mencius to devise a policy for them. However, Chen Bainian, Qian Xuantong, and Liu Bannong[3] swear they are talking nonsense.

Those articles refuting them in *New Youth* are enough to make one's blood run cold. This is the twentieth century, and dawn has already broken on mankind. If *New Youth* were to carry an article debating whether the earth were square or round, readers would almost certainly sit up. Yet their present arguments are pretty well on a par with contending that the earth is not square. That such a debate should continue today is enough to make anyone's blood run cold!

Though constitutional monarchy is no longer discussed, the spiritualists still seem to be going strong. But they have failed to satisfy another group, who continue to shake their heads and mutter: "Men are growing more degenerate every day." These, in fact, have thought up a different remedy, which they call "extolling chastity."

For many years now, ever since the failure of the reformists and the call for a return to the past, devices like this have been generally approved: all we are now doing is raising the old banners. Moreover, in step with this, writers and public speakers keep singing the praises of chastity. This is their only way to rise above those who are "growing more degenerate every day."

Chastity used to be a virtue for men as well as women, hence the references to "chaste gentlemen" in our literature. However, the chastity that is extolled today is for women only—men have no part in it. According to contemporary moralists, a chaste woman is one who does not remarry or run off with a lover after her husband's death, while the earlier her husband dies and the poorer her family, the more chaste it is possible for her to be. In addition, there are two other types of chaste woman: one kills herself when her husband or fiancé dies; the other manages to commit suicide when confronted by a ravisher, or meets her death while resisting. The more cruel her death, the greater glory she wins. If she is surprised and ravished but kills herself afterward, there is bound to be talk. She has one chance in ten thousand of finding a generous moralist who may excuse her in view of the circumstances and grant her the title "chaste." But no man of letters will want to write her biography and, if forced to, he is sure to end on a note of disapproval.

In short, when a woman's husband dies, she should remain single or die. If she meets a ravisher, she should also die. When such women are praised, it shows that society is morally sound and there is still hope for China. That is the gist of the matter.

Kang Youwei had to use the emperor's name; the spiritualists depend on superstitious nonsense; but upholding chastity is entirely up to the people. This shows we are coming on. However, there are still some questions I would like to raise, which I shall try to answer according to my own lights. Moreover, since I take it that this idea of saving the world through chastity is held by the majority of my countrymen, those who expound it being merely their spokesmen who voice something that affects the whole body corporate, I am putting my questions and answers before the majority of the people.

My first question is: In what way do unchaste women injure the country? It is only too clear today that "the country is faced with ruin." There is no end to the dastardly crimes committed and war, banditry, famine, flood, and drought follow one after the other. But this is owing to the fact that we have no new morality or new science and all our thoughts and actions are out of date. That is why these benighted times resemble the old Dark Ages. Besides, all government, army, academic, and business posts are filled by men, not by unchaste women. And it can hardly be because the men in power have been bewitched by such women that they lose all sense of right and wrong and plunge into dissipation. As for flood, drought, and famine, they result from a lack of modern knowledge, from worshipping dragons and snakes, cutting down forests, and neglecting water conservancy—they have even less to do with women. War and banditry, it is true, often produce a crop of unchaste women; but the war and banditry come first, and the unchaste women follow. It is not women's wantonness that causes such troubles.

My second question is: Why should women shoulder the whole responsibility for saving the world? According to the old school, women belong to the yin,[4] or negative element. Their place is in the home, as chattels of men. Surely, then, the onus for governing the state and saving the country should rest with the men, who belong to the yang, or positive element. How can we burden weak females with such a tremendous task? And according to the moderns, both sexes are equal with roughly the same obligations. Though women have their duties, they should not have more than their share. It is up to the men to play their part as well, not just by combating violence but by exercising their own masculine virtues. It is not enough merely to punish and lecture the women.

My third question is: What purpose is served by upholding chastity? If we grade all the women in the world according to their chastity, we shall probably find that they fall into three classes: those who are chaste and should be praised; those who are unchaste; and those who have not yet married or whose husbands are still alive, who have not yet met a ravisher, and whose chastity therefore cannot yet be gauged. The first class is doing very nicely with all these encomiums, so we can pass over it. And the second class is beyond hope, for there has never been any room for repentance in China once a woman has erred—she can only die of shame. This is not worth dwelling on either. The third class, therefore, is the most important. Now that their hearts have been touched, they must have vowed to themselves: "If my husband dies, I shall never marry again. If I meet a ravisher, I shall kill myself as fast as ever I can." But what effect, pray, do such decisions have upon public morality, which, as pointed out earlier, is determined by men?

And here another question arises. These chaste women who have been praised are naturally paragons of virtue. But though all may aspire to be saints, not all can be models of chastity. Some of the women in the third class may have the noblest resolutions, but what if their husbands live to a ripe old age and the world remains at peace? They will just have to suffer in silence, doomed to be second-class citizens all their lives.

So far we have simply used Old World common sense, yet even so we have found much that is contradictory. If we live at all in the twentieth century, two more points will occur to us.

First of all: Is chastity a virtue? Virtues should be universal, required of all, within the reach of all, and beneficial to others as well as oneself. Only then are they worth having. But in addition to the fact that all men are excluded from what goes by the name of chastity today, not even all women are eligible for this honor. Hence it cannot be counted a virtue, or held up as an example. . . . When a rough man swoops down on one of the weaker sex (women are still weak as things stand today), if her father, brothers, and husband cannot save her and the neighbors fail her too, her best course is to die. She may, of course, die after being defiled; or she may not die at all. Later on, her father, brothers, husband, and neighbors will get together with the writers, scholars, and moralists; and, no whit abashed by their own cowardice and incompetence, nor concerned about how to punish the criminal, will start wagging their tongues. Is she dead or not? Was she raped or not? How gratifying if she has died, how shocking if she has not! So they create all these glorious women martyrs on the one hand and these wantons universally condemned on the other. If we think this over soberly, we can see that, far from being praiseworthy, it is absolutely inhuman.

Our second query is: Have polygamous men the right to praise chastity in women? The old moralists would say, of course they have: the mere fact that they are men makes them different from other people and sole arbiters of society. Relying on the ancient concept of yin and yang, or the negative and the positive, they like to show off to women. But people today have had a glimpse of the truth and know that this talk of yin and yang is absolute gibberish. Even if there are dual principles, there is no way of proving that yang is nobler than yin, the male superior to the female. Besides, society and the state are not built by men only. Hence we must accept the truth that the two sexes are equal. And if equal they should be bound by the same contract. Men cannot make rules for women that they do not keep themselves. Moreover, if marriage is a sale, swindle, or form of tribute, a husband has no right even to demand that his wife remain faithful to him during his lifetime. How can he, a polygamist, praise a woman for following her husband to the grave?

This ends my questions and answers. The moralists' case is so weak it is strange it should have survived to the present time.

To understand this, we must see how this thing called chastity originated and spread, and why it has remained unchanged.

In ancient society women were usually the chattels of men, who could kill them, eat them, or do what they pleased with them. After a man's death, there was naturally no objection to burying his women with his favorite treasures or weapons. By degrees, however, this practice of burying women alive stopped and the conception of chastity came into being. But it was mainly because a widow was the wife of a dead man whose ghost was following her that other men dared not marry her—not because it was thought wrong for a woman to marry twice. This is still the case in primitive societies today. We have no means of ascertaining what happened in China in remote antiquity; but by the end of the Zhou dynasty (1066–77I B.C.) the retainers buried with their masters included men as well as women, and widows were free to marry again. It appears then that this custom died out very early. From the Han (206 B.C.–A.D. 220) to the Tang dynasty (618–907) no one advocated chastity. It was only in the Song dynasty (960–1279) that professional Confucians[5] started saying "Starving to death is a small matter, but losing one's chastity is a great calamity." And they would exclaim in horror when they read of some woman in history who married twice. Whether they were sincere or not we shall never know. That was when men were beginning to grow "more degenerate every day," the country was "faced with ruin," and the people were in a bad way; so it is possible that these professional Confucians were using women's chastity to lash the men. But since this type of insinuation is rather contemptible and its aim was far from clear, though it may have resulted in a slight increase in the number of chaste women, men in general remained unmoved. And so China, with "the oldest civilization in the world and the highest moral standard," "by the grace of God and the will of Heaven" fell into the hands of Sechen Khan, Oljaitu Khan, Kuluk Khan,[6] and all the rest of them. After several more changes of rulers, the conception of chastity developed further. The more loyalty the emperor demanded of his subjects, the more chastity the men required of the women. By the Qing dynasty (1644–1911) Confucian scholars had grown even stricter. When they read in a Tang dynasty history of a princess who married again, they would thunder in great indignation: "What is this! How dare the man cast such aspersions on royalty!" Had that Tang historian been alive at the time, he would certainly have been struck off the official list, to "rectify men's hearts and mend their morals."

So when the country is about to be conquered, there is much talk of chastity, and women who take their own lives are highly regarded. For women belong to men, and when a man dies, his wife should not remarry; much less should she be snatched from him during his life. But since he himself is one of a conquered people, with no power to protect his wife and no courage to resist, he finds a way out by urging her to kill herself. There are rich men, too, with whole bevies of wives, daughters, concubines, and maids, who cannot look after them all during times of trouble. Confronted by rebels or government troops, they are absolutely helpless. All they can do is to save their own skin and urge their women to seek a glorious death, for then they will be of no interest to the rebels. Then when order is restored, these rich men can saunter back to utter a few encomiums over the dead. For a man to remarry is quite in order anyway, so they get some other women and that is that. This is why we find works like *The Death of Two Virtuous Widows* or *The Seven Concubines' Epitaph*. Even the writings of Qian Qianyi[7] are filled with accounts of chaste women and praise of their glorious death.

Only a society where each cares solely for himself, and women must remain chaste while men are polygamous, could create such a perverted morality, which becomes more exacting and cruel with each passing day. There is nothing strange about this. But since man proposes and woman suffers, why is it women have never uttered a protest? Because submission is the cardinal wifely virtue. Of course a woman needs no education: even to open her mouth is counted a crime. Since her spirit is as distorted as her body,[8] she has no objection to this distorted morality. And even a woman with views of her own has no chance to express them. If she writes a few poems on moonlight and flowers, men may accuse her of looking for a lover. Then how dare she challenge this "eternal truth"? Some stories, indeed, tell of women who for various reasons would not remain chaste. But the storytellers always point out that a widow who remarries is either caught by her first husband's ghost and carried off to hell or, condemned by the whole world, becomes a beggar who is turned away from every door till she dies a wretched death.

This being the case, women had no choice but to submit. But why did the men let it go at that? The fact is that after the Han dynasty most mediums of public opinion were in the hands of professional Confucians, much more so from the Song and Yuan dynasties onward. There is hardly a single book not written by these orthodox scholars. They are the only ones to express opinions. With the exception of Buddhists and Taoists who were permitted by imperial decree to voice their opinions, no other "heresies" could take a single step into the open. Moreover, most men were very much influenced by the Confucians' self-vaunted "tractability." To do anything unorthodox was taboo. So even those who realized the truth were not prepared to give up their lives for it. Everyone knew that a woman could lose her chastity only through a man. Still they went on blaming the woman alone, while the man who destroyed a widow's reputation by marrying her or the ruffian who forced her to die unchaste was passed over in silence. Men, after all, are more formidable than women, and to bring someone to justice is harder than to utter praise. A few men with some sense of fair play, it is true, suggested mildly that it was unnecessary for girls to follow their betrothed into the grave; but the world did not listen to them. Had they persisted, they would have been thought intolerable and treated like unchaste women; so they turned "tractable" and held their peace. This is why there has been no change right up till now.

(I should mention here, however, that among the present champions of chastity are quite a few people whom I know. I am sure there are good men among them, men with the best intentions, but their way of saving society is wrong. To go north they have headed west. And we cannot expect them, just because they are good, to be able to end up north by going due west. So I hope they will turn back.)

Then there is another question.

Is it difficult to be chaste? The answer is, very. It is because men know how difficult it is that they praise it. Public opinion has always taken it for granted that chastity depends upon the woman. Though a man may seduce a woman, he is not brought to book. If A (a man) makes advances to B (a woman) but she rejects him, then she is chaste. If she dies in the process, she is a glorious martyr: A's name is unsullied and society undefiled. If, on the other hand, B accepts A, she is unchaste; again A's name is unsullied, but she has lowered the tone of society. This happens in other cases, too. A country's downfall, for instance, is always blamed on women. Willy-nilly they have shouldered the sins of mankind for more than three thousand years.

Since men are not brought to book and have no sense of shame, they go on seducing women just as they please, while writers treat such incidents as romantic. Thus a woman is beset by danger on every side. With the exception of her father, brothers, and husband, all men are potential seducers. That is why I say it is difficult to be chaste.

Is it painful to be chaste? The answer is, very. It is because men know how painful it is that they praise it. Everyone wants to live, yet to become a martyr means certain death—this needs no explanation. A chaste widow, however, lives on. We can take her grief for granted, but her physical existence is also a hard one. If women had independent means and people helped each other, a widow could manage on her own; but unfortunately the reverse is the case in China. So if she has money, she is all right; if she is poor, she can only starve to death. And not till she has starved to death will she be honored and her name recorded in the local history. Invariably the records of different districts contain a few sections headed "Women Martyrs," a line or half a line for each. They may be called Zhao, Qian, Sun, or Li, but who cares to read about them? Even the great moralists who have worshipped chastity all their lives may not be able to tell you offhand the names of the first ten martyrs of their honorable district; so alive or dead, such women are cut off from the rest of the world. That is why I say it is painful to be chaste.

In that case, is it less painful not to be chaste? No, that is very painful too. Since the public looks down on such women, they are social outcasts. Many of the tenets carelessly handed down by the ancients are completely irrational, yet the weight of tradition and numbers can crush undesirable characters to death. God knows how many murders these anonymous, unconscious assassins have committed since ancient times, including the murder of chaste women. They are honored after their death, though, by mention in the local histories, while unchaste women are abused by everyone during their lifetime and suffer meaningless persecution. That is why I say their lot is also very painful.

Are women themselves in favor of chastity? The answer is: No, they are not. All human beings have their ideals and hopes. Whether high or low, their life must have a meaning. What benefits others as well as oneself is best, but at least we expect to benefit ourselves. To be chaste is difficult and painful, of profit neither to others nor to oneself; so to say that women are in favor of it is really unreasonable. Hence, if you meet any young woman and in all sincerity beg her to become a martyr, she will fly into a passion, and you may even receive a blow from the respected fist of her father, brothers, or husband. Nevertheless, this practice persists, supported as it is by tradition and numbers. Yet there is no one but fears this thing "chastity." Women fear to be crucified by it, while men fear for their nearest and dearest. That is why I say no one is in favor of it.

On the basis of the facts and reasons stated above, I affirm that to be chaste is exceedingly difficult and painful, favored by no one, of profit neither to others nor oneself, of no service to the state or society, and of no value at all to posterity. It has lost any vigor it had and all reason for existing.

Finally I have one last question.

If chastity has lost any vigor it had and all reason for existing, are the sufferings of chaste women completely in vain?

My answer is: They still deserve compassion. These women are to be pitied. Trapped for no good reason by tradition and numbers, they are sacrificed to no purpose. We should hold a great memorial service to them.

After mourning for the dead, we must swear to be more intelligent, brave, aspiring, and progressive. We must tear off every mask. We must do away with all the stupidity and tyranny in the world which injure others as well as ourselves.

After mourning for the dead, we must swear to get rid of the meaningless suffering that blights our lives. We must do away with all the stupidity and tyranny that create and relish the sufferings of others.

We must also swear to see to it that all mankind know true happiness.

Notes

1. Kang Youwei (1858–1927), who led the 1898 reform movement, in 1918 published an article declaring that China was not yet ripe for democracy.

2. Chen Duxiu (1880–1942), then chief editor of the magazine *New Youth*, published an article there refuting Kang Youwei's ideas.

3. In 1918 *New Youth* carried articles by these three professors at Beijing University inveighing against the spiritualist school and advocating a return to the past.

4. Certain Confucians claimed that all phenomena resulted from the interaction of the positive principle yang and the negative principle yin.

5. The neo-Confucians of the Song dynasty, self-styled champions of morality.

6. All the emperors during the Yuan dynasty (1279–1368) had Mongolian titles. Sechen Khan is better known by his personal name Khubilai.

7. 1582–1664. Minister of ceremony at the end of the Ming dynasty, he was a traitor who welcomed the Manchu invaders.

8. This refers to the practice of binding women's feet.

3
Is This Also a Human Being?

Ye Shengtao (February 14, 1919)

Originally published in *New Tide*, vol. 1, no. 3, February 14, 1919.

She was born into a peasant family and had neither the privilege of being a lady who could dress in silk and satin and order servants around nor any education about ideas such as the "Three Obediences and Four Virtues" or "Fraternity and Equality." To put it bluntly, she was simply treated as an animal. Not long after her birth, when she started to speak and could walk around, she was already helping her parents to pick up grains of rice left behind in the paddy fields and to find and collect wild vegetables. When she was fifteen, she was married off by her parents. It is supposedly the fate of a woman, and it is better sooner than later—otherwise, her parents will not get a good deal on her because they will have paid more expenses for her food and clothing. On the other hand, it was not so bad for her husband's family to have some extra help in the fields, especially during the busy seasons on the farm. She was not a full farmhand, but she was no less useful than half a cow. In less than a year, she gave birth to a son while knowing next to nothing about the facts of life. She felt as if it was only yesterday that she was sleeping in her mother's arms; but now, most strangely, she herself was holding her own baby in her arms. Her child had no cradle to sleep in, no soft clothing to wear, and no access to sunshine or fresh air. The infant could only sleep in his mother's arms at night and in a dark corner in the house in the daytime. Within six months, her child died; she cried bitterly because she had never felt so heartbroken in her life. Her mother-in-law cursed her for being a bad mother and causing the death of the baby. Her father-in-law blamed her for being an inauspicious woman who was killing off his patriline. Her husband said nothing, except that he would not give a damn about how many of his children would die as long as he kept winning at his gambling. Poor woman! She could only cry by herself all day long, without even trying to understand what all that was about.

One day, when she opened her trunk, she found that the black cotton jackets she brought over as part of her dowry were gone. Only later did her husband confess while drunk that he had pawned her clothing. Winter quickly returned; the cold west wind was bone chilling. She plucked up her courage and begged her husband to buy back her jackets, but only got two slaps on her cheeks. To be slapped on the face was nothing new in her life; the only thing she could do was to cry. That day, she cried again, but her mother-in-law yelled at her: "Crying again? You are certainly going to cry our entire family to death!" Upon hearing that, she cried even more sorrowfully. Enraged by her crying, her mother-in-law picked up the laundry club and hit her hard on her back. Her husband added two more slaps on her face.

Brutally beaten, she began to worry about her future—tomorrow, the day after tomorrow . . . she was scared. The very next morning, before daybreak, she quietly left the house and felt lucky that her husband was not awake. The west wind cut like daggers and her face hurt badly. But she felt that it still felt better than her husband's palms and so she was content. Almost in one breath, she ran about ten miles and did not stop until she came to a riverside. There were passenger boats on the river.

Finally, a boat arrived and she quickly got on. The passengers aboard all seemed to be psychics who could tell instantly why she had run away from home. They told her: "It must be your own fault that you could not get along with your family and that they gave you a hard time. They may have wronged you, but you are a young woman and should learn to tolerate and endure. If you behave so capriciously, you will have a lot more to suffer in the future. Now that you have run away from home, whom are you going to rely on? It is best to return home with this boat." She lowered her head and said nothing about their comments, which drew the attention of some of the other passengers. One of them mocked her, saying: "Who knows what she is up to? Probably, there is another man waiting for her in town." The crowd laughed and jeered. She just turned a deaf ear to them.

She got to town and found a domestic service agency that recommended her for work as a maid in a good family. Thus her new life began. Although she had to work from morning till night, it was not as strenuous as working in the fields. Also, there was no one to scold or beat her. She felt happy, emancipated, and utterly content with the new life, except for the fact that she often missed her dead child at night.

One day, at the market, she ran into a man who happened to be a former neighbor; she was really frightened. In less than three days, the anticipated misfortune occurred: her father-in-law came rushing in and yelled at her: "You ran away, hey! Now I have found you! See where you can hide now. If you are smart, you will follow me home." She was too scared to speak and could only try to hide behind the back of her mistress, overwhelmed by the situation. Her mistress called the father-in-law in and said to him: "Your daughter-in-law is now serving in my house, and her contract has not expired yet. How can I let her go?" Her father-in-law was dumbfounded and could only threaten her by fiercely saying: "Come back home immediately when the contract expires. If you try any monkey business again, we will disown you and sell you anywhere we want. Or better yet, we will simply break your legs."

She was totally terrified by the threat, fearing that this haven here would be soon replaced by hell. Her eyes were swollen with crying; and she lost her appetite and energy. Her master was a sympathetic man; and knowing that, according to the law, it was already possible to get a divorce in those days, he asked her: "Are you willing to divorce your husband?" She replied, "Of course." So her master wrote an appeal on her behalf about her past suffering and her current intentions. The appeal was to be sent to the magistrate, but her mistress said to the husband: "It is indeed a good idea for her to file a divorce; but she may not necessarily work for us all her life. Once she leaves us, and is out of work, what will happen to her? Her natal family should take her back. But can her parents do that?" Her mistress's remarks dampened her master's chivalry, and then the latter simply uttered: "That's right; what can we do?"

A few days later, urged by her father-in-law, her own father came. When her mistress asked him: "Is there any way you can rescue your daughter?" Her father said: "She has married into this family, so her fate is doomed. Any cursing or beating is completely beyond my control. I am here today simply to pass a message from her father-in-law that she should return to her husband." However, under the protection of her mistress, she refused to go back with her father.

Sometime later, her parents-in-law asked one of their neighbors to deliver the message that her husband was seriously ill and needed her to take care of him. As one would expect, she was unwilling to return; so her mistress rejected the request for her. Another four days later, her own father returned to tell her: "Your husband has died. If you still refuse to go back, I would not be able to face all the folks and fellow villagers. You have to come with me!" Though scared and unwilling, she thought to herself, "No one here will support me if I refuse to go home even under these circumstances."

She returned home and was quite saddened to see her dead husband lying stiff on the bed. But then, she thought, "He was the one who cursed and beat me." Her parents-in-law did not bother to ask her to cry and wail, and they did not even bother her with all the mourning rituals. Instead, they sold her to another family for 20,000 copper coins. To her own father and parents-in-law, it was the best and most reasonable thing to do; after all, when the field no longer needs to be cultivated, the cattle should be sold. She was just such a cow—an animal without any thoughts or feelings; when she was no longer of any use, she ought to be sold. And sold she was, to pay off the funeral expense and fulfill her last obligation to her late husband.

4
Emancipating Women by Reorganizing the Family

Zhang Weici (August 10, 1919)

First published in *Weekly Review*, no. 34, August 10, 1919, under the name Wei Ci.

The word "woman" contains a long history of tragedy. In foreign countries as well as in China, women have been subject to all sorts of social, legal, and economic restrictions for thousands of years. Women have had to depend upon men completely, and obey them. Everyone knows about Chinese laws and customs regarding women, so we need not belabor them. But even in various European countries that supposedly respect women, the laws also treat women very unequally. According to Roman law, women were completely dependent on men.

After marriage, they became the property of their husbands. Before marriage, they were completely under the control of their fathers. If her father died, a woman became the ward of her immediate relatives, and if there were no immediate relatives, she became the ward of her clan as a whole. Women had no share in any of the rights guaranteed by law. According to English common law, women have no right to inherit property, and a married woman and her husband can only be counted as one person. Women are not legally recognized. There is not enough room to write about the other kinds of inequalities; I am just mentioning a few of the most egregious ones.

China is a land where famous teachings about rites, etiquette, bonds, and virtues prevail. We have all kinds of ways to limit women's freedom, prevent women from developing their abilities, and strip away their personalities. We know how to do this to the utmost perfection. Having been subjected to poisons that have been handed down for thousands of years, our women lose their own consciousness and become superb playthings for men. The few among them who receive society's utmost praise are only the ones who know how to be "virtuous wives and good mothers." Having been taught for thousands of years, this kind of system has never been challenged and is not regarded by anyone as unreasonable. On the contrary, it is generally accepted as a system based on "the laws of heaven and earth." But recently some people have been exposed to new ideas, and they have developed a new kind of thinking. They not only think that this old system treats women very inhumanely, but also that men suffer from this system (for example, men suffer unhappiness in marriage and unhappiness in the family) and that society has also been greatly affected (for example, society suffers the economic losses resulting from women not working). Furthermore, when this thinking is compounded with Western influence, these people are even more likely to compare and to dissent. Gradually, "woman" becomes an issue. "Woman" becomes an issue because, in accordance with laws and customs, society's treatment of women and men is too unequal. Women face regulation and restriction everywhere, and enjoy no freedom anywhere. Therefore, most people see the emancipation of women as the means to resolve the woman question.

But the issue of women's emancipation is easy to resolve. Shanghai's *Weekly Review* raised the issue of "Where does the project of emancipating women begin?" and drew many suggestions. My friend Hu Shi responded that "women's emancipation should of course begin with the emancipation of women; there is no other way." If emancipation were the only thing women needed, if women had all the other rights (including the right to work, the right to vote, and the right to freedom from patriarchal restrictions), then the woman question would be the easiest issue to resolve. Though today there are many who oppose the expansion of women's rights, these basic rights should not be denied to women any longer. Today, it is patently impossible to continue to use traditional customs and habits to limit women's freedom and to imprison them in the family. It is no longer possible to claim that women must remain under the control of their parents or husbands, since patriarchal control has already become a fact of the past. Even if it is said that women's duties are in the home, that so-called home must be a new kind of home, totally different from the home of the past and the home of the present.

Therefore, the emancipation of women is both essential and quite feasible. But even after women are emancipated, the woman question will still not be completely resolved. President Lincoln of the United States could issue an order to emancipate the black slaves held in the southern states, and the Russian Emperor Alexander II could write an order emancipating serfs who had been enslaved for hundreds of years. But the question of blacks remains a problem in America even today, and the question of peasants and land was a major reason for the recent Russian Revolution.

I think the most difficult part of the woman question concerns how to raise women's status to meet the demands of the new society after women are emancipated. It has always been the case that women have only what others give them; the emancipated woman must seek for herself what she needs. It has always been the case that women are forever under others' control—as they say, women "obey the father in the natal family, obey the husband after marriage." The emancipated woman must take care of herself. It has always been the case that women have inhabited the tiniest world, under the care and protection of others. The emancipated woman will enter the wide world without anyone's care or protection. She knows very little about the circumstances of this wide world. Even men do not understand clearly what her relationship with this wide world is. In any case, the woman question should be handled in the same way all questions about the transformation of society are handled: first comes emancipation, and then comes construction. Between emancipation and construction, there is a big gap. This big gap can be called the period of "letting go": a drifting and uncertain transitional period. The women of Europe and America are currently at this stage. Our Chinese women will soon be at this stage too.

Many people say that women and men will be equal after women are emancipated: Whatever men do, women will also be able to do. Women will be able to take men's actions as models for their own. But women are, after all, women; they cannot just imitate men. When it comes to love and children, women's attitudes are different from those of men. Women certainly cannot, in trying to become men, repudiate the special temperament that is natural to women. Even if women could do this, it would be extremely foolish, because this world already has enough men.

What I mean is that in the future the work of the majority of women should consist of using artistic and scientific methods to reform the family. This kind of work is actually not narrow in scope, and this method is not in fact one that will return women to the situation they were in prior to emancipation. In the family of the future, there will be opportunities to develop all kinds of natural abilities, and women will be able to enjoy all kinds of benefits. It will be necessary for women to increase their participation in politics, since the family is intimately related in all kinds of ways to the city government, the provincial government, and the central government. The area of education is also pretty much in women's hands. This includes more than primary school education; it also includes that most important period between infancy and school enrollment. Even though women of the future will have many duties at home, they will not have to do everything. Women's duties can be subject to the division of labor, so that each person will have one specialized duty. Today there are many chores that are done by each family on its own, but in the future these chores can be done by a group, or ten groups, of families organized into a collective. Today's families are completely based on a kind of "individualism," so each family has its own kitchen, each family washes its own clothes, and each family raises its own children. Yet the women of each family are ignorant about many kinds of situations, and must lead muddle-headed and disorganized lives. The economic losses that result are truly incalculable. The collective management of housework I am talking about is actually not a utopian system; there are already in the present some successful examples of similar things. In the past, before there were schools, everyone had to teach their own children, and the home was the school. After schools were established, everyone sent their children to school because a private education at home could not compare at all with a school education. It is also this way with hospitals. I think that the management of household chores can follow the example of schools and hospitals.

If we can smash this "individualism" completely and use the division of labor to apportion household chores one by one and let each chore be the special social responsibility of one family, then most women will be able to work at jobs. Once women have divided labor among themselves, they will be able to get wages. Women will be able to get monetary compensation for the value of their work only if they stop doing everything there is to be done in the house. If work were divided, with different people doing different work, then everyone would have to pay monetary compensation, and this would be to everyone's advantage. A woman does not get wages for cooking her own food, but she will be able to get wages if she cooks for a neighbor. So if women apply the principles of the division of labor and collective organization to the family, they will be able to get wages, and thus economic independence.

Only then will women be truly emancipated. As it is today, women have to do all the household work. Not only do they lack specialization, they also have to wait till they have families of their own before they can contribute their work. A woman has to wait until she has found someone who loves her before she can develop her nascent abilities. But once women have specialized skills they will be able to do the work of specialists, and they will be able to start doing household work even before they get married. A kindergarten teacher will not have to wait till after she gives birth to start teaching children. Only in this way will women be able to have a position and a career in this world. Their character and their self-respect will also be significantly enhanced because they will truly be able to do some very useful things. They will be able to marry for love, perhaps because they want children of their own, or perhaps because they want to enjoy the happiness of family life, and not because they will become women without identities if they do not marry.

Today we have already concluded that women's narrow-mindedness is a big obstruction to social evolution, and that women's "individualism" is an obstruction to collective life. Why is it that so many people are hesitant and indecisive, and so many people always want to abandon the masses and try to act on their own? The reason is precisely that they have been subject to the influence of several women in their families. These kinds of women have very narrow vision, and only know about their own immediate interests. Small children are even more susceptible to their influences. Small children are constantly surrounded by models of the solitary family right when they are most impressionable. As time passes, they begin to think that the most important duty in life is to the family, not to the outside world. This is why a democratic system is so hard to establish. It is precisely because we are all raised in the smallest of worlds.

Based on women's economic and spiritual subservience, small children develop their understanding of gender relations. The masses all know about the influence parents have on small children. A child may be able to absorb a father's psychological devaluing of female children even while inheriting all of the father's good disposition. This influence is usually not the kind that we would want. It results when fathers recklessly throw their weight around the house, while small daughters learn in their homes only how to obey and how to serve "noble" men, and at the same time think that their relationship to the world is truly unimportant. This kind of upbringing is just what produced our people today: people who know nothing about the principles of democracy, but only calculate their own interests from morning till night.

Therefore the way to emancipate women is necessarily to make the family part of society. To have careers, women must first have some sort of specialized skills. Once women have specialized skills, they must make a joint effort to work together. The "individualism" of the old family must be eliminated. The affairs of the new family must be conducted cooperatively by an organization of many families.

5
How Can We Honor Women?

B. E. Lee (October 1919)

Originally published in English in *Chinese Recorder*, October 1919, as notes from a speech. The *Chinese Recorder* was published monthly at the American Presbyterian Mission Press in Shanghai, China.

First, girl slaves must be emancipated. We all know how often they are ill-treated. But even though they are not ill-treated, it is a sin against humanity to keep slaves. Lincoln said, "Slavery is a violation of eternal right." As a human being, born exactly the same as her mistress, why should she be taken as a slave? Is it because she was unluckily born into a poor family, and ugly poverty deprives her of the sacred right to personal freedom? Democracy cannot tolerate such an idea. The Americans gave up their lives for the freedom of the colored people; can we suffer the girls of our own race to be tortured under the yoke of slavery?

Similar to girl slaves we have in some parts of China foster daughters-in-law (Tang Hsi-fu, the rearing of prospective daughters-in-law in the home), a queer and wicked custom. The notorious cruelty of the mother-in-law of such has made the phrase "treated like a foster daughter-in-law" a national saying to signify any cruel treatment of a young girl. Now, even if we leave out of account all the evil consequences of such a misused life to a future family, the lack of freedom in marriage alone should be sufficient cause to abolish such a custom.

Young girls are mothers of the next generation. If the mothers are slaves, how can their offspring be fit for free citizenship? They cannot fit a democracy because the crooked nature of their mothers will still live in them. The habit of fear, a dependent disposition, lack of self-respect, and the absence of high principles will be their heritage. Can we allow the race to thus degenerate? We must emancipate girl slaves and abolish the custom of foster daughters-in-law.

Second, concubinage should be prohibited. Polygamy is a heinous crime! It is a custom of savages, and a shame to the civilized! Never has there been a greater abuse of human beings than this black custom. It is as wicked as slavery, if not worse. In the twentieth century when sex equality is the golden rule, the vile custom of concubinage should long ago have been abolished!

And yet those so-called learned and high-class men, as soon as they have money, marry concubines and consider it glorious! With such citizens, how can China be a true Republic? Dare we tolerate this custom? Are we not ashamed to let concubinage tacitly go on without starting a crusade against it? We can trace numerous social evils to this bad custom, and we almost never pass a day without hearing or witnessing these evils. How many rascals and bad people in society are born of concubinage! How much official corruption is its product!

How many family troubles are its consequence! How much deterioration of morality is its fruit! Wipe out concubinage, and see how much more pure China will be. Let us fight against it, fight to the end until China is relieved of this national shame.

Lastly, prostitution must be annihilated. Is man a beast? Alas! the beast has its instinct to guide it away from lustful abuse. Here many men are worse than beasts! Prostitution is a worldwide crime. It is a great humiliation to mankind. Nature recognizes the sin and gives a deadly punishment to warn men from committing it. But how obstinate and foolish men are! They are bondsmen of passion, and slaves of lust. Just think of the fat officials, the sacred members of the parliament, the majestic leaders of society, the professed patriots, the learned teachers, the opulent merchants—all of them their "glorious" hours in houses of ill fame! Can a nation of such moral corruption be called civilized? Such is China and many other nations. O wicked world, I would empty the oceans to wash thee clean! But that only means another deluge, and when the land is dried, thou art as dirty as ever. I would burn up all thy filth! But then I should destroy thee altogether. Repent thou and rise above thy sins. Be pure and noble that thou, though small, mayest become the head of the family of inhabitable worlds. Now America has awakened and taken the lead in fighting against this sin. Let China be the second, nay, the first to clear off this evil. We have the best women of the world in China, and if we men were but willing to suppress prostitution, we could easily accomplish it in a short time!

In a word, let us show our manhood; respect women, and respect them not only by words but by deeds.

6
A Refutation of Yang Xiaochun's "Against Public Childcare"

Yun Daiying (April 8, 1920)

Originally published in the *Beacon of Learning Supplement* to the *Current Affairs Newspaper*.

On March 1, Yang Xiaochun's "Against Public Childcare" was published in the *Beacon of Learning* column. At first glance, Mr. Yang's argument appears seamless and formidable, based as it is on various investigations and statistics. A more careful examination, however, reveals that his argument is flawed in many ways. I will now refute Mr. Yang's argument point by point. I welcome comments and criticism from readers and from Mr. Yang himself.

Mr. Yang said that the family is the starting point of organized human society and the basis of developed societies. Lower animals lack societies because they lack families. Birds and beasts lack enduring families, so they also lack enduring societies. Barbarian families lack the perfect stability of civilized families, so barbarian societies are likewise very undisciplined and loosely organized.

I concede that all of Mr. Yang's examples are true. But this does not mean that the family is the key factor in the development of social instincts; rather, we can only say that the family exists because of the development of social instincts. Thus, the evolution of the family is not the reason society evolves; instead, it is a result of the development of social instincts. The evolution of the family is just one aspect of the evolution of society. The family evolves just as all other aspects of society evolve. Because of this, it is an error to say that society cannot exist without the family. The creation and continued existence of society depends on social instincts, not on the family. Social instincts depend on human consciousness about humankind's evolutionary adaptation to its environment. Mr. Yang said that the family is the key factor in social development, but how do we know that the family was not created and developed by social instincts? How were families created if not by social instincts? Even without families, society can still develop.

Mr. Yang said that society would produce more criminals if it did not have families. In 1904, American population statistics indicated that 64 percent of the criminal population consisted of single people. The situation in other countries is fairly similar. This suggests that family life prevents crime.

Here, Mr. Yang merely quoted statistics without giving the reasons behind those statistics. Some might think that single people are more likely to commit crimes because they live without the concern of families or the tempering effects of the opposite sex. Yet this is a very superficial view. If economic oppression did not exist, sane people would not readily resort to crime. Mr. Yang did not think about what kind of people this 64 percent were, or why they were single. Were they not people who suffered from economic oppression? On the one hand, economic oppression compelled them to stay single; on the other hand, economic oppression caused them to commit crimes. Thus, single status and crime were both the result of economic oppression. Yet Mr. Yang ignored the reason for people's single status, and mistakenly assumed that single status causes people to commit crimes. This is another error.

Mr. Yang said that without families, many people would be poor and unable to attain self-sufficiency. People without families tend to be lazy. Widows, widowers, singles, and childless people comprise a large proportion of the poor in every nation.

I think it should be clear to the reader that Mr. Yang has reversed cause and effect here. People lack families because of poverty and laziness, but Mr. Yang mistakenly assumed that the absence of families causes poverty and laziness. I think I need go no further.

Mr. Yang said that without families, more people would be prone to early death. He based this claim on Richmond Mayo-Smith's[1] report about a thousand German men and women who had died between the ages of forty and fifty during the period 1876–1880. In this sample, the ratio of men who had never married to men who had married was 26 to 5; the ratio of women who had never married to women who had married was 15 to 4; the ratio of divorced men to married men was 14 to 2; the ratio of divorced women to married women was 11 to 4; the ratio of widowers to men whose wives were alive was 29 to 9; the ratio of widows to women whose husbands were alive was 13 to 4.

I think this error is of the same kind as the previous error about people without families being more likely to commit crimes. It is true that people without families are more likely to die because they do not have people to take care of them when they are ill. But we must remember that the poverty of people without families constantly exposes them to all kinds of hazards, deprives them of suitable sanitation, and prevents them from engaging in suitable recreation. These are all reasons for their high death rate. Thus, even though the statistics prove the truth of the phenomenon Mr. Yang talks about, we cannot say that this proves that the interpretation Mr. Yang advocates is also correct.

Mr. Yang said that public childcare would directly damage the family. Love between husbands and wives is inconstant, so without children to cement their relationship, husbands and wives will readily get angry at and turn against each other. In every nation, childless couples comprise the largest proportion of couples that divorce (in America they comprise three out of every four couples that divorce).

I believe that public childcare will directly damage the family. But I have already shown that Mr. Yang's arguments about the advantages conferred by the family and the harm caused by a lack of family are fallacious. Thus, Mr. Yang has no reason to oppose public childcare. As for the issue of divorce, I believe that husbands and wives should have the freedom to divorce if they feel that divorce is necessary. For the sake of their children, most men and women suppress their anger and gulp down their sobs in order to save their miserable marriages. This certainly should not be happening. Therefore, I think that if only Mr. Yang could get rid of his traditional idea that "divorce is a misfortune," he would rightly see that public childcare is needed. Bertrand Russell said, "It is truly unreasonable when husbands and wives are expected to stay married to each other all their lives, or when they cannot separate unless they present some reason besides the mutually agreed-upon desire to separate." Bernard Shaw said, "First, divorce should be a private matter. It should be as easy as marriage. Second, divorce should be granted even if only one party asks for it, without asking the reason for divorce or asking for the permission of the other party. Third, those with the power to grant divorces should not try to prevent divorces from occurring; rather, they should only handle arrangements for alimony. Fourth, marriage cannot be used as a punishment; if you disapprove of a couple's behavior, punish them to the full extent of the law, but do not force them to stay married to each other forever."[2] Of course, when Bernard Shaw mentioned alimony, he was addressing socioeconomic inequalities between men and women.

Mr. Yang said that children are happy by nature, so families with children are full of the joy of life. Would not public childcare reduce the joy of life? The establishment of public childcare facilities would disempower women, since, in old-fashioned families, childrearing is the source of women's empowerment. According to convention, women who do not bear children are despised.

I think that those who strongly advocate public childcare facilities but do not talk about other aspects of reform should pay attention to this portion of Mr. Yang's argument. Of course I believe in public childcare facilities. But public childcare facilities are only one aspect of the project of overall reform, or perhaps we might call it the first step of the project of overall reform. If we only try to establish public childcare facilities without recognizing the need to transform all other aspects of the system, these facilities will do more harm than good. When people can work freely and do not suffer pressure in their daily lives, everyone will be able to achieve self-fulfillment. Why, then, will they have to depend on ingenuous children for happiness and the joy of life? When women are completely emancipated, have economic independence, and do not suffer from domestic burdens, why will they still have to depend on childrearing to avoid scorn? When the joy of life and women's empowerment necessarily depend on children, those who do not bear children are miserable. Does Mr. Yang think that this kind of misery is appropriate? Or that we should content ourselves with children as a small comfort for dull lives and as a shady means for women to attain power? Why should we not have public childcare?

Mr. Yang said that people raise other's children the way they raise calves, so no one can give a child as much love and devotion as the child's own mother. Also, the milk of wet nurses is limited; a few women's milk cannot feed a whole bunch of babies. Is cow's milk as good as a human mother's milk?

Mr. Yang's claims about the pros and cons of letting public childcare facilities raise children may not sound unreasonable. But love and devotion alone do not make for good childrearing. Ordinary parents love their children, but they still sacrifice countless children to backward and unreasonable childrearing practices. The work of running public childcare facilities, on the other hand, would be entrusted to capable and efficient experts. Of course society would not entrust such work to people who are not responsible, devoted, and meticulous. If public childcare workers cannot be as trustworthy as the child's own parents, why do we say that schoolteachers are more trustworthy than the child's own parents when it comes to the child's education? Why do we trust doctors more than our own family members when we go to the hospital? How can we say that the staff members of public childcare facilities certainly cannot be as trustworthy as a child's own mother when we also say that teachers and doctors are all more trustworthy than one's own family members? Now let us discuss the question of whether a wet nurse's milk or cow's milk can be as good as the milk of one's own mother. I think those of us who talk about public childcare should pay attention to this question. When S.J. Baker, MD,[3] became the director of New York's Division of Child Hygiene, New York City achieved the lowest infant mortality rate of all the large cities in the world. She said, "A mother's milk is the most appropriate food for her infant. The mother's body is equipped with the ability to facilitate her infant's natural rate of development. The mother's milk always contains the ideal blend of all the nutrients that should be in infants' food. Infants who drink their mother's milk during their process of gradual growth and change do not lose the benefits of this ideal nourishment. They develop very healthily. They develop straight teeth and strong physiques. They learn to walk relatively early. They seldom have intestinal problems and are unlikely to catch laryngitis. When they do get sick, they are better able to resist disease, fight off their illnesses, and recover easily."[4] Because of my personal respect for Baker, I find it easy to believe that these statements she made are trustworthy. Also, it is to be expected that the mysterious workings of the Creator would make the mother a perfect match for her child. But this should not stop us from establishing public childcare. Right after the infant is born, the mother could receive guidance from a public childcare facility about how to nurse her infant. At some time during the period between when the infant is a month old and when the infant is weaned, the mother should be required to go to the public childcare facility to learn the best way to nurse her infant. Or the mother could work nearby and nurse her baby, while letting specialists take care of her baby the rest of the time. This would free mothers from the burden of raising children and at the same time prevent their ignorance from doing long-lasting damage to their children. Thus, public childcare facilities are still feasible. We cannot say that the issue of nursing is resolved just because nursing is the inevitable responsibility of the mother herself. No one can replace the mother at duties that are inevitably her own. There are some duties, such as childbirth, that must necessarily be fulfilled by women themselves, even though they are burdensome. Breastfeeding is one such duty. But it is possible to reduce women's burden with external assistance.

Mr. Yang said that statistics for Paris show that children living in public childcare facilities suffer death rates four times higher than the usual death rate for children.

Here, Mr. Yang is really speaking too indiscriminately. Parisian public childcare facilities are obviously a different issue than the public childcare facilities we are talking about. Born to poverty-stricken families, the children in Parisian public childcare facilities are constantly exposed to all sorts of prenatal and postnatal factors that contribute to a high death rate. How can we say that this is the fault of public childcare? How can we say that public childcare causes their high death rate?

Mr. Yang said that childrearing is an ability inherent in women, and also the most important duty of humankind. Women do not need to work very hard at learning how to rear children because childrearing is an inherent ability. Because childrearing is a duty, everyone should do it. How can educated mothers be worse than public childcare facilities?

I do not disagree much with Mr. Yang on this point. But I also think that it is too economically inefficient to have all women expend their energy on this one identical task of childrearing. Even though childrearing is an ability inherent in women, scientific methods of childrearing can be satisfactorily implemented only by those with special training. Not everyone can do it. After all, when humankind builds society on the basis of mutual assistance, it is possible to entrust what one could do oneself to specialists who can do it even better. The education of children has always been a most vital duty of humankind. Yet it can be transferred from fathers to teachers, so why can we not transfer the work of childrearing from mothers to public childcare facilities?

I think Mr. Yang has advanced the above arguments partly because he has not clearly discerned what is cause and what is effect, and partly because he thinks that public childcare facilities will be just like today's orphanages. I believe in public childcare facilities because they are part of the proper way of human life, and because they can help humanity achieve the proper way of life. Unlike Shen Jianshi, I am not asking for public childcare facilities supported by donations; unlike Luo Jialun,[5] I am not asking for maternity subsidies for pregnant women. Public childcare is not just a social policy or social reform movement carried out for the sake of expedience. Rather, I think that public childcare is an integral part of a society where the principle of "to each according to need, from each according to ability" prevails. The establishment of public childcare in small organizations will help those organizations develop, and help all of humankind evolve toward a proper way of life. This is the goal toward which we should strive today.

In an article published in *Golden Mean*,[6] Chen Zhengmo[7] also raised three objections to public childcare. First, the destruction of the concept of lineage will reduce people's willingness to work hard, and thus hinder the evolution of humankind. Second, people might give birth to too many children if they know that they will not be responsible for caring for those children. Third, the destruction of the concept of descendants will lead women to use contraception to avoid the hassle of pregnancy. His first and third objections assume that his concept of "the true meaning of life" should be used to make humans "slaves to doctrine." His second objection emphasizes that people should avoid early marriage and control their desires. Moreover, he argues, some women might bear many children, but some might bear few children, and some might bear no children at all. He claims that when people use their brains too much, their reproductive abilities diminish, and when society becomes civilized, husbands and wives may have different bedrooms for the sake of convenience, thus reducing the number of children born.

I am not very satisfied with Mr. Chen's arguments. I think that it is human nature to work (I will explain this in another essay). If people comprehend the true relationship between the individual and society, they will be able to work even harder, with an awakened consciousness. As for women using contraception to avoid the hassle of pregnancy, I think that this is the situation in all societies based on systems of private ownership. But if women get free prenatal care and free childcare and do not suffer economic oppression, I believe that the natural instinct to procreate will prevent most women from using contraception to avoid a negligible inconvenience to themselves. As for the fear of too many births, I think that, in the future, when men and women are completely emancipated, the alluring mystique of sex will diminish, and humans will naturally stop being the sex maniacs they are today. Furthermore, even if there are too many births, there will certainly be some people who will practice contraception or family planning for the sake of society with the same kind of dedication demonstrated by today's social reformers. Thus, I believe that public childcare depends on the complete emancipation of humankind and the awakening of humanity's social consciousness, not on humanity's enslavement to doctrines.

I look forward to the day when committed people will gain a clear understanding of the true meaning and proper methods of public childcare, and work hard to make it a reality. Public childcare is necessary for human happiness and a proper way of life. I believe that we should start with communal life, and then establish public childcare on the basis of communal life. Public childcare will enable communal life to achieve internal fulfillment and external development.

Notes

1. Richmond Mayo-Smith (1854–1901) was a professor of political economy and social science at Columbia University who used statistics to study economic and demographic questions.

2. Bernard Shaw's words appear here as translated from the Chinese, not as they originally appeared in English.

3. Sara Josephine Baker (1873–1945) was an American physician who contributed significantly to public health and child welfare in the United States. Baker became the assistant commissioner of the New York City Health Department in 1907. The following year, she established the Division of Child Hygiene, the first public agency solely devoted to child health and a model for similar agencies around the world. She introduced public school health measures, midwife training schools, and baby health stations that dispensed both milk and advice. Baker helped to found the American Child Hygiene Association in 1909, and in 1911 she organized the Babies Welfare Association, later the Children's Welfare Federation of New York. After her retirement in 1923, she became a consultant to the federal Children's Bureau and a representative on child health issues to the League of Nations. She published over 250 popular and scholarly articles and five books on child hygiene (*Encyclopaedia Britannica* 1996).

4. S.J. Baker's words are here translated from the Chinese rather than taken from the original English.

5. Luo Jialun (1897–1969) was one of the principal student leaders of the May Fourth Movement at Beijing University. He helped found *New Tide* magazine on January 1, 1919, translated Henrik Ibsen's influential feminist play *A Doll's House* into Chinese, and is credited with being the first to use the term "May Fourth Movement" in print. He went on to serve as president (1928–1930) of Qinghua University and then as president (1932–1941) of the Nationalist-controlled Central University (Boorman and Howard 1971, 428–431; Chow 1960, 349; Schwarcz 1986, 15–16, 113).

6. *Golden Mean* was a monthly magazine founded in Beijing in 1919 (Chow 1963, 50).

7. Chen Zhengmo was born in 1894 in Hubei and graduated from Beijing University in 1923. He later became an official in the Nationalist government (Cavanaugh 1982, 23).

7
Freedom of Marriage and Democracy

Lu Qiuxin (June 15, 1920)

Originally published in *New Woman*, vol. 2, no. 6, June 15, 1920.

I have recently heard that a good number of people who are normally open-minded, sensible, and quite influential in society still have deep doubts when it comes to the issue of freedom of marriage. In their opinion, marriages prearranged by parents are indeed no longer in tune with the spirit of our era; yet still, it would not be appropriate if the parents sit idle and give complete freedom to their children. It is best, according to them, to have the parents choose the bride or the bridegroom and then get consent from their children. This method, frankly speaking, still runs counter to the spirit of our era and is akin to the idea of constitutional monarchy advocated by Liang Qichao.

It is already 1920—the ninth year of the Republic of China! Democracy, democracy! This is the word that has been repeated millions of times by those gentlemen, both verbally and in print. Imagine if someone said that feudal monarchy is no good but a republic does not make sense either, so the best solution must be constitutional monarchy. Those gentlemen would surely be indignant at such a fallacy, and curse that that person must be completely insane to advocate constitutional monarchy in the era of the Republic. As supporters of the Republic and of democracy, these gentlemen would do the right thing in condemning such a person; and such a person would deserve it.

When it comes to discussing marriage, however, these gentlemen have clearly forgotten democracy and are only interested in the idea of constitutional monarchy. In all fairness, I don't believe that those gentlemen have indeed forgotten about democracy and are truly interested in establishing constitutional monarchy. It is only because of their deep love for their own children and for the younger generation that they, out of too much concern and deliberation, have made such a ridiculous mistake. Now that I have raised the issue, they will probably also laugh at themselves for having joined the ranks with those sticks-in-the-mud, such as Senator Jiang Xunru from Zhejiang, who, being a most conservative person, does not have any concept about the mechanism of the democratic age. However, I have to make it clear that I do not mean to belittle any of you gentlemen. I only wish to discuss this issue, which none of you have addressed in a way that makes sense.

I believe that freedom of marriage is necessary in a democratic society. Semi-free marriages are against the principle of democracy. To be a citizen of the Republic, one has to accept the concept of freedom of marriage; to support democracy, one has to support freedom of marriage. Below, I will compare three marriage systems with three political systems:

I. Marriage systems:
1. Marriage completely arranged by the parents, without the consent of the children.
2. Marriage arranged by the parents with the consent of the children.
3. Free marriage between the man and woman, without any interference from a third party.

II. Political systems:
1. Monarchy.
2. Constitutional monarchy.
3. Democratic republic.

We can easily see that the consensual arranged marriage in item 2, part I, between "completely arranged marriage" and "free marriage" is analogous to constitutional monarchy, that is between "monarchy" and "democratic republic." To put it more clearly, we can see:

Completely arranged marriage—monarchy
Consensual arranged marriage—constitutional monarchy
Free marriage—democratic republic

Now we would like to ask: Is there room for the so-called "consensual arranged marriage" in a democratic republic? The answer is obviously no. The former is absolutely not in accordance with the latter; and the two are, in fact, opposed to each other. If democracy allows "consensually arranged marriages" to exist, then it will also accept "completely arranged marriages." Advocacy and support of "consensual arranged marriage" is intended to overthrow democracy and topple the Republic. In other words, to support democracy and the Republic, it is necessary to oppose "consensual arranged marriages" and to advocate "free marriages." On this note, I sincerely hope that all of us will see clearly, cast away any doubts, and try our best to promote progress as our era demands.

There is another theory that China traditionally practiced the "completely arranged marriage" and is now progressing toward "consensual arranged marriage." If one tries to skip a step in the process by jumping into "free marriage," one would be committing a mistake of over-zealousness and hastiness and would be doomed to failure. In any business, one ought to consider feasibility and not be engaged in empty talk about ideals. I strongly believe that this kind of argument is definitely erroneous. China was under the Manchu monarchy until the

Revolutionary Alliance led by Dr. Sun Yat-sen, who, in the name of the Three Principles of Democracy, founded the Republic of China in 1911. But before that, there was a big debate between *The Republic* (a paper produced by Chinese intellectuals living in Tokyo) and Liang Qichao, Yang Du, and others, who resolutely opposed democracy and advocated the introduction of constitutional monarchy into China. The reason given by advocates like Liang Qichao and Yang Du was also that to jump from monarchy to republic was to skip a step in the natural historical process and would be doomed to failure. At that time, the majority of the elite in China agreed with Liang and Yang and demanded constitutionalization by the Qing government. But the idea failed because of the Huanghua Gang Uprising and the Wuchang Revolution; as a result, the Republic was founded and democracy brought to China. This eloquently proved that skipping a historical step is technically feasible and that the idea of constitutional monarchy advocated by Liang and Yang is absolutely absurd. It was politically possible to advance from monarchy to republic—this was not empty talk about ideals. So, when it comes to the marriage system, why can't we advance from "absolutely arranged marriage" to "free marriage"? This should not be applicable to political systems alone. Certainly not! We all support democracy and have heard what Dr. Dewey said about democracy. According to him, the essence of democracy has two components: one is freedom, and the other is responsibility. Consequently, we should all bear responsibility for promoting freedom of marriage. Talk about over-zealousness and hastiness and talk about reconciliation and compromise should cease, because they are only repeating what the lackeys of Liang Qichao have been prattling about.

Additionally, some have pointed out that several young people who advocate the abolition of marriage also cited the example of China's direct advance from monarchy to democracy when confronted with critics who argued that their ideal was not practical. Is not democracy more relevant to their argument than to mine? After all, which is more analogous to democracy—freedom of marriage or the abolition of marriage? Aren't you mistaken? My reply is: Dear Sirs, I am not mistaken. When they related the abolition of marriage to democracy, those young people did not mean to say that the abolition of marriage is what democracy requires. They simply borrowed the concept of democracy owing to their want of examples to illustrate their viewpoint. Dear Sirs, you need to bear in mind that the abolition of marriage is a step further than freedom of marriage—an antifamily step that would lead the future away from democracy to anarchism. Rather unwillingly, these young people had to use democracy as an expedient device because they could not find anyone who supported anarchism. Certainly, they were not referring to the abolition of marriage as democracy itself. Obviously, advocating the abolition of marriage is at odds with democracy; how can these two be compared?

In sum, it is not difficult to see that, under democracy, one advocates freedom of marriage and under anarchism, one advocates the abolition of marriage. The two should never be mixed. Now that we are all citizens of the Republic, please do not talk about the so-called "consensual arranged marriage" again. It is my sincere wish that all of us will just remember freedom of marriage and democracy.

Long live freedom of marriage!

Long live democracy!

8
Public Childcare and Public Dining Halls

Tang Jicang (August 10, 1920)

Originally published in *New Woman*, vol. 3, no. 3, under the name Ji Cang.

If men and women are to be equal, women must first attain the ability to be economically independent. This major step is urgent and necessary. Our discussion naturally begins with the question of jobs. To get jobs, women must have skills and time. Skills can be learned, but because of contemporary social customs, women's time constraints make it hard for them to get jobs. After women marry and have children, they must take care of their children from morning till night in order to qualify for the title of "virtuous mother." Since we need "three meals a day," all the burden of cooking falls to women. They must assume this burden in order to attain the titles of "primary giver" and "good wife." Whatever the size of their family, most women have no free time after a long day of housework. Only the women of a few wealthy families can afford to hire wet nurses and cooks. But most of those hired are uneducated, so even these wealthy women feel uneasy if they do not supervise the work of those they hire. With all these burdens, can women find time to leave the home to work in society? Thus, when we talk about women's emancipation, we come to two urgent questions. We should start trying out ways to address these questions; there is no time to lose. These are the question of public childcare and the question of public dining halls.

Public childcare means allowing children to be raised in communally established facilities. Everyone should discuss this complicated issue in preparation for the much-awaited day when public childcare becomes a reality. I will discuss some of the questions that come to mind. Some say that maternal nature is such that no one can take care of children with as much devotion as their mother. Therefore, it seems that public childcare facilities would be inappropriate. I say that the way the old society has done things has caused many problems and must necessarily be reformed. Of course, at first we feel uncomfortable with many aspects of the reforms because we are not used to them. Public education is one such reform. But I should address the fact that there are already many orphanages across the country. Though I have not personally investigated them, I have heard people say that most children in these orphanages are not treated well. Thus, these children suffer a high death rate, and even the survivors grow up with weak bodies. This is truly atrocious. When we set up public childcare facilities, we certainly cannot use the same methods used by these orphanages. Childcare facilities should be like kindergartens and elementary schools. In setting up childcare facilities, we should use new methods and expend even greater effort. Those who work at childcare facilities must be split into a day shift and a night shift. Otherwise, children who kick out their quilts or wet their beds for a few nights will soon become ill, and may even suffer chronic illness for the rest of their lives. This is no small thing! Childcare facility workers should be trained as nurses and nannies. Most importantly, it is necessary to enhance their consciousness so that they will care about their work and treat the children like their own. If we set up childcare facilities like this, I think society will start having a bit more faith in them. If our achievements are great, then society's faith in childcare facilities will increase. A few of the new residential arrangements currently advocated are already starting to sprout up. New, specially arranged residential quarters are urgently needed, but there are currently too few of these. The improvement of domestic life is an even more pressing matter. Therefore, we should spread new residential arrangements throughout the country, to old-fashioned families in every corner of the country. I am also considering new residential arrangements here because they are very much related to the question of how children eat and sleep. Currently, all families still depend on men. Except for men in families with property, there are only two kinds of men: those who work at home and those who migrate elsewhere to work. Public childcare and public dining halls would of course be convenient for men who work in their home villages. As for those who work outside their home villages and have brought their families with them, their homes must also be near their workplace. Family organization today is often complex, and there are a good number of migrants. Public childcare facilities and public dining halls would make it easier for people to have families; furthermore, things would become much easier if women would also be able to work a little and make their home anywhere. Consequently, the new residential system would gradually spread throughout society. We often say that childbearing is the only real reason women are more encumbered than men. So we should stipulate whenever possible that women get special treatment and protection during the weeks right before and after childbirth. After a few weeks, mothers can still nurse their babies as before. Whether the mother has to be the one to put the children to bed is a question that should be handled according to the situation. Mother's milk could also be stored so that babies can be bottle-fed in the childcare facility; if this is not enough, there may be other ways to supplement their nursing. In any case, the childcare facilities should try the methods that seem the simplest; if these are not suitable, they should adjust their methods as needed. I hope there will be as many childcare facilities employing these methods as there are kindergartens and elementary schools today. As far as the relationship between a mother and her child is concerned, I believe that generally about 80 or 90 percent of it can be preserved in the childcare facilities. These facilities would offer more benefits than harm. Even if they do some harm, it will be easy to correct. Therefore, I am convinced that childcare facilities are a prerequisite for women's emancipation.

Now let us turn to the issue of public dining halls. A public dining hall would serve neighbors from a common public kitchen. Breakfast, lunch, and dinner would all be served in the public dining hall, and individual families would never have to start their own cooking fires again. Public dining halls are much simpler to set up than public childcare facilities. Everyone just has to realize that public dining hall meals would be just like family meals, except that they would derive from cooperation and a division of labor. Those who work in the dining halls would be trained for that purpose; they would not be restaurateurs trying to make money. Or, people could take turns working in the dining halls. These dining halls would be even more careful about cleanliness and nutrition than individual households are. It would be even better if prices can be adjusted in accordance with seasonal fluctuations. Public dining halls are another prerequisite for women's emancipation.

Public childcare facilities and public dining halls are not new inventions of the twentieth century. As early as three thousand years ago in Europe's Greek Confederation, there was a state called Sparta that also had public childcare facilities and public dining halls. Unfortunately, the exact details of their rules and regulations are lost to us today. Even if we can make a rough guess at how they did things, we should still adjust their methods to fit the different circumstances that prevail today. For instance, the "nationalization of land" has recently become an important question. Yet this very principle can be found in ancient Chinese history, in the form of the field system of the Three Dynasties and in the form of field redistribution during the Later Wei dynasty.[1] This demonstrates that human yearnings and ideals have not changed very much. The new questions that have been raised in the past one or two years are mostly questions that have been addressed by others before. Therefore, I ask everyone not to fear trying out "new things" just because they are rarely done today. We need only think clearly about the reasons we want to do these things, and separate what we should do from what we should not do. Everyone should unite in determination to do what needs to be done; empty words do not benefit anyone. This is what deserves our attention the most; therefore, I am pointing it out especially, and concluding on this point.

Note

1. Tang Jicang refers to state-run land redistribution programs implemented during China's Three Dynasties period (A.D. 220–280) and under the Northern Wei (A.D. 386–534).

9
Love and Socializing Between Men and Women

Yang Zhihua (July 1922)

First published in *Women's Critic*, a supplement of the *Republican Daily*, July 26, 1922.

There stood several young men, who all wore new-style clothes, hats, and shoes, and usually spoke and wrote in a brand new language and fancy style. Suddenly, one of them came up to me and said: "Your relationship with so-and-so is already known to us all. Aha, you two are in love!" I simply laughed. If he had been smart, he would have instantly known what my laughter meant. What did I laugh at? I simply laughed at his "newness" and the fact that he was new on the outside but old on the inside. His mixture of old and new is even older than the old and dirtier than dirt. Then he continued to ask me: "Why don't you tell us more about it, since you two are indeed in love?" Once again, I laughed coldly. He had no idea.

How many people who are supposedly engaged in the New Culture Movement these days truly mean business? Far too many of them are just wearing masks! As it is, there are more destroyers than builders; if this continues, our future is really in grave danger!

Open socializing between men and women is a very important issue. There has been a lot of public demand for that since the May Fourth Movement. Unfortunately, it has not been easy to carry out. Why not? In my opinion, it is due to the obstacles created by the men and women involved. On the one hand, they advocate open socializing between men and women; on the other hand, they are doing things to hinder it. This is a real self-contradiction; it is like blocking one's own way with rocks.

This is where the obstacles lie.

First, when a man and a woman start to socialize by speaking and writing to each other, going to the parks together, or studying together, people jump to the conclusion that this young man and this young woman are in love, even though they are actually just friends. Consequently, some young men and women succumb to these outside pressures and speculations, go ahead and push themselves into the "business of love," and then have sex. After that, they break up, agonize, and part ways. The whole process usually lasts a very short time because their relationship has the wrong foundation to begin with. This kind of love is caused by outside pressure, so it is not true love. It is not a personal choice, so it usually does not last long. It is certainly not a good thing for society when couples separate, though divorce is an expedient means to deal with problems caused by the old marriage system. Any society that allows people to copulate and then casually separate is a primitive one and exists only in periods of barbarism. Now that such things happen in our society, it is no wonder that those old moralists feel disgusted.

As I have shown, this situation results from the fact that some people who have been steeped in the old tradition resent and make a fuss about socializing between men and women. This is an objective obstacle.

The second is a subjective obstacle—one that is caused by the men and women themselves. Often, one feels excited when one meets a stranger of the opposite sex. When this happens, people behave strangely, assuming that the purpose of socializing with someone of the opposite sex is to "love and marry." For the sole purpose of speeding up the game of love, they discard their personal integrity and try all sorts of tricks to seduce the opposite sex. They never question whether love should be achieved that way and whether this kind of union between the sexes is natural or everlasting. This is completely wrong! This kind of union has nothing to do with love. It is nothing but animal desire. With this kind of animalistic socializing going on, it is no wonder that those old moralists curse the absurdity of the New Culture Movement and prevent their own children from going to public gatherings.

Third, there are some who tend to misunderstand the intention of the other party, assuming that even the slightest agreement in language and thought signifies "love." They then seek love without trying to understand the other party. Suffering from "unrequited love," many of them end up becoming ill, insane, or suicidal. Those who are smarter may come back to their senses in time. Observation of these kinds of encounters may cause pessimism and loneliness in other people, and keep them from going out and socializing.

The above are the obstacles that hinder the socializing between men and women.

Love is sacred and should not be spoken of lightly. It is a union of character. Anybody who misinterprets the concept of character, fails to distinguish between the part and the whole, or fails to understand the significance of character is not qualified to talk about "love."

I respect my own and others' character. If I actually fall in love with someone, I will not be afraid to talk about it. If not, however, I will certainly curse those who don't respect the character of others. Who can sway my will? Who can force me? Who would dare to control me? I have the right to control my own life and would never allow anybody else to control me. I sincerely advise young people: Raise your consciousness, never take lightly your own character or others', never try to destroy our New Culture Movement, and avoid hindering our progress. It is my hope that there will be more discussion on socializing between men and women. I also welcome comments and criticisms.

10
The Debate over "Love and Open Socializing Between Men and Women"

Yang Zhihua (August 11, 1922)

Originally published in *Women's Critic*, a supplement to the *Republican Daily*, August 11, 1922.

Some lack knowledge of how to use an axe, and therefore want the handles of other people's axes to fall off. Some lack lovers, and therefore want to destroy the love of others. Some lack the strength to support a cultural movement, and therefore capitulate to the opposition. Who are they to call others "hypocrites" and "idiots"? They would do better to reflect on themselves, and think about what they themselves deserve.

A week ago, the *Beacon of Learning* supplement to *Current Affairs* carried a certain gentleman's column entitled "On the article 'Love and Open Socializing between Men and Women' published in *Women's Critic*." Due to illness, I could not reply until now.

Anyone acquainted with both that gentleman and me knows the purposes of his article. They are twofold: destruction and self-gratification.

To be frank, he resorts to libeling and villifying others because he himself cannot find a lover. He is motivated by the most selfish reasons to destroy the happiness of others. In his article, he says, "A destroyer must also have some constructive ideas, and a builder must also have some destructive schemes." In dealing with other people, I myself have always been very honest, and have never resorted to schemes; therefore, I have expected the same of other people. Unfortunately, this gentleman has used a certain scheme to coerce and destroy. What he is really trying to say is that his destructiveness also embodies some constructive ideas, and that he must resort to destructive schemes to build up his ideas. I did not know this until today!

Love requires the consent of both parties, and there is no room for a third party. The interference of others is absolutely unnecessary. The application of coercion to love is the most despicable of all. Anyone who does it knows nothing about love, and he who knows nothing about love is not qualified to talk about whether love is conditional or unconditional. This gentleman alleges in his article that as long as two people know and care about each other, love does not depend on the amount of time they have spent together. However, this gentleman did the opposite of what he said. The way he treated me attests to that.

I have always been very kind and loyal to my friends, whether male or female. I never believed that any of my friends could be a hypocrite. That is how I have treated this gentleman. In a surprise move, however, he misunderstood me and tried to press me into a romantic affair with him. I honestly told him that I was unwilling. But he just made it worse by spreading the rumor that he and I were romantically involved. I had to confront him about that; then he told his friends that I wanted to tempt and use him for reasons of my own. On the other hand, he still kept writing me intimate letters, asking me to divorce my husband and marry him. He said, "I truly love you and hope you will love me in return. I am an honorable man. Please pity me and show mercy on me." Knowing that he has become obsessed with unrequited love, I could only behave coldly toward him. However, he continued to misunderstand me, then started to hate, curse, and slander me. These are the facts. He knows nothing about love and has no respect for love. How can one tolerate this? Additionally, he wrote in his article, "Love is a necessity of life and an indication of life force. Just as when one worships and prays to God or Buddha, one has to continue to do so even if one's prayers are not answered. If one wants to raise birds or grow plants, one will never stop doing so simply because the plants and birds do not reciprocate. To love is the same—one cannot stop loving simply because one's love is not requited." Here he contradicts himself. In the beginning of his essay, he claims that love should be conditional; then later on, he apparently advocates unconditional love. That proves that he knows nothing about love and takes love too lightly. Human beings are not gods, Buddhas, plants, or birds. A human being has a mind that thinks, and a sense of dignity. A human being cannot be manipulated. How can we compare a human being with senseless clay or wooden sculptures? Love involves two parties and cannot be coerced. Otherwise, it is disrespectful to the other person's dignity and thus disrespectful to one's own dignity!

"Flirting"[1] is a special term used to describe the brazen dalliances of hypocritical parasites, a behavior that is denounced by society as immoral. But this gentleman takes this kind of behavior as "love." He says, "We know that in society there are some young men and women who try to seduce the opposite sex by wearing fancy clothing and using specially rehearsed language. That is what people call 'flirting.' But wealth, fame, erudition, and personality could also seduce people. So I can conclude that 'flirting' is nothing but a bad name a few old moralists and intellectuals gave to the proletarian underdog's expression of love." In reality, the true, uneducated proletarians have to work from morning till night and hardly have time for the game of "flirting." Hiding under the flag of the proletariat, this gentleman openly advocates "flirting" and insults not only knowledge, reputation, and personality but also the uncorrupted proletariat. His writing, originally meant to be published in one of those trashy magazines, now serves to show the true colors of those who occasionally call themselves socialists, thus thoroughly disheartening those who had regarded him as a friend. I, for one, would never have imagined that he could fall so low. We have been forced to coin the term "Neo-hooliganism," which, I hope, can serve as a good warning. We young people should guard against words and actions that would place us into this category. We should all support the New Culture Movement. One needs to refresh one's thinking constantly. The old social tradition dies hard and constantly tries to pull us back with its evil claws. Therefore, it is unavoidable for us to make mistakes, and we are seldom aware of those mistakes we ourselves make. We should wholeheartedly welcome anyone with clearer vision who is willing to guide us; otherwise, we could easily destroy our bright future with our egotistical oversight.

Nowadays, there are some who appear to be activists, but who, in reality, often encumber and encroach upon the human rights of others. Instead of examining their own behavior, they slander and defame others. They should certainly lose their right to free speech. Freedom of speech should not impede others' right to freedom. Freedom should go hand in hand with responsibility, and anyone who pursues freedom should be aware of this. The last thing we need is to have people who refuse to correct their own mistakes and try to entice others into returning to the old path under a brand new name. There is no room in our society for those who fervently advocate indulgence in animalistic desire, resort to highhandedness, and hinder the freedom of others. I truly hope that those who do this will mend their ways and try to be good members of our new society; otherwise, they will either lose their right to speak to the public or surrender to the reactionary forces. Such a demonstration of weakness would be a profound misfortune indeed!

Note

1. The original Chinese term *diaobangzi*, (literally, "hanging your arm out") has a much more negative connotation than the English term "flirting."

11
My View on the Issue of Divorce

Yang Zhihua (July 25, 1922)

Originally published in *Women's Critic*, a supplement to the *Republican Daily*, July 25, 1922.

There are so many people in the world, but there are no two people who share exactly the same natural inclinations. Each person has different strengths and weaknesses. Some like to move around; others like to stay put; some like food; others like clothing; some like to study; others like to do other things. Furthermore, there are differences even among those who like to move around and among those who like to stay put. And among those who like to study, some prefer to study literature, whereas others prefer to study science. The same goes with those who like to do other things. People's character, thinking, will, and behavior are all different, even though some might have a few things in common. On top of that, there are only one or two out of a thousand who even have a few things in common. It is no wonder that there are often conflicts between human beings!

Love, whether between friends, siblings, or husband and wife, may eventually turn problematic, and that leads to mutual dissatisfaction and eventually a breakup. It is relatively easy to break up with your friends or siblings, but because of the intimacy of marriage, it is more difficult to break up with your spouse. Divorce is a truly a delicate issue.

In our society today, there are quite a few people who believe that they are practicing what we call "free love." But the question whether they are indeed in love with each other remains. If people do not marry out of true love, what difference is there between their marriage and those arranged or coerced marriages? There should not be the slightest doubt that couples are allowed to divorce if their marriage was not freely willed or if it is lacking in true love. In my opinion, even couples who originally married out of true love should be allowed to divorce. To force an estranged couple to share the same bedroom would only cause immoral and unnatural behavior. How love begins and ends is beyond our control and comprehension. Love is like life itself—to lose one's love is to lose one's life. We see so many men in society who visit brothels or obtain concubines because they do not love their wives. But we women can only lead a lonely, sad, and painful life if we do not love our husbands. How many women are there who are numbed or die because of their husbands and their unhappy marriages! Because of traditional morality, it is unthinkable for those who survive to demand a divorce. Those women may commit adultery; but what fun is that?! Thus, it is much better to just get a divorce. They should try to rely on their own strength, but society should also lend them a helping hand.

I have stated that people have different inclinations, and that these differences may produce disagreements and even mutual resentment between husbands and wives. Even those whose love is free, natural, and long-standing go through some rough times. In the beginning, courting or married couples tend to demonstrate their similarities rather than their differences. Consequently, their love becomes more and more passionate, thus rendering them unable to see each other's shortcomings; meanwhile, others may see the potential problems but not be in a position to interfere. This is usually the root cause of a broken relationship. If the love of a courting couple is true, natural, sustained, and based on mutual observation, however, their marriage is more likely to survive the shortcomings revealed afterward, because the couple will probably understand and forgive each other. This kind of marriage may last longer than those based on a love that is superficial, not entirely free and natural, and lacking in a long period of mutual observation. Nonetheless, though this kind of marriage may not be so fragile, it may still last only a bit longer than other marriages. I think that a couple should simply divorce, when their marriage can no longer last.

If divorce is the result of dissatisfaction, then the intention of divorce is to seek satisfaction. But does seeking satisfaction mean seeking another love? If so, can one be assured that the new love is satisfactory? Most likely not! As I said earlier, people have different experiences, worldviews, ways of thinking, and behavior. So their relationship may fall apart despite their passionate love. The second marriage or relationship may fall apart even more easily than the first one. Therefore, I think it is not necessary to have another love or marriage after divorce. It matters little even if one lacks financial independence; as long as one has good health, there will always be life. All of us have our own natural strength; why should one rely on other people and suffer?

12
The New Year's Sacrifice

Lu Xun (February 7, 1924)

Originally published in the Shanghai periodical *Eastern Miscellany*, vol. 21, no. 6, in March 1924. This translation by William A. Lyell was published in 1990 by the University of Hawaii Press in *Diary of a Madman and Other Stories*, pp. 219–241. It is reprinted with permission from the University of Hawaii Press.

When you come right down to it, the windup of the old Lunar Year was what the end of a year really should be. To say nothing of the hubbub in the towns and villages, the very sky itself proclaimed the imminent arrival of the New Year as flashes of light appeared now and then among the gray and heavy clouds of evening, followed by the muffled sound of distant explosions—pyrotechnic farewells to the Kitchen God.[1] The crisper cracks of fireworks being set off close at hand were much louder, and before your ears had stopped ringing, the faint fragrance of gunpowder would permeate the air. It was on just such an evening that I returned to Lu Town. I still called it home, even though my immediate family was no longer there, a circumstance that forced me to put up at Fourth Old Master Lu's place. Since he is my clansman and a generation above me, I really ought to call him "Fourth Uncle."

An old Imperial Collegian and follower of neo-Confucianism,[2] he seemed little changed, only a bit older than before, though he still had not grown a beard as one might have expected. Upon seeing me, he recited the usual social commonplaces; commonplaces concluded, he observed that I had put on weight; that observation having been made, he began to denounce the new party. I knew, however, that this was by no means intended as an indirect attack on me, for by "new" he had meant the reformers of twenty years back, people like Kang Youwei.[3] Even so, as we continued to chat, my words and his never seemed to jibe, and before long I found myself alone in his study.

I got up quite late the next day, and after taking lunch, went out to visit some relatives and friends. I spent the third day in exactly the same way. They did not seem much changed either—a bit older, that was all. In every household people were busily preparing for the ceremony known as the "New Year's Sacrifice."[4] In Lu Town this was the most important of all the ceremonies conducted at the end of the year. With great reverence and punctilious observance of ritual detail, people would prepare to receive and welcome the gods of good fortune, and to ask them for prosperity during the coming year.

Chickens and geese would be killed; pork bought; and the meats washed with a diligence and care that left the arms of the women red from the soaking. Some women kept on their locally made bracelets—braided strands of silver—even as they washed. On the last day of the year, once the meats were cooked, chopsticks would be thrust at random into the various dishes prepared from them. This was the "ritual offering" that would bring down bountiful blessings during the new year. At the Fifth Watch, just before dawn on New Year's Day, the various dishes would be set out, candles lit, incense burned, and the gods of good fortune respectfully invited to descend and enjoy the feast. The actual execution of the ceremony was exclusively the province of men.

Once the ceremony was completed, then of course still more firecrackers would be set off. Year by year, family by family, as long as people could afford the expenditure, the ritual had always been performed in this manner. And this year, of course, was no exception.

The sky grew even darker. By afternoon it had actually begun to snow. From horizon to horizon, blending together with the soft mists and general atmosphere of urgent activity, snowflakes as large as plum blossoms danced through the air, catching Lu Town off balance and throwing it into a state of hopeless disarray.

By the time I got back to Fourth Uncle's study, the roof tiles were white and the study so brightened by the reflected light of snow that the red ink-rubbing hanging on the wall stood out with unusual crispness. The rubbing consisted of the single character meaning "long life" and had been written by Venerable Founder Chen Tuan.[5] There had been a pair of scrolls flanking it, but one of these had fallen off the wall and now lay loosely rolled up on the long table under the rubbing. Its mate still hung on the wall and read: *Having completely penetrated the principle of things, the mind becomes serene.*[6] Aimlessly I went over and rummaged through the pile of old-fashioned stitched books on the desk by the window: an incomplete set of the *Kang Xi Dictionary,* a copy of *Collected Commentaries to "Reflections on Things at Hand,"* and a copy of *A Lining to the Garment of the "Four Books."*[7] Then and there I decided to leave the next day. Furthermore, when I thought about how I had run into Sister Xianglin[8] on the street the day before, I realized it would have simply been impossible for me to remain in Lu Town with any peace of mind.

It had happened in the afternoon, immediately after I had paid a visit to a friend of mine on the east side of town. Leaving my friend's place, I caught sight of Sister Xianglin down by the riverbank. Her eyes were intense and focused on me. I could tell she wanted to have a word.

Among the people I had run into on this visit, I can safely say that no one had changed as much as she; the gray hair of five years back was now entirely white. No one would have taken her for the woman of forty or so that she was. Her face was sallow with dark circles around the eyes, and what was more, even the expression of sadness that she used to wear had now disappeared altogether. Her face seemed to be carved of wood. Only an occasional eye movement hinted that she was still an animate creature. In one hand she carried an empty bamboo basket; a broken bowl lay inside it—empty. With the other hand she supported herself on a bamboo pole that was taller than she and had started to split at the bottom. It was obvious that she had become a beggar, pure and simple. I stood still, waiting for her to accost me and ask for money.

"So, you've come back," she began.

"Yes."

"Just the man I've been lookin' for. You know how to read books. You've been out there in the world and must've seen a thing or two. Now tell me . . ." A bright light suddenly glowed in her heretofore lifeless eyes. Never imagining that she would begin by saying this sort of thing, I just stood there in astonishment.

"Tell me . . ." She came a few steps closer, lowered her voice as though sharing a secret, and continued in tones of great urgency: "Is there *really* a soul after a body dies?"

I was aghast at the question. When I saw how her eyes were riveted upon me, I became so fidgety you would have thought that someone had thrown a handful of thorns down the back of my gown. I was even more on edge than when, back during my school days, a teacher would pop an unexpected question, look straight at me, and wait for the answer.

I had never really cared one way or the other about whether souls existed or not, but that was not my problem. My problem was what would be the best answer to give *her* right then and there? I hesitated for a moment to give myself time to think. I knew that people in these parts did, as a rule, believe in ghosts, but now *she* seemed to doubt—or perhaps "hope" would be a better word—seemed to hope that they existed, and yet, at the same time, seemed to hope that they did not. Why add to the suffering of a poor woman already at the end of her rope? For her sake it would probably be best to say that they did exist.

I hemmed and hawed: "Well, perhaps they do. Probably. The way I see it—."

"Then there's gotta be a hell too, right?"

"What! A hell?" Taken off guard by the question, I became evasive.

"Well, logically, I suppose there ought to be, but then not necessarily either. Who has the time to bother about that sort of thing anyway?"

"But if there is, then dead kin are all gonna meet again, right?"

"Hmmmm . . . Let's see . . . your question . . . your question is . . . uh . . . will they meet again?"

At this point I began to see that, for all the good it did me, I might just as well have remained uneducated, for despite all my stalling, despite all my brainwracking, I had been unable to stand up to three questions posed by this simple woman. Suddenly I turned timid and searched around for a way of nullifying whatever I had said up to this point. "Well, you see. . . . To tell the truth, I can't say for sure. As a matter of fact, I can't even say for sure whether there are souls or not." Taking advantage of a lull in her persistent questioning, I strode away and beat a hasty retreat to Fourth Uncle's house.

Anxious at heart, I began to mull it all over in my own mind. "That may well have been a dangerous sort of answer to have given her," I thought to myself. "To be sure, it's probably just because everyone else is so caught up in preparations for the New Year's Sacrifice that she's become so keenly aware of her own isolation—but still, could there be anything more to it than that? Could it be that she has had some sort of premonition? If there is anything more to it and something regrettable happens as a result, then I shall be partially responsible because of what I said. . . ."

By the time I got to this point, I couldn't help but laugh at myself. After all, what had happened was nothing more than a chance occurrence and could not possibly have any great significance. Yet, against all reason, I had insisted on analyzing it in painstaking detail. Was it any wonder that certain people in educational circles had accused me of being neurotic?[9] What was more, I had told her in no uncertain terms that I couldn't "say for sure," nullifying everything I had said before. "Even if something *does* happen," I thought, "it will have nothing to do with me."

Can't say for sure—what a wonderfully useful expression! Dauntless youngsters, wet behind the ears, will often plot a course of action for an indecisive friend, or even go so far as to help someone choose a doctor. When things don't turn out well, then of course they've only succeeded in making enemies.

If, on the other hand, you conclude everything you say with a *can't say for sure,* you always remain comfortably free and clear no matter *how* things turn out. After meeting with Sister Xianglin on the street that day, I began to appreciate the necessity for some such formula. I hadn't been able to get along without it even when talking with a simple beggar.

Nonetheless, I continued to feel uneasy. Even after a good night's sleep I couldn't get her out of my mind. It was as though I had a premonition of disaster. The wearisome atmosphere of my uncle's study melded with the gloom of the snow-filled skies to intensify my anxieties. "Might as well leave and go back into the city tomorrow," I thought to myself. "Shark's fin cooked in clear broth costs only a dollar a bowl at the Fuxing—good food at a bargain price.[10] Wonder if it's gone up by now? The friends I used to go there with, of course, have long since scattered to the four winds, but I can't afford to pass up that shark's fin soup even if I do have to eat alone. . . . Well, I'm definitely going to clear out of here tomorrow, come what may."

I had often seen things that I hoped wouldn't turn out the way I anticipated, begin, one after the other, to turn out exactly the way I was afraid they would. Now I began to worry that this business of Sister Xianglin would fit the mold. And sure enough, strange things began to happen. Toward evening, I heard people discussing something-or-other in the inner rooms. Before long, the conversation ended, and all I could make out was the sound of Fourth Uncle pacing back and forth. He began to yell. "Not a minute sooner and not a minute later, had to pick exactly this time of year! You can tell from that alone what bad stock we're dealing with!"

At first I was merely curious as to what it was all about, but then I began to feel downright uneasy, for Fourth Uncle's words seemed to have something to do with me. I poked my head out the door, but there was no one around whom I could question. I was on pins and needles until just before supper, when a temporary servant, taken on for the holidays, came into my room to make tea. I finally had my chance.

"Who was Fourth Old Master so mad at just now?"

"Sister Xianglin, who else?" Brief and to the point.

"What *about* Sister Xianglin?" I asked apprehensively.

"She's aged away."[11]

"Aged away?" My heart constricted into a tight knot and felt as though it would jump out of my body. The color probably drained out of my face too, but from beginning to end, the servant kept his head down and tended to the making of the tea, unaware of my reaction. Forcing myself to be calm, I continued with my questions.

"*When* did she die?"

"When? Last night, or maybe it was today. I can't say for sure."

"What did she die of?"

"*What* did she die of? Poverty, what else?" He answered in flat, unemotional tones; still not raising his head to look at me, he left the room.

Surprisingly, however, my own agitation turned out to be but a momentary thing, for right after the servant left, I felt that what was bound to happen had already come and gone. Without even having to resort to a *can't say for sure* or adopting the servant's formula for dismissing the whole thing—Poverty, *what else?*—I gradually began to regain my composure. And yet, I still felt an occasional pang of guilt.

With Fourth Uncle in stern attendance, dinner was served. I wanted to learn more about Sister Xianglin's death, but I knew that although Fourth Uncle had read that *ghosts and spirits do but natural transformations of the two powers be*,[12] he still harbored many superstitions and would not, under any circumstances, be willing to discuss anything related to sickness or death as the time for the New Year's Sacrifice drew near. If such subjects had to be broached, then one would be expected to employ a substitute language of roundabout phrases in discussing them. Unfortunately, I did not know the proper phraseology and therefore, although there were several moments when I thought about asking something, in the end I didn't. As I looked at the stern expression on my uncle's face, it suddenly occurred to me that he might well be thinking that I, too, "not a minute sooner and not a minute later, had to pick exactly *this* time of year" to come and disturb his peace of mind, and that I too was "bad stock." Deciding that I had better set his mind at rest as soon as possible, I told him I would leave Lu Town in the morning and go back to the city. He made a very perfunctory bow in the direction of trying to dissuade me. We finished the meal in gloomy silence.

Winter days are short. Snowy skies shorten them even more, and thus by the time our meal was over, the shades of evening had long since enshrouded the entire town. By lamplight on this New Year's Eve, people were bustling about in every home as they prepared for the following day.

Outside the windows of those same homes, however, all was lonely silence. Large snowflakes fell on a blanket of white that was already piled thick on the ground. I even seemed to hear a faint rustling sound as they touched down, a sound that made me feel the silence and loneliness all the more intensely. As I sat there in the yellowish glow of an oil lamp, my thoughts turned to Sister Xianglin.

With nothing left, with no one to turn to, she had been tossed onto a garbage heap like a worn-out toy that people are tired of seeing around. And yet, until only a short time before, Sister Xianglin had at least managed to maintain her physical form even amid the refuse. People happy in their own lives had no doubt thought it odd that she chose to continue such an existence.

Well, now at last Wuchang had swept her away without leaving the slightest trace.[13] I didn't know whether souls existed or not, but in the world we live in, when someone who has no way to make a living is no longer alive, when someone whom people are sick of seeing is no longer around to *be* seen, then one cannot say that she has done too badly, either by herself or by other people. Sitting in silence, listening to the faint rustle of snowflakes, and thinking these thoughts, gradually and quite unexpectedly I began to feel relaxed.

As I sat there, the bits and pieces of Sister Xianglin's story that I had either witnessed or heard about secondhand came together and painted a portrait of her life.

She did not come from Lu Town.

At the beginning of winter one year they decided to change maids at Fourth Uncle's place. And so it was that Old Lady Wei, acting as go-between, led a new servant into the house.

Hair tied back with a piece of white wool, she wore a black skirt, a blue lined jacket with long sleeves, and over that a sleeveless vest of light blue. She looked to be twenty-six or twenty-seven and was on the whole rather pale, though her cheeks were rosy. Old Lady Wei called her Sister Xianglin and said she was a neighbor of her mother's. Because her man had died, Sister Xianglin had come out to look for a job. Fourth Uncle frowned at that, and Fourth Aunt knew the reason: he objected to hiring a widow. But at the same time she also noted that Sister Xianglin looked quite presentable, seemed sound of limb, and what was more, kept her eyes submissively averted and said nothing at all—very much the hardworking servant who knows her place. And so it was that despite Fourth Uncle's frown, Fourth Aunt decided to give her a try.

During this trial period, from one end of the day to the other, Sister Xianglin worked so hard that one would have thought being unoccupied depressed her. Moreover, she was quite strong, easily a match for any man. And so on the third day things were finally settled: Sister

Xianglin would be taken on as the new maid at five hundred coppers a month.

Everybody called her Sister Xianglin. No one asked her family name, but since the go-between was from Wei Family Hill and had said that Xianglin lived close to her mother's place, it is safe to assume that Sister Xianglin's name was Wei too. She did not like to talk much; when people asked questions of her she would speak, but even then she did not volunteer very much.

Back where she had come from, she had had a very strict mother-in-law, and a brother-in-law who was only ten, just big enough to gather firewood. She had lost her husband back in the spring. Ten years younger than she, he had been a fuel gatherer too. Bit by bit this came out over a period of two weeks or so. That was all anyone knew of her.

The days passed quickly, but Sister Xianglin's pace slackened not one whit. She was very fussy about her work, to which she gave her all, but was not in the least particular about the food she ate. People began saying that over at Fourth Old Master Lu's place they had hired a maid who was more capable than a hardworking man.

And when the end of the year came, she single-handedly cleaned the entire house, straightened up the yard, killed the geese and chickens, and worked straight through the night to prepare the ritual offering that would assure the Lu household of blessings in the year to come. That New Year, Fourth Uncle was actually able to get by without hiring any part-time help at all. Despite all these demands on her energies, Sister Xianglin seemed quite contented. Traces of a smile began to appear at the corners of her mouth, and her face began to fill out as well.

Just after the New Year, she came back from washing rice down by the river one day with all the color drained from her face. She said that she had seen a man skulking around off in the distance on the opposite bank, a man who looked a lot like an elder cousin of her husband. She was afraid he might well be looking for her. Fourth Aunt was a bit suspicious, but when she tried to get to the bottom of things, Sister Xianglin immediately clammed up. When Fourth Uncle heard about it, he frowned and said: "Doesn't look good. She's probably a runaway." Before long, Fourth Uncle's conjecture was confirmed.

A few weeks later, just as everyone was gradually beginning to forget the incident, Old Lady Wei suddenly reappeared. She had in tow a woman who looked to be somewhere in her thirties. This, she announced, was Sister Xianglin's mother-in-law.

Although the woman looked like a hillbilly, she had a certain natural poise and was a good talker as well. After the usual formalities, she apologized for the intrusion and announced she had come to fetch her daughter-in-law back. She pointed out that it was now Beginning-of-Spring, a busy season for farmers. Since everyone back home was either too young or too old, they were shorthanded and in sore need of Sister Xianglin.

"Since it's her mother-in-law who wants her to go back, what can we say?" opined Fourth Uncle.

Sister Xianglin's wages were totaled up: one thousand seven hundred and fifty coins. When she first started to work, she had told Fourth Aunt to keep the money for her and had not touched any of it. Now the entire amount was handed over to her mother-in-law, who also took care to gather up all of Sister Xianglin's clothes. By the time the mother-in-law had thanked everyone and gone on her way, it was already noon.

It was not until some time after they had left that Fourth Aunt cried out in alarm: "The rice! Wasn't Sister Xianglin preparing the meal?" Fourth Aunt was probably a little hungry by then and had remembered the lunch. Thereupon she and Fourth Uncle went to look for the rice basket. She tried the kitchen first, then the hall, and finally Sister Xianglin's bedroom— no trace anywhere. Fourth Uncle went outside to look, but didn't see it anywhere out there either. It was not until he had gone all the way down to the river that he caught sight of the rice basket, neatly placed on the bank, a head of cabbage still beside it.

According to some people who saw what happened, a white-canopied boat had moored on the river that morning, the canopy closed tightly all the way around so that no one could tell what was inside. At the time nobody had taken any particular notice of it anyway. But then later on, when Sister Xianglin had come down to wash the rice, two men had jumped out just as she was about to kneel down on the riverbank. One of them had grabbed her in his arms and, with the help of the other, dragged her into the boat. Sister Xianglin had screamed a few times, but afterward there was no sound at all. They had probably gagged her. Soon after that, two women emerged from the boat. One of them was Old Lady Wei. No one had recognized the other. A few villagers had tried peeking through the canopy, but it was so dark inside they weren't able to see very clearly. They had, however, made out Sister Xianglin's form lying on the floor, all tied up.

"Despicable! But still . . ." said Fourth Uncle.

Fourth Aunt had to boil the luncheon rice herself that day. Her son, Ah-niu, made the fire. After lunch, Old Lady Wei came back again.

"Despicable!" said Fourth Uncle to her.

"What in the world do you think you're doing? You've got your nerve coming here again," said Fourth Aunt angrily as she washed the rice bowls. "You were the one who brought her here to us, and then you turn around and join up with those people to come and snatch her away! And what about all the commotion you kicked up in the neighborhood while you were doing it? What are you trying to do, make a laughingstock of our family?"

"Aiya . . . aiya, I was really taken in. I made a point of gettin' back to you today to get this cleared up. Okay then, Sister Xianglin comes to me lookin' for a place. Now how was I to know that it was behind her mother-in-law's back? Let me tell you, Fourth Old Master and the Missus, I'm just as sorry as I can be. All said and done, I slipped up and wasn't as careful as I should've been. Now I've gone and done wrong by two of the best clients I've got. Lucky for me that you've always been bighearted, understandin' folks, not the kind to get picky with ordinary folks like me. Well, never you mind. I'll get you a *really* good maid this time to make up for it. . . ."

"But still . . ." said Fourth Uncle.

And thus ended the Sister Xianglin affair. Before long, she was entirely forgotten.

Only Fourth Aunt ever mentioned her again, and that was only because she was not happy with any of the maids she hired afterward. Most were either lazy or the kind who would try to eat you out of house and home—and some were both. When exasperated with one of them over this or that, she would often say to herself: "I wonder how she's doing now?" What she really meant was that she hoped Sister Xianglin would somehow come back. By Newstep of the following year, however, she had given up all hopes of that.[14]

Toward the end of Newstep a comfortably tipsy Old Lady Wei showed up at Fourth Uncle's place to wish everyone a belated Happy New Year. She said she had gone back to Wei Family Hill to spend a few days with her parents, and this was why she was late in coming to pay her respects. In the course of the conversation, of course, the subject of Sister Xianglin came up.

"Sister Xianglin?" began Old Lady Wei expansively. "Her turn for good luck's rolled round again. Long before that mother-in-law of hers ever came over here to snatch her away, she'd fixed it up to marry her off to the sixth son of the He family over in He Family Hollow."

"Aiya! What kind of mother-in-law would *do* a thing like that?" asked Fourth Aunt in shock.

"Would you listen to that! Dear, dear lady, you really *do* sound like a rich-family wife! Up there in the hills, for poor families like us, it's no big deal. Sister Xianglin had a younger brother-in-law up there, you know. Well, he needed a wife too, right? If they hadn't married Sister Xianglin off, where would they have come up with the money to get him a bride? That mother-in-law of hers is one sharp cookie. A real planner too, that one. That's how come she married Sister Xianglin off to somebody way back in the hills. Now if she'd sold her to somebody right there in the village, how much money would *that* bring? But you're not gonna find too many girls willin' to marry way back into the hills. That's why she came out of the deal with eighty strings of cash in hand! Just think, the wife she got for her younger son only cost her fifty Take out the cost of the weddin' and stuff, and she still had more'n ten strings to the good. Now that's what I'd call plannin', wouldn't you?"

"And did Sister Xianglin actually go along with it?"

"What's that got to do with it? Fuss? Sure, anybody'd put up some sort of fuss. But in the end they just get hog-tied, stuffed into a bridal chair, and carted off to the man's house.[15] As a rule, all you've gotta do then is slap on a weddin' cap, force 'em through the ceremony, then lock 'em up in a room with the new man, and that's that.

"But Sister Xianglin was somethin' else—kicked up a rumpus the likes of which nobody'd ever seen. Folks said it was more than likely 'cause she'd worked in a family that had book learnin' and wasn't just your run-of-the-mill widow bein' remarried. Let me tell you, Missus, us go-betweens have seen a lotta this kind of stuff. When second-timers marry, some'll scream and holler; some'll try to do themselves in; some'll raise such a ruckus after they get to the groom's place that you can't even get 'em through the ceremony; you'll even find some who'll bust up the weddin' candies.

"But Sister Xianglin topped 'em all. Hear tell she wailed and cursed every step of the way. By the time they got her there, she'd shouted herself so hoarse she couldn't even talk. They had to drag her out of the bridal chair. But even with two strong men and her brother-in-law thrown in, all holdin' on to her for all they were worth, they *still* couldn't get her through the ceremony. Then when they let their guard down for just a split second—Aiya, may Buddha preserve us!—before anyone knew what was up, she slammed her head on the corner of the incense table. Made a hole so big the blood just gushed out. They slapped a couple handfuls of incense ash on the hole and wrapped her head in some red cloth. But even with all that they still couldn't stop the blood. Clear up to the time when they got her—and they had everybody fallin' over everybody else tryin' to do it—got her and the groom into the bride-room and locked it from the outside, she kept cursin' for all she was worth. Aiya! That was really, really. . . ." She shook her head, looked down, and stopped there.

"And then what happened?" Fourth Aunt went on with her questions.

"The way I heard it, she didn't get up the next day," answered Old Lady Wei, raising her eyes.

"And then?"

"Then? Well, then she got up. Toward the end of the year she had a kid, a boy. He was two this New Year's.[16] Past few days when I was at my folks' house, someone went out to He Family Hollow and saw the two of 'em. The kid was nice and chubby and the mom was all filled out too. Better yet, now she's got no mother-in-law over her. She's got a good strong man who knows how to work, and the house is theirs free and clear. Her turn for good luck has rolled around again for sure!"

After that, Fourth Aunt never mentioned Sister Xianglin again.

But one year in the fall—it must have been a New Year or so after Sister Xianglin's "turn for good luck rolled round again"—to everyone's complete surprise, there she stood once again in the main hall of Fourth Uncle's house. Her bamboo basket, shaped like a water chestnut, lay on the table, and her small bedroll was under the eaves outside. She was much the same as she had been the first time: hair tied back with a piece of white wool; black skirt and blue lined jacket with long sleeves; and sleeveless vest of light blue. But her cheeks had lost the slightly rosy touch that had once relieved her general pallor. She kept her eyes averted; the spirited gleam that once had lit them was now gone, and traces of tears showed in their corners. Just as the first time, too, it was Old Lady Wei who led her in. Assuming an exaggerated air of compassion, the old woman prattled on and on.

"*Like a bolt out of the blue*—there really is somethin' to those words. That man of hers was a husky young guy. Who would've ever expected a young horse like that would lose his life to typhoid. As a matter of fact, he *did* get over it, but then later on he went and ate a bowl of cold rice, and it came onto 'im again. Luckily he left a son behind and Sister Xianglin's someone who knows how to put in a good day's work. Gatherin' firewood, pickin' tea, raisin' silkworms—no problem. She should've been able to hold things together. Who would've even thought that with spring almost over there'd still be wolves comin' round the village. Well, with no rhyme or reason one *did* come along, and dragged her son right off.

"Now she's got nothin' left but herself. Her brother-in-law came and took the house back. Drove Sister Xianglin out.[17] She's really at the end of her rope now. Nothin' left for it but to come here and see if her old employers can help out. The good part is that she's got nothin' to tie her down now. As luck would have it, the Missus is lookin' for a maid right now, and so I decided to bring her over. I thought since Sister Xianglin knows her way around the place, it'd be much better for the Missus to get her back than to have to break in someone new. . . .

"I was real dumb, real dumb," began Sister Xianglin as she raised her expressionless eyes. "All I knew was that when it snows and the wild animals can't find anything to eat up there in the hills, sometimes they'll come into the villages. But I didn't know they could show up in springtime, too. I got up bright and early, opened the door, filled a little basket with beans, and told our Ah-mao to go outside, sit by the door, and shell 'em. He always minded, did everything I told him. Well, he went out and I went to the back of the room to split firewood and wash the rice. I put the rice in the pot and was gettin' ready to steam the beans on top. 'Ah-mao!' No answer. I went out and all I saw was beans scattered all over the ground, but our Ah-mao was nowhere to be seen.

"Now it wasn't like him to go and play at other kids' houses, but I asked all over anyway. Sure enough, nobody'd seen him. That's when I got good and worried, begged folks to go out and make a search. Right down till the bottom half of the day, they looked everywhere. Finally, they came to a holler and found one of his little shoes hangin' on some brambles. They thought he was a goner then for sure, that most likely he'd met up with a wolf. They kept on goin' and sure enough, there he was, lyin' in the den of a wolf. His belly was open and his insides all eaten out. Still had that little basket clutched tight in his hand." She kept on talking, but now she was sobbing so that she could no longer get an entire sentence out.

At first, Fourth Aunt had been somewhat hesitant, but after hearing out Sister Xianglin's own telling of what had happened, she too became a bit red-eyed. She thought for a moment and then told Sister Xianglin to take her blanket and bedroll to the servant's room. As though just relieved of a heavy burden, Old Lady Wei heaved a sigh of relief. Sister Xianglin also looked more relaxed than when they had first arrived. Without waiting to be shown the way, she took the basket and bedding to her room, and once again Sister Xianglin worked as a maid in Lu Town.

To be sure, the family still called her Sister Xianglin, just as they had before, but her situation was far different this time. She had not been back more than a few days or so when her employers noticed that she was not so quick on her feet as she had once been and that her memory had gone downhill too. Furthermore, from one end of the day to the other, there was never so much as the trace of a smile on her corpselike face. When talking to her now, Fourth Aunt revealed considerable dissatisfaction in her tone of voice.

When she first came back, Fourth Uncle frowned as might well have been expected, but in view of the difficulties he and his wife had endured in finding a good replacement, he did not seriously oppose her return. However, he did warn Fourth Aunt privately: "People like her may seem quite pitiable, to be sure, but one must remember that they do have a deleterious influence on the morals of society.[18] While it may be permissible to let her help out with the housework, she must have absolutely nothing to do with the family sacrifices. You will have to prepare all the sacrificial offerings yourself; otherwise they will be tainted and our ancestors will not accept them."

In Fourth Uncle's house, the family sacrifices had always been the most important event of the year by far, and always in the past Sister Xianglin had been busiest during the period when they were conducted. This year, however, she had not been given a thing to do. Of her own volition, she took a table and placed it in the center of the room, tied the tableskirt around the edge, and even remembered to arrange the chopsticks and wine cups just as she had done before.

"Sister Xianglin, *leave those alone!* I'll set the table!" Fourth Aunt cried out in alarm. Completely at a loss, Sister Xianglin drew her hands back, and then went to fetch the candlesticks.

"Sister Xianglin, *put those down!* I'll get them." Again the tone of voice was one of alarm.

Aimlessly she walked around the room for a bit, but since there was nothing for her to do, she finally walked out the door in a state of utter bewilderment. The only thing she was allowed to do during this entire day was to sit by the stove and tend the fire.

The people in the village still talked with her and called her Sister Xianglin, just as they had before, but their tone of voice had changed and the smiles on their faces had turned cold. When she met up with them, she paid no heed to any of this but simply stared off into space and recited that same story, which she could not put out of mind either by day or by night.

"I was real dumb, real dumb. All I knew was that when it snows and the wild animals can't find anything to eat up there in the hills, sometimes they'll come into the villages. But I didn't know they could show up in springtime, too. I got up bright and early, opened the door, filled a bamboo basket with beans, and told our Ah-mao to go outside, sit by the door, and shell 'em. He always minded, did everything I told him. Well, he went out and I went to the back of the room to split the firewood and wash the rice. I put the rice in the pot and was gettin' reedy to steam the beans on top.

"I yelled, 'Ah-mao!' No answer. I went out and all I saw was beans scattered all over the ground, but our Ah-mao was nowhere around. Then I got really worried. I begged people to go out and make a search. By the bottom half of the day, some of 'em came to a holler and found one of his little shoes hangin' on some brambles. They thought he was a goner then for sure, that most likely he'd met up with a wolf. They kept on goin' and sure enough, there he was, lyin' in the den of a wolf. His belly was open and his insides all eaten out. Still had that little basket clutched tight in his hand." At this point tears would be streaming down her face and her voice broken with sobs.

Her story was actually quite effective, for by the time she got to this point, even the men would put aside their smiles and wander off in embarrassed silence, while the women would immediately shed their disdainful looks and, seeming to forgive her somewhat, would join their tears with hers.

The few old ladies who had not heard Sister Xianglin tell her sad tale in the streets and alleyways would make a special point of running her down so that they, too, might have a chance to hear her heart-rending recitation. When Sister Xianglin reached the point where she began to sob, they too would release tears that had been welling up in the corners of their eyes, sigh for a bit, and then walk away, contentedly evaluating the details of her story in a great flurry of chatter.

Sister Xianglin told her tragic tale over and over again. Before long, everyone in town knew it down to the finest detail. Even in the eyes of the most pious old Buddhist ladies, not so much as the trace of a tear was anymore to be seen. Later on, it even got to the point where everyone could recite it word for word. And so it was that people eventually grew so sick of hearing her story that their heads ached at the mere mention of it.

"I was real dumb, real dumb," she would begin.

"Right, all you knew is that when it snows and the wild animals can't find anything to eat up there in the hills, they'll come to the village." They would cut her off immediately and get away as quickly as possible.

Stunned, she would stand there, mouth agape, and stare after their retreating forms. And then she would walk away as though she too felt there wasn't any point to it. And yet, against all reason, she still wanted to tell people the story of her Ah-mao. She began searching out opportunities to bring it up: whenever anyone mentioned a small basket, or beans, or someone's child, she would try to fit her story into the conversation. Whenever she saw a two- or three-year-old, she would look at the child and say, "Oh, if only our Ah-mao was still alive, he'd be just about that big too. . . ." The child, in turn, would usually be frightened by the look in her eyes, grab its mother's clothing, and pull her away. At this point, Sister Xianglin would again be left standing alone, and finally she too would sense the awkwardness of the situation and wander away.

After a while, everyone became aware of this quirk of hers, and whenever there was a child in the immediate vicinity, someone would look at her with a smile that was not really a smile and ask, "Sister Xianglin, if your Ah-mao was still livin' he'd be just about that big too, wouldn't he?" By now everyone had long since chewed and savored the taste of her tragedy, had long since worked it into pulp, flavorless and ready to be spit out. She may not have been aware of this herself, but she did sense something cold and sharp in their smiles and knew there was no point in speaking. She would simply glance at them, but utter not one word in reply.

Lu Town had always celebrated the New Year, and this year was no exception. Things began to pick up after the twentieth day of the twelfth lunar month. But this year, even after they had taken on a temporary male servant, there was still too much to do at Fourth Uncle's place and too little time to do it in. And so it was that Mother Liu was hired to lend a helping hand. As a pious Buddhist who kept to a vegetarian diet, however, she believed in preserving life and refused to butcher the chickens and geese. She was willing to help only with the washing of the sacrificial utensils. At this, the busiest time of the year, not being allowed to do anything except tend the fire, Sister Xianglin found herself almost completely idle.

And so it was that she was sitting by the stove one day, watching Mother Liu work. A light snow was beginning to fall. As though talking to herself, she sighed and said, "I was real dumb, real dumb. . . ."

"There you go again, Sister Xianglin," said Mother Liu, looking at her impatiently. "Okay, then, let me put it to you this way. Wasn't it at that second weddin' that you bashed in your head and got yourself that scar there?"

"Uh, uh. . . ." Sister Xianglin became evasive.

"Okay, then let me try another one on you. Since you went to all that trouble, how come you finally gave in?"

"Who, me?"

"Yeah, you. I think way down deep you must'a wanted to, or else—"

"Now wait just a minute, you don't know how strong he was."

"Don't believe a word of it. I just can't see how a woman as strong as you are couldn't hold him off if you wanted to. Down deep you *wanted* to give in, and then you turn around and lay it on his bein' strong."

"Well, I'd . . . I'd just like to see you try and hold him off." Sister Xianglin smiled.

Mother Liu roared with laughter, making the corners of her mouth go back so far that her deep wrinkles shrunk together and transformed her face into a walnut. Her wizened little eyes glanced at the scar and then fixed Sister Xianglin with such a stare that she became quite ill at ease, stopped smiling, turned away, and gazed at the snow.

"Sister Xianglin, you really came out on the short end of the stick on that one," said Mother Liu enigmatically. "If you'd only put up more of a fight, or just bashed your brains out and been done with it, you'd have been all right. But now? Without even gettin' to spend two years with that second man, you've ended up committin' a big sin. Just think, later on when you die and go to the underworld, the ghosts of those two men are gonna fight over you. Which one will you give yourself to then? Yama, Great King of the Underworld, will have only one choice—saw you in half and give each of 'em his piece. The way I see it, you've really gotta . . . well, I think you've gotta find some way of guardin' against that as soon as you can. Why not go to the temple and donate money for a doorsill. Then that doorsill will be your body. Thousands'll step on it and tens of thousands'll walk over it. That way you'll make up for all your sins and you won't have to suffer after you die."

At the time, Sister Xianglin said nothing in reply, but in all likelihood she was extremely depressed, for the dark circles around her eyes when she got up the next morning bespoke a sleepless night. After breakfast, she made her way to the temple at the west end of town and asked if she could donate a doorsill. At first, the priest in charge was adamant in his refusal. It was only when Sister Xianglin became emotional and was on the verge of tears that he reluctantly agreed. The price was set at twelve strings of cash, a thousand to the string.

Since everybody had long since become bored with the story of Ah-mao, she had not been able to find anyone to talk to in a long time. But now, once word of her conversation with Mother Liu spread abroad, people began to take new interest. Once again, they would stop her on the street and inveigle her into a chat. Now of course, in view of the new wrinkle that had been added, people's interest focused entirely on the scar.

"Sister Xianglin, how come you finally gave in?" one of them would ask.

"What a shame you had to bash your head in for nothin'," another would chime in while staring at her scar.

Aware of their smiles and tone of voice, she probably realized they were making fun of her, and so she would just stare at them without saying a word. Later on, she got so that she would not even turn her head when people called her.

Bearing that scar, which everyone now considered a mark of shame, tight-lipped and silent from morning to night, Sister Xianglin ran the errands, swept the floor, prepared the vegetables, and washed the rice. It was not until a year was almost out that she took from the hands of

Fourth Aunt all the wages she had let accumulate and exchanged them for twelve Mexican silver dollars. She asked for time off to go to the west end of town. Then, well within the space of time it takes to eat a meal, she was back. She appeared relaxed and happy, and there was even an unaccustomed spark of life in her gaze. She seemed in very high spirits as she told Fourth Aunt how she had just donated a doorsill at the Earth God's temple.

When the winter solstice came and it was time to carry out the ancestral sacrifices, she became particularly energetic. Seeing that Fourth Aunt had already set out the sacrificial foods, Sister Xianglin got Ah-niu to help her move the table to the center of the hall. Then, with complete self-assurance, she went to get the wine cups and the chopsticks.

"Sister Xianglin, *leave those alone!*" shouted Fourth Aunt frantically.

Sister Xianglin jerked back her hand as though it had been scorched. Her face began to darken. Nor did she go and fetch the candlesticks. She just stood there, utterly lost. It was only when Fourth Uncle came with the incense and told her to get out of the way that she finally left the room. The change in her this time was immense. The next day there were again deep circles around her eyes and she was more listless than she had ever been before. What was more, she became very timid: she was afraid of the night; she was afraid of dark shadows; she was afraid of people, even her own employers. In everything she did, she was as skittish as a mouse away from its nest in daylight. Often she would just sit motionless and blank, lifeless as a wood-carved doll. Before half a year was out, her hair began to turn gray and her memory slipped dramatically, even to the point where she often forgot to wash the rice.

Sometimes, with Sister Xianglin right there in the room, Fourth Aunt would say, as though issuing a warning: "Wonder what's come over Sister Xianglin? It really would have been better not to keep her when Old Lady Wei brought her back."

But such warnings had no effect. She stayed the same, and it was painfully obvious that there was no hope she would ever again become the alert and nimble Sister Xianglin of old. They thought of getting rid of her at this point, of sending her back to Old Lady Wei, but while I was still in Lu Town, at any rate, this remained just talk. Looking back, though, it is apparent that they must have let her go sometime later on.

But was it right after leaving Fourth Uncle's place that she became a beggar, or had she gone back to Old Lady Wei first? There was no way to tell.

Startled into wakefulness by the loud roar of fireworks going off close by, I focused my eyes on a yellow patch of light the size of a human head—the glow of the oil lamp. I heard the sharp and rapid pow-pow *pow-pow-pow* of entire strings being set off. Fourth Uncle's family was indeed in the midst of celebrating the New Year and I realized it must have been close to the Fifth Watch. In my drowsiness I was also vaguely aware of the faint but continuous sounds of various other kinds of explosions going off all around me in the distance, sounds that wove together into a skyful of dense and resounding clouds. Thickened by flakes of snow, they held all of Lu Town in their enfolding arms. Wrapped in this comforting symphonic embrace, I too was filled with a deep sense of well-being and felt wholly free of worldly cares. All the worries and concerns that had plagued me from morning till night the day before had been totally swept away by the happy atmosphere of the New Year. I was conscious of nothing except that the various gods' of heaven and earth were enjoying the ritual offerings and all the incense that burned in their honor. Comfortably tipsy by now, they staggered through the sky and prepared to shower the people of Lu Town with infinite blessings.

Notes

1. Toward the end of the twelfth lunar month, the kitchen god of each household, King Stove (Zao Wang), ascended to heaven and reported the doings of the family to the Jade Emperor. A paper image of the god was burned (the ascension), and he was given a royal firecracker farewell to ensure that he would have nothing but good news to report about the family.

2. "Imperial Collegian" (*jiansheng*) might refer to someone actually placed in the Imperial College (*guozijian*) at Beijing, or to someone, like Fourth Uncle, who had been proclaimed "qualified" to be there. The title could either be earned through examination or bought. Neo-Confucianism is the school of Confucianism, somewhat puritanical and heavily influenced by Buddhist metaphysics, which dominated scholar-official circles in China from 1313 onward, the year when it was declared the orthodox ideology for interpretation of the classics in the civil service examinations. Its authority went virtually unchallenged until 1905, when the examination system was officially abolished.

3. Kang Youwei (1858–1927) was among those reformers at the turn of the century who sought to modernize China while retaining the Imperial government. At

the time this story is set (somewhere between 1919 and 1924), people of the narrator's age and educational background would have considered Kang Youwei outdated and reactionary.

4. *Zhufu*, the ceremony described in this story, was unique to the area around Lu Xun's native Shaoxing.

5. A historical figure of the Five Dynasties period (907–959) who lived as a mountain recluse and, according to the tradition, became a Daoist Immortal.

6. An important neo-Confucian concept divided the universe into form or principle (*li*), and substance (*qi*). Contemplation of "forms" led to serenity (the influence of Buddhist meditation is apparent) and would eventually result in enlightenment. The narrator, we should remember, views these ideas as outmoded claptrap.

7. The dictionary was compiled under the reign of the Kang Xi emperor (1661–1722), hence its name. *Reflections on Things at Hand* (Jinsilu) is a collection of writings by four neo-Confucians of the Northern Song (960–1126); it has been translated into English by Wing-tsit Chan (New York: Columbia University Press, 1967). *A Lining to the Garment of the "Four Books"* is a Qing Dynasty (1644–1911) commentary on the *Four Books of Neo-Confucianism: The Analects of Confucius, The Mencius, The Great Learning,* and *The Doctrine of the Mean.*

8. "Sister" (*sao*) is a polite term of address for married women.

9. This reflects charges that were leveled at Lu Xun himself, who, at the time he wrote this story, was working in the Ministry of Education and teaching part-time as well.

10. "Clear broth" means there is no soy sauce in the recipe.

11. It would be unlucky to pronounce a word meaning "die" during the New Year period, hence the circumlocution.

12. The two powers are *yin* and *yang* (the female and male principles in nature); the quotation is from *Reflections on Things at Hand*, the work whose commentary lies on Fourth Uncle's desk (see note 7).

13. Wuchang (the name means literally "nothing is permanent") was a deity who, despite a rollicking sense of humor, played the role of grim reaper. A local Shaoxing saying went: "When you see Wuchang arrive, you'll not be long alive" (*Wuchang yidao xingming nantao*). Lu Xun devoted a reminiscence to Wuchang and even included some of his own sketches of him. This is included in *Zhaohua xishi* (Dawn Blossoms Plucked at Dusk). A translation appears in *Selected Works of Lu Hsun* (4 vols.), vol. I, pp. 377–386. Translated by Yang Hsien-yi and Gladys Yang. Peking: Foreign Languages Press, 1956–1960.

14. New step (*xinzheng*) is the period that includes the first fifteen days of the lunar year.

15. A bride would be sent to her new home in a sedan chair supported between long poles that were carried on the shoulders of two bearers.

16. His age would be counted as "one" immediately at birth and "two" at the following New Year.

17. Sister Xianglin was not driven out as long as her son, a blood heir to her dead husband's family, was still alive.

18. Fourth Uncle is a hidebound traditionalist: a widow would be bad enough, but a remarried widow is simply beyond the pale of decency.

13
My Marriage

Ye Shengtao (October 29, 1930)

This is part of an essay originally published in *Magazine for Middle School Students*, October 29, 1930.

I had never met my wife and had not even written a letter to her before the wedding, because ours was an arranged marriage. Fortunately, we fell in love with each other after marriage. My wife and I were both teachers; although separated, we managed to write to each other often—writing letters and waiting for replies became our two passions. Now we have been married for fourteen-odd years, and we are still in love. It would be hard for us to say what we see in each other; we only know that we are a compatible couple and it is hard to imagine another couple more compatible than we are.

Of course, a marriage like ours is like a risky lottery game. That my wife and I happen to be such a happy couple is a blessed accident. As superstition would have it, ours was indeed a marriage arranged by the Old Man in the Moon at the White Cloud Temple by the West Lake.[1] I feel most fortunate that I never had to suffer from insomnia in the pursuit of a wife and that I never had to go through what most courting couples go through, be it joy or pain. Of course, it is still hard for me to say whether it is worth it for everyone to risk partaking in a lottery-like marriage just because it turned out that I was extremely lucky. But, in this case, a great deal of time and energy had been indeed saved for doing other things during my youth.

It is absolutely understandable that nowadays people would not bother to risk partaking in such a lottery-like marriage. Premarital love has become a commonly accepted norm. Of course, I have no intention of challenging this norm. Its popularity is widely accepted, after all. Here, I would only like to make some comments on those who believe in love above all else. When they are pleased and happy, they indulge in lovey-dovey talks, write love letters and poems to each other, and go to films and scenic spots. But, when displeased or dissatisfied, they go crazy, cry their hearts out, and again resort to writing poems (that are full of exclamation marks), claiming that they are the most miserable people in the world. Some would even go so far as to jump into the Huangpu River. To me, it is rather sad that one would give up one's entire life for love. This kind of love is a privilege belonging to the children of the rich and famous alone. Born "with a silver spoon in their mouth," these young men and women spend the filthy money of their wealthy parents or ancestors and enjoy the high social status that was prepared for them even before they were born. To them, this world of ours is full of peace and prosperity and free from any social problems. When one is placed in such a leisurely and carefree position, one inevitably engages in the game of love and contrives some joys and pains to fulfil one's otherwise blank and boring life. But if young people who are not endowed with such a mixed blessing want to follow suit, they will only hinder their own progress and weaken themselves.

Love exists as long as life exists, but there are many kinds of love in life. Down with the love of those playboys and playgirls!

Note

1. The legend goes: All good marriages are arranged by Yuexia Laoren. Yuexia Laoren ("The Old Man in the Moon") is a mythological figure who is supposed to tie a couple's feet with his "red string"—akin to "Cupid's bow" in Roman mythology—for a happy marriage (*Dictionary of Classical Allusions*, p. 211).

Part Two

The New Women Martyrs

Editors' Introduction

Biographies of women martyrs were a widespread genre in late Imperial China. These biographies—the object of Lu Xun's derision in "My Thoughts on Chastity" (essay 2)—generally extolled the virtues of women who committed suicide to preserve their chastity when threatened with rape or widow remarriage. They were honored by gazetteers and officials as exemplars who gave their lives to uphold dominant, patriarchal values. In the May Fourth era, however, activists adapted the "woman martyr" genre to honor women who gave their lives for very different values. As they sought to mold particular tragedies into symbols of social problems and solutions, these activists created a new kind of woman martyr: the young woman who seeks emancipation but encounters pressures (usually related to marriage) that lead to her death.

This section presents a sample of the heated discussions that followed the deaths of Li Chao, Miss Zhao (Zhao Wuzhen), Xi Shangzhen, Liu Hezhen, and Yang Dequn, all of whom died on the path of the "New Woman." Miss Zhao resorted to suicide as a means of resisting marriage. The motives behind Miss Xi Shangzhen's suicide were less clear, but they had to do with outrage at her boss's mismanagement of her money and his demand that she be his concubine. Li Chao died of tuberculosis, but, according to Hu Shi, her ultimate cause of death was the social, emotional, and economic pressures placed on her by her family, pressures that weakened her to the point where she succumbed to the illness. In telling her story, Hu Shi also mentions another woman—Chen Wenhong, the sympathetic wife of Li Chao's stingy brother—who attempted suicide after conflicts with her husband that were partly due to disagreement over what to do about Li Chao. Liu Hezhen and Yang Dequn were killed by soldiers while participating in a demonstration.[1]

Chinese history and literature are replete with instances of suicide as the last and often the only resort of women in unbearable circumstances (Brown 1997; Rosenblum 1992; Witke 1967; Wolf 1975; Yap 1958). The essay by Ida Kahn (essay 37 in this collection) mentions numerous women who slit their throat but were nursed back to health by Christian doctors. For many women, suicide was not only a means of escape but also a means to take revenge on their oppressors by bringing them social disgrace and supernatural misfortune. Indeed, Miss Zhao's suicide succeeded in bringing social disgrace and financial catastrophe to both her natal family and the family of the man to whom she was betrothed (Gilmartin 1995, 26–27). Xi Shangzhen's suicide also managed to cast suspicion on her boss and presumed oppressor, though he seemed to have more defenders than Miss Zhao's oppressors did. The deaths of Liu Hezhen and Yang Dequn served to intensify outrage at the warlord regime responsible, though they also served as a warning that demonstrators would not be spared, even if they were female. The death of Li Chao is rendered heroic primarily by Hu Shi's powerful biography; without his persuasive attribution of her death to family pressures and the social injustices underlying them, she may have been counted as just another random case of tuberculosis.

Despite the differences in the circumstances of their deaths, the new women martyrs were portrayed with certain common themes. Those who eulogized them emphasized that they represented far larger numbers of women in a similar plight, that a terribly flawed social system was at fault for their deaths, and that the correction of these flaws was necessary to prevent further such deaths. The new women martyrs were particularly useful as symbols because they could no longer speak for themselves or their motives, and public knowledge about the facts of each case was limited to a few sensational details, leaving the rest for the activist to construe in accordance with his or her particular agenda. The essays in this section provide an important glimpse at the link between the ideas advocated by these activists and the harsh realities that inspired them. They also demonstrate the perils that awaited many women who followed the path to emancipation so boldly advocated in essays like those that appear in this book. They serve now, as they served then, as dramatic illustrations of the daily obstacles faced by women who sought emancipation in the May Fourth era.

Note

1. Liu Hezhen and Yang Dequn were killed by warlord Duan Qirui's soldiers in Beijing when they, along with others from Beijing Normal Women's College, participated in a six-thousand-person demonstration against the Chinese warlord regimes' failure to resist the foreign powers' Taku Ultimatum. The soldiers killed forty-seven protesters, including six women, in what became known as the March Eighteenth Incident (Gilmartin 1995, 146).

14
The Question of Miss Zhao's Personality

Mao Zedong (November 18, 1919)

First published in *Public Interest*

The day before yesterday, I wrote a commentary in which I said that the cause of Miss Zhao's death was entirely determined by her circumstances, that is, by the society in which she lived and by the two families, those of her own parents and of her fiancé. Consequently, I would like to say a few words about the personality of Miss Zhao.

Someone asked me whether Miss Zhao had a personality or not. I said that I had two replies, one, that Miss Zhao did not have a personality of her own; the other, that she did have a personality.

What did I mean by saying that Miss Zhao did not have a personality? If Miss Zhao had had a personality, she would not have died. Why not? Having a personality requires respect from those one deals with. Its prerequisite is freedom of the will. Was Miss Zhao's will free? No, it was not free. Why wasn't it free? Because Miss Zhao had parents. In the West, the free will of children is not affected by the parents. In the Western family organization, father and mother recognize the free will of their sons and daughters. Not so in China. The commands of the parent and the will of the child are not at all on an equal footing. The parents of Miss Zhao very clearly forced her to love someone she did not want to love. No freedom of will was recognized at all. If you do not want to love me, but I force my love on you, that is a form of rape. This is called "direct rape." Their daughter did not want to love that person, but they forced their daughter to love that person. This, too, is a kind of rape, which is called "indirect rape." Chinese parents all indirectly rape their sons and daughters. This is the conclusion that inevitably arises under the Chinese family system of "parental authority" and the marriage system in which there is the "policy of parental arrangement." For Miss Zhao to have had a personality of her own she would have had to have a free will. For her to have a free will, her parents would have had to respect her and accede to her wishes. If Miss Zhao's parents had respected her, had acceded to her wishes, would she have been put into that cagelike bridal sedan chair in which she finally committed suicide? But it is now a fact that this happened. Thus, my first reply is that Miss Zhao did not have a personality of her own.

Why do I also say that she did have a personality? This is with reference to Miss Zhao herself. Although Miss Zhao lived for twenty-one years in a family that did not allow her to have a personality, and for twenty-one years her father and mother kept her from having a personality, in that last brief moment of her twenty-one years, her personality suddenly came forth. Alas, alas, death is preferable to the absence of freedom. The snow-white knife was stained with fresh red blood. The dirt road of Orange Garden Street, splashed with blood, was transformed into a solemn highway to heaven. And with this, Miss Zhao's personality also gushed forth suddenly, shining bright and luminous. Consequently, my second reply is that Miss Zhao did indeed have a personality of her own. Thus, my conscience forces me to utter the following two sentences:

1. All parents who are like the parents of Miss Zhao should be put in prison.
2. May the cry of all humanity fill the heavens, "Long live Miss Zhao!"

15
Concerning the Incident of Miss Zhao's Suicide

Mao Zedong (November 21, 1919)

First published in *Public Interest*.

In recent days there have been many commentaries on the incident of Miss Zhao's suicide, and I too have written a few comments on it that have been published in this city's *Dagong bao*. This is a public event that concerns all mankind, and leaving aside those who advocate extreme individualism and living alone, everyone should pay attention to it and study it. But Chinese women should devote particular attention and study to it. Because for the several thousand years that perverse customs based on the [Confucian] rites have prevailed in China, women have had no status in any area of life. From politics, law, and education, to business, social relations, entertainment, and personal status, women have always been treated very differently from men, and relegated to the dark corners of society. Not only are they denied happiness, they are also subjected to many kinds of inhumane mistreatment. That this incident of a woman being driven to suicide should occur at a time like this, when the truth is very clear and there are loud calls for the liberation of women, shows just how profound are the evils of our nation's society. Today we need not express more pity for the deceased, but rather we should look for a method that will thoroughly correct this problem so that from now on such a tragedy as this will never happen again. But before we look for a method, we must first search for the controlling root causes of this domination.

Let us consider why it is that women have been bullied by men and have not been able to emancipate themselves [fanshen]¹ for thousands of years. Regarding this point, we must examine the question of what, in the last analysis, are the defects of women? Looked at superficially, women have a lower level of knowledge than men, and are weaker willed than men. Women have deep emotional feelings, and when the emotions well up, one's conscious awareness recedes. In this respect, they are psychologically not the equals of men. Also, women are physically somewhat weaker, and to this must be added the suffering and painful difficulty of walking with bound feet. These are the physiological defects of women. Actually, none of these are inherent defects. Generally speaking, the psychological processes of women are not much different from those of men. This has already been proven by the fact that the effects of education in all countries show no differences based on gender. The last two items of physical weakness are the result of custom. The binding of women's feet was not practiced in antiquity and cannot be regarded as a basic biological defect. The search for any inherent biological deficiency in women finally comes down solely to the question of childbearing.

The relationship between men and women should, according to the contemporary view, center on "love," and apart from love, must not be governed by "economics." Thus the contemporary position is, "Each is economically independent, sharing the fruits of love." Before modern times, this was not the case. No one knew of the principle "Love is sacred." In the relationship between men and women, love was considered to be only secondary, while the core relationship remained economic, and was thus controlled by capitalism. In antiquity, eating was a simple affair. People picked fruit and caught wild animals and fish, and were easily satisfied. Men and women were equals, and economically women asked nothing of men and men asked nothing of women. Men and women sought of each other only "love." Thus woman sometimes, on the contrary, used her physiological strengths (physiologists say that in sexual physiology women are stronger than men) to control men. Later, as population increased, and food supplies became inadequate, the competition for survival made it necessary to emphasize work, and with this arrived the terrible age in which women became subjugated to men.

In doing physical labor, women are not inherently inferior to men, but because women cannot work during the period of childbearing, men took advantage of this weakness, exploited this single flaw, made "submission" the condition of exchange, and used "food" to shut them up. This then is the general cause that has kept women subjugated and unable to emancipate themselves. On the one hand, what member of the human race was not born of woman? Childbearing by women is an indispensable element in the survival of humanity. That men should have forgotten this supreme act of benevolence, and on the contrary should have wantonly and unscrupulously oppressed women, merely for the sake of petty economic relationships, is truly a case of resuming evil for good. On the other hand, childbearing is an extremely painful event. "The pangs of childbirth" is a term that frightens every woman who hears it. Despite the medical discoveries that have changed the "difficulty of childbirth" into the "ease of childbirth," we should show great reverence and compassion. How can we instead take advantage of trivial economic benefits to press the other down?

Having presented the "reasons" above, we can now turn to the "methods." The methods by which women can become free and independent and never again be oppressed by men may in general be listed as follows:

1. A woman must never marry before she is physically mature.
2. Before marriage, at the bare minimum, a woman must be adequately prepared in knowledge and skills to live her own life.
3. A woman must prepare herself for living expenses after childbirth.

The above three items are the basic prerequisites for a woman's own personal independence. In addition, there is a further condition of "public child support," to which society should pay close attention. If women themselves are able to fulfill the above three conditions, and if society, for its part, provides for the public rearing of children, then marital relationships centered on love can be established. This will depend on the efforts of all of us young men and women!

Note

1. This is the term used after 1946 to characterize the transformation of the lives of the peasants as a result of land reform, which William Hinton took as the title of his book on the subject.

16
Commentary on Miss Zhao's Suicide

Tao Yi (November 21, 1919)

Originally published in *Women's Bell Special Edition*, no. 1, under the name Si Yong.

No one who has heard about Miss Zhao's suicide can avoid tears and heartache. Her death was too painful. Why would anyone be willing to die, much less die in such an agonizing way, unless she felt there was no other way out? Who would have thought that such a tragedy would be enacted before our eyes today, just when cries for women's emancipation are on the rise? Why was there no place in all the world for this one woman? Why was she forced to her death? What was at the root of this? Alas! Is it not this vile marriage system? This vile marriage system has also smothered countless other young women to death. I refer only to young women because a young man has some room for discussion about the girl his parents betrothed for him. Thus, there were many answers to the *China Times'* question, "What should today's young man do about the woman his parents betrothed for him?" A young man has complete freedom to decide whether to marry his betrothed or break off the betrothal. But a young woman has no freedom to decide anything other than whether to hang herself; she has no possible answer besides the words "I would rather die." No matter how strong she is, she cannot resist those time-honored bright lights of Confucianism and paternal authority. If she tries to resist, she will immediately be slapped with the labels "unchaste" and "unfilial," and there will be nowhere on earth for her to go. Miss Zhao was clearly unwilling at the time the betrothal was made, but her parents did not seek her consent. Afterward, it was not as if her parents did not know that she had expressed her opposition. Indeed, they even knew that she was willing to die rather than go through with the marriage; that was why they searched her for weapons right before she entered the bridal sedan. They clearly knew that she was unwilling; they clearly knew that she would rather die. Alas, this young woman was unwilling from the start, totally unwilling; it was impossible for her to seek a life for herself, so she sought death instead. Even death itself was nearly out of her reach. If her parents went so far as to search her right before she entered the sedan, one can only imagine what the security measures must have been like when she was living at home. Alas!

"What should today's young woman do about the man her parents betrothed for her?" Didn't Mr. Wen Tian raise this "question" in the *China Times* news column and ask for young women to respond? Through her death, Miss Zhao became the first to offer a response to this question. Miss Zhao is dead, but I think there are countless women like her in the world, as well as countless parents like her parents. When faced with the same problem, must death be their only means of resolution? Is there any other way to save them? Must parents hold fast to that kind of "no resistance to tradition will be tolerated" attitude and force their daughters down the path of suicide? Or is there room for discussion? I can only pray and hope every day for a satisfactory answer.

Though we should not say that Miss Zhao died "for love of freedom," we must recognize her as "one who sacrificed herself to reform the marriage system." If she were just a passive person trying to protect her own freedom, then why did she not commit suicide at the time she hid the knife, or while she rode in the sedan with her family to her sister's home? Why did she wait till she was in her bridal clothes, and sitting in her bridal sedan, to commit suicide? I doubt that so many people would have known about her suicide or felt so deeply troubled by her death if she had killed herself a day earlier, when she was dressed as a regular daughter, sitting in a regular sedan! When this free spirit declared war on the demon of despotism, she may have sounded an alarm to awaken ordinary people to the realization that the days of the monstrous practice of selling women against their will are numbered. At this point I feel neither exhilaration nor discouragement, but I feel as if I hear countless voices crying out for freedom—sacrifice—struggle. We must make our own choices—my ears are inundated with the cry that we must make our own choices. I cannot help but cry out with my pen, "Long live freedom!" It is the glory of humankind's future!

17
"The Evils of Society" and Miss Zhao

Mao Zedong (November 21, 1919)

First published in *Public Interest*.

My friend Mr. Yinbo,[1] in his editorial comments published the day before yesterday in this paper, criticized my article, "Commentary on Miss Zhao's Suicide," saying that I had placed all the blame on circumstances, letting Miss Zhao off scot-free, and that this was not right. He wrote, "The action of Miss Zhao was a weak and negative action. Such actions must never, never be advocated." I am basically in total agreement with this positive critique, forcefully put forward by Mr. Yinbo. On the question of the suicide of Miss Zhao, I had originally intended to criticize her on several different small points. Among the several small points that I was considering, one was precisely "against suicide." Mr. Yinbo's view and my view are really identical.

In the end, however, I cannot let "society" off. No matter how weak you might say Miss Zhao's act of committing suicide was, you cannot say she "died without cause." And the "cause" of her death, to one degree or another, indisputably did come from outside of herself, from society. Since society contains "causes" that could bring about Miss Zhao's death, this society is an extremly dangerous thing. It was able to cause the death of Miss Zhao; it could also cause the death of Miss

Qian, Miss Sun, or Miss Li. It can make "women" die; it can also make "men" die. There are still so many of us who today have not yet died. We must be on our guard against this dangerous thing that could find the occasion to inflict a fatal blow on us at any moment. We must protest loudly, warn and awaken those fellow human beings who are not yet dead, and cry out, "Society is evil!"

I said that there were three factors that drove Miss Zhao to her death. One was her parents' family, one was her fiancé's family, and one was society. Ultimately, both her parents' family and her fiancé's family are part of society. Her parents' family and her fiancé's family are each one component of society. We must understand that the parents' family and the fiancé's family are guilty of a crime, but the source of their crime lies in society. It is true that the two families could themselves have perpetrated this crime, but a great part of their culpability was transmitted to them by society. Moreover, if society were good, even if the families had wanted to perpetrate this crime, they would not have had the opportunity to do so. For example, if the Zhao family had heard that Madame Wu, the prospective mother-in-law, was bad, the go-between, Fourth Madame She, would have insisted that it was not true. If this had taken place in Western society, there would have been no system of go-betweens to force them together, and no lies to trick them. Or again, if this had been in Western society, and Miss Zhao's father had slapped her in the face when she refused to get into the sedan chair, she could have taken him to court and sued him, or she would have resisted in some way to protect herself. Or yet again, when Miss Zhao wanted the Wu family to change the date, the wife of the eldest brother of the Wu family had the right simply to "refuse adamantly," and the other side was forced to accept this "refusal" and go ahead with the marriage. All these are dirty tricks peculiar to the evil society of China.

Mr. Yinbo wonders why Miss Zhao didn't just run away, and he says that it would have been possible for her actually to do this. I say, true enough, but first let me raise a few questions, after which I shall present my view.

1. Within the city of Changsha there are more than forty peddlers of foreign goods. Within a 30-*li* radius of Shaoshan Village where I live, there are seven or eight peddlers of mixed foreign and domestic goods.[2] Why is this?

2. Why is it that all the toilets in the city of Changsha are for men only, and none for women?

3. Why is it you never see women entering a barber shop?

4. Why is it single women are never seen staying at hotels?

5. Why is it you never see women going into teahouses to drink tea?

6. Why is it that the customers hastening in and talking business in such silk shops as the Taihefeng or in stores selling foreign merchandise such as Yutaihua are never women, always men?

7. Why is it that of all the carters in the city not one is a woman, they are all men?

8. Why is it that at First Normal School outside South Gate there are no women students? And why are there no male students at Old Rice Field First Normal?

Anyone who knows the answers to these questions will understand why it was that Miss Zhao could not run away. The answers to these questions are not difficult. There is only one general answer, that "men and women are extremely segregated," that women are not allowed a place in society. In this society, in which "men and women are extremely segregated" and women are not allowed a place, even supposing Miss Zhao had wanted to run away, where would she have run to?

To those who say that there are examples in this world of those who have run away, I again reply, yes there are. Once more, I will give you an example. "In our village of Shaoshan, there is a young woman of eighteen named Mao who is both intelligent and good looking. She was married to a man named Zhong who was both extremely stupid and extremely ugly. This young woman was extremely unwilling. Finally she threw off her husband and had an affair with the son of a neighbor named Li. In August of this year she ran away from her home to exercise the freedom to love."

You certainly must think that this was very good. But . . .

"In less than two days, she was surrounded by some other people who notified her family. Her family then sent someone to catch her."

Just being caught wouldn't have been so bad.

"She was dragged home, where she was beaten very severely and locked in an inner room, where, as before, she was left with her stupid husband to fulfill that 'most proper' marital relationship."

This still wasn't much.

"Zhang San says, 'She deserved to be beaten. She ran away. She's shameless.'"

"Zhang Si[3] agrees. 'If you don't beat her now, when will you! If a family produces a girl like this, it's really a miserable disgrace to their whole clan.'"

This Miss Mao should be seen as putting into practice a positive view of things. Not afraid of danger or stopped by difficulties, she did everything possible to struggle against the evil demon. But what was the result? As far as I can see, she got only three things: she got "caught," she got "beaten," and she got "cursed."

If we look at it in this perspective, how could Miss Zhao have done anything else but commit suicide? Alas for Miss Zhao! Alas for the evils of society!

After I had finished writing the draft of this article, I saw the critique of Mr. Rulin.[4] He also emphasizes the aspect of society, on which our views agree. But from the standpoint of Miss Zhao, as to whether or not there were other means by which she could have fulfilled her free will, and what the relative value of the different means might be, I will discuss that next time. Any further details on what Miss Zhao's personal name was, or what school she graduated from, or whether she had bound or natural feet, would be most welcome.

Notes

1. Peng Huang.

2. The peddlers to whom Mao alludes were those who brought cotton cloth, particularly that used for women's undergarments and for children's clothes, to people's homes. The point of this reference is that, unlike the men referred to under item 6 in the list, who hung about silk shops, women were sequestered in their houses and could only wait for the peddlers to come to them.

3. Zhang San and Zhang Si (literally "Third Brother" and "Fourth Brother" Zhang) are names like John Doe or Bill Smith commonly used in Chinese to represent typical individuals.

4. Mr. Rulin is believed to be Xiao Rulin (1890–1926), a native of Hunan Province. After the 1911 Revolution, he became editor in chief of the Changsha *Junguomin ribao* (National Military Daily), and was deputy chief of the office of Governor Tan Yankai in 1917. The *Dagong bao* published his article, "My Views on the Suicide of Miss Zhao," on November 19, 1919.

18
The Biography of Li Chao

Hu Shi (December 1, 1919)

Originally published in *New Tide*, vol. 2, no. 2.

Li Chao did not do many great deeds in her life. My research into her correspondence and activities suggests that her life story was merely this:

Li Chao (born Weibo,[1] also known as Weibi and Puzhen) was from Jinzizhuang Village in Wuzhou County, Guangxi Province. Both her parents died early, so she had only two elder sisters, the older named Weijun and the younger named ————.[2] Her father had a concubine named Sister Fu. Li Chao was raised by Sister Fu. Her parents had adopted a nephew[3] as their heir because they had no son. His name was Jipu and he was also known as Weishen.

Li Chao came from a large and wealthy family. She received a few years of education hanging around her uncle's office while he was a county official. This is why her essays and letters are fluent and clear.

In 1911, she entered Wuzhou Normal School for Women. She graduated with high marks. In 1915, she organized a women's Chinese literature study group. But her friends scattered after a year and she alone stayed at home. She found life in her old-fashioned family uninteresting and wanted very much to go out and pursue her studies. She entered Guangzhou's Advanced Public Normal School for Women, then entered Jiefang Academy, then entered a Christian missionary school, and finally entered the Public Normal School for Women. She found Guangzhou's women's schools unsatisfactory and was determined to come to Beijing's National Advanced Normal School for Women. In July 1918, she finally got her travel fare together and headed for Beijing. She began auditing classes when she first entered in September, and then matriculated as a regular student. That winter, she fell ill. She was weak from the start, and nothing was going well for her. This spring, her illness intensified, and her doctor diagnosed it as tuberculosis. She moved into Shoushan Hospital to recover, but her illness only worsened. She died in a French hospital on August

16. She was twenty-three or twenty-four years old when she died (her age at death was recorded as twenty, but this is erroneous).

These facts seem irrelevant and unimportant. Traditional essayists would certainly not deem her worthy of a biography. Even if they granted her a biography, it would only say stock phrases about how she was "born intelligent, naturally filial and amicable, praised by friends and relatives, eager to study, unfortunately not fated to live, a pity indeed." No reader would believe this kind of stilted essay. But when Li Chao died, her friends collected all her writings and found a lot of her correspondence. Her fellow villager Su Jiarong collected her letters, which vividly illustrated a life of ambitions and hardships. When I read this collection, I felt strongly that this short-lived, unknown woman was worth a full-length biography. Her story would not only move people to sympathy and admiration, but also capture the attention of concerned people throughout the nation, and arouse discussion. Therefore I think that a biography of this woman is much more significant than that of any great general.

When Li Chao first decided to go to Guangzhou, she wrote her stepbrother a letter:

Half a year has gone by since I[4] stopped going to school. I feel bored at home. Of course I have tried to study on my own. But I am just not smart enough to do that. When I came to sophisticated ideas I could not understand, there was no one to ask. Studying without a teacher is fruitless in the end. All the students have high praise for Guangzhou's Advanced Public Normal School for Women. It is a well-run school with an excellent faculty. Also, it does not require tuition. If I live on campus, I will only have to pay five *yuan* per month for food. And the school rules will ensure that I graduate in only two years. . . . Guangdong is right next to our province; if I go by ship, I can get there in one day. . . . I will need no more than 100 *yuan* per year. Even though our family's annual income is not very high, we could still afford such a small sum. It wouldn't be too hard, would it? . . . I hope you won't mind. . . . I feel I was born at the wrong time, with misfortune in childhood and poverty now that I am older. . . . I continue living only because my parents gave me life and I feel I should not waste it. As long as I have one breath left in me, how can I not seek an education? The world has changed so much in recent years and education is extremely important for women as well as men. Though I am slow and ignorant and cannot compete with others, I am still young and want to use my time to improve myself. If I could just be fortunate enough to learn a few ideas, I won't regret my life. Then I would be happy. As for everything else, such as wealth, I already see through it. Although I can't claim to be able to ignore it completely, I accept my fate. . . . If you could give me the money . . . I would be grateful for the rest of my life. Even my parents would be smiling in heaven. I am full of anxiety as I write to you to ask for this. Please write back soon.

This letter may be written in rather polite language, but one can sense that it carries the sound of sobbing. Now let's look at a letter she wrote to a close friend:

I believe you already received the short letter I wrote to you last time. I don't know if you have permission to lend me money. I am on pins and needles. It may not seem like an emergency to you, but my life hangs on this. . . . In past years, my family has had so many misfortunes. You can well imagine what I've faced. Ever since Jipu remarried, we have had a lot of quarrels. Now we all hate each other even more. We are living together, but we think differently. That's why quarrels keep breaking out. Even when I'm not involved in the quarrel, I can hear them making sarcastic remarks about me. I can't get even one peaceful day. Last year, I could go to school, so I could still get by. But now, since I left school, I live at home and have no means of escape. . . . I have to live in the midst of gossip. . . . I never wanted to get stuck here in Wuzhou. I am not seeking wealth and glory; I just want peace and happiness. My environment is already very difficult; on top of that, my family quarrels a lot. I have no confidante here. I've been sick and tired of Wuzhou for a long time.

One can well imagine the darkness of the old-fashioned family mentioned in this letter. But when I take a closer look at this letter, I think it does not even touch on the real source of her suffering. At the time, Li Chao was already twenty years old, but still not engaged. Her brother and his wife were very unhappy about this. They wanted to get her to marry out so they could get her property. Li Chao had "no confidante here." Only Weijun[5] and her husband Ou Shousong were willing to help her. Li Chao's correspondence included two letters that Li Chao had written on behalf of Weijun.[6] One letter read:

Our parents died too early, leaving only the three of us. . . . Of the three of us, Li Chao was the only one who lost all her support while she was still very young. She won't be able to achieve anything when she grows older. When she looks forward, she cannot see what is in store for her. She doesn't know how she'll end up. Every time I think of this, I can't eat or sleep. My sister is different from my brother, who just loves money. My sister just loves to study. So they often quarrel. I am sad that we have such an authoritarian family that might prevent my sister from pursuing her dream. Li Chao often worries about this. She is even weaker than before. She gets a headache every time she thinks about these problems. . . . Please take note of her plight. I would also be grateful if she could marry a worthy man. Our parents in heaven would smile. . . .

This letter reveals Li Chao's most unspeakable suffering. She wanted to go out to study in order to avoid an arranged marriage. Her brother did not want her to go far away, like a bird escaping her cage. He feared that she would stay single all her life and remain an eyesore in her natal home.

Li Chao asked her brother for permission to study in Guangdong, which was just a day's steamship ride away, but he would not have it. He wrote to her in reply:

Sister: You want to go to Guangzhou for an education. I don't care about the money or about how far it is, but our ancestors have always been country folks and we all grew up in the village; not one of the women in our village or nearby villages has gone away for school. You would be the first. The villagers would be unhappy and blame you for it. They would criticize you for doing something unheard of. Even if you don't care about village gossip, Fifth Uncle is the eldest man of the lineage, and Second Aunt is the eldest woman of the lineage. It would not be right for a maiden like you to go off to faraway Guangdong without asking their permission. If they hear the constant gossip that would result, they would blame me. The responsibility is too great for me to bear. I really cannot recommend to the elders that a girl like you go somewhere far away. I even resorted to asking Sister Fu[7] to plead on your behalf. But neither she nor anyone else dared to do this, and Sister Fu also disapproves of your going far away. But my responsibility will be too great if someone does not go and ask the elders for permission. If you still want to go to Guangdong after reading this letter, you will have to get permission from the elders yourself.

In this letter, Jipu used all sorts of threats to suppress his sister. This is a prime example of the tyranny of the lineage system.

But Li Chao could not be fazed, and she left for Guangdong anyway. She went to several academies in Guangzhou. Her brother was
furious and refused to write to her. On July 5, 1917, his wife Chen
Wenhong wrote in a letter:

> . . . Ji Pu said to Ninth Kinsman, "She refuses to obey me, so I refuse to
> write to her. She's off in Guangdong, and I don't know whether she is
> studying or living in a hotel and lying to us in her letters.[8] I won't let
> her get away with it!" He spoke so harshly. . . . I can't think of anything
> you can do, except to return to Wuzhou, and end the sorrow you've
> caused our family. Why cause sorrow to the family?

Then, on the seventeenth day of the fifth lunar month,[9] Chen
Wenhong wrote again to Li Chao:

> . . . It's been less than half a year, and you've already changed schools
> several times in Guangdong. You've made the family very angry. Now
> that you want to go to yet another school to study Chinese literature, I
> fear the family will be even angrier. . . .

We can see from these letters how Li Chao was treated by everyone
in her family.

Once Li Chao had left, she refused to return, and her family could
do nothing about it. They could only use the clever tactic of cutting off
her financial support. During the two years Li Chao was in
Guangzhou, she depended on her sister-in-law Chen Wenhong, her
brother-in-law[10] Ou Shousong, her cousin[11] Weiji, her kinsman Li
Dianwu, her cousin[12] Boyuan, and her cousin Wanzhen[13] for help with
tuition. On the thirtieth day of the ninth lunar month, Weiji wrote to Li
Chao that "Jipu was often very angry at me for giving you money." Ou
Shousong even had to borrow money to contribute to Li Chao's tuition. You can imagine how all this made Li Chao feel.

Li Chao changed schools several times while in Guangzhou because
she never quite found a satisfactory school. Then her friend Liang
Huizhen wrote a few letters to her from Beijing's Advanced Normal
School for Women, encouraging her to come to Beijing to study. Li
Chao was like a bee inside a house, flying around frantically, but
always moving toward the light. Having heard about how good
Beijing's Advanced Normal School for Women was, she sent her old

writings to Liang Huizhen and asked her to forward them to Fang Huan, principal of that school, so that Li Chao could apply to transfer there. She also asked someone from her village who was working as an official in Beijing to put in a good word for her. Principal Fang accepted Li Chao as a class auditor. But her family tried many tactics to stop her. How could they let her go to faraway Beijing?

At first Li Chao tried to hide her plans from her family. She wanted to get some money together and then go. During the winter of 1917, Li Boyuan wrote to Li Chao:

> . . . Your sister-in-law Chen Wenhong loves you dearly, but her husband is very harsh and limited your budget to 120 *yuan* per year. . . . Your sister-in-law was very anxious and had to say a lot of good things on your behalf in order to get you the money. Now that she has learned that you are going to Beijing, she may change her mind. . . .

Later, Li Chao's family heard of her plans to go to Beijing. On November 7, 1917, her sister-in-law Chen Wenhong wrote:

> Recently, we got a letter from you saying that you won't be coming home and that you are determined to go north. I was very unhappy when I heard this. Why are you doing this? I think this is making me look bad. You're hurting me. Your brother, uncles, and aunts have scolded me ever since you went to Guangdong, saying it was all my idea. Recently, my husband beat me. And your stepmother (Sister Fu) was also scolded and often got into quarrels. All this was because of you. If you love me, you'll realize how hard this trip would be on us. Please think it over carefully, please. . . .

At the time, Li Chao's family wanted to marry her off to prevent her from going far away. Over the next few months, Li Chao got many letters about prospective marriages. She rejected them all. She was adamant about going to Beijing, and tried to borrow money from every friend and relative she could think of. But, though her family was wealthy, her brother refused to be the guarantor for her loans, so no one dared to lend her money. On May 22, 1918, her older sister Weijun wrote to a kinsman living in Guangzhou:

> . . . I heard that Li Chao wants to go to Beijing to study. This should be very good. But Jipu and Fifth Uncle Juting[14] think that a few characters are all the education women need. It is impossible for her to fulfill her desire of going to Beijing alone. Even if she could borrow money from

others to fulfill her own ambition, she would not be able to repay it later. . . .

This was the most effective way to deal with Li Chao. On June 28, Boyuan wrote to her:

> . . . Your sister-in-law Chen Wenhong said she won't give you money anymore because she thinks you'd use it to go to Beijing. We could get the money together for you, but Chen Wenhong has said that she would hold Wanzhen and me responsible if you use it to go to Beijing. . . . She is very angry at you. She said [you] don't understand her good intentions. She will not repay the loan you got from Dianwu. All this may be hard on you, but it is even harder on her.

This letter shows that even Li Chao's understanding sister-in-law Chen Wenhong also had plans to cut her off.

At that point, Li Chao was both anxious and angry, and she had been ill for a few months. Afterward, her brother-in-law Ou Shousong promised to take full responsibility for her tuition. Ou Shousong was a good person of the rarest kind. He wrote to her:

> . . . If you have decided to go to Beijing to study . . . I approve. I will try to the best of my ability to provide you with the 80–90 *jin*[15] you need every year. . . . I don't think Jipu will continue to be so uncaring.

With Li Dianwu's loan and Ou Shousong's promise to pay her tuition, Li Chao managed to go to Beijing in July. At first she was only a class auditor at Beijing's Advanced Normal School for Women, but soon she was accepted as a regular student. Her brother Jipu and his wife Chen Wenhong not only refused to give her money but also wrote to Ou Shousong telling him not to give her money either. Mr. Ou wrote to Li Chao on September 5, 1918:

> . . . It may be that Jipu just doesn't have enough money to spare these days. Yesterday I received a letter from Xuan'er saying that not only was Chen Wenhong unhappy and unwilling to give you money, but also that Jipu ordered me not to give you money. I already wrote back to him to ask him not to be so unfeeling. I also said that if he does not send you money, I will take full responsibility for your tuition. I already owe about three thousand *yuan*. Pinyuan[16] is very poor, and every year I

find that my income is not enough to repay my debts. Unlike Jipu, I can't spare the money. I am now managing to eke out enough money to send to you, but it's pretty incongruous that your family can't afford to do this for you. . . .

This letter was asking why Li Chao's brother and sister-in-law could not send her money even though their family was relatively wealthy. Actually, Li Chao's brother Jipu was an adopted son, and he stood to inherit everything. Who would have thought that this stubborn sister would refuse to marry early and instead want use of the family money to pursue her studies? Their greatest fear was that Li Chao would remain single all her life, and remain an eyesore in her home for the rest of her life. Therefore, Ou Shousong continued to write letters to Li Chao urging her to declare an intention to marry, in order to ease the worries of her brother and sister-in-law. On September 5, Mr. Ou wrote:

. . . In my last letter, I unambiguously asked you to try to get engaged as soon as possible, because they will not have a day's peace until you make this declaration. . . . If you don't marry, your sister and I will be blamed for the rest of our lives, and we could say nothing in our defense. This is why last year in Guangdong I kept asking you when you plan to marry. You should have declared the exact year you will complete your studies, and promised that at that time you will resign yourself to immediately marrying whoever is chosen for you, no matter what he is like, and accept your fate without complaining. Otherwise, you should have said that you plan to shave your head, become a nun, and stay single all your life. If you had made it clear then, things would be easier for Jipu to handle, and you would not be in so much trouble now. Now there seems to be no way out; no one knows how much longer you will need tuition support.

He wrote to her again in September:

. . . It's good that you are studying, but we don't know what your goal is. You're getting older, and I'm very worried. . . . Jipu believes that it is not beneficial for you to study all your life. Even if you don't care about him, you should think of me, and decide on this and tell me soon. . . .

Li Chao was extremely grateful for Ou Shousong's kindness. These letters were written with the utmost sincerity, so Li Chao responded very sincerely as well. Her reply was this:

. . . You have helped me so much with my education, despite your own financial troubles. I don't know how I could ever repay your kindness and I will never forget what you've done. . . . When I first came to Beijing, I wrote to my brother before saying that I would be in Beijing no longer than two to three years before returning. Then they could suggest potential matches so that I may decide on who to marry. If you tell me to get betrothed now, I wouldn't dare to object, but the marriage itself will have to wait till after I have graduated. I know that everyone in the family suspects that I want to remain single all my life, and that's why I set things straight to relieve their worries about that. It had never occurred to me that this would be an issue today. They think my studies have been expensive, and that my education will never end, so they have tried to find ways to stop me. My family is not very wealthy, but still we have enough annual income to take care of my studies. I only spend two to three hundred *yuan* per year; how could this be too much? And this is the inheritance my parents left me. The men of the family can spend the family money at will, so why can't I use it on something as legitimate as an education? It is truly unfair to say that I am using too much money. After thinking long and hard about why my brother wants to stop me, I've come to realize that it is because he is very stingy, and also because he doesn't think women should be educated. These are the only reasons he is making such a big fuss about this. . . .

Li Chao said: "And this is the inheritance my parents left me. The men of the family can spend the family money at will, so why can't I use it on something as legitimate as an education? It is truly unfair to say that I am using too much money." These words describe the cause of her death. Why did she have to be a woman? Just because she was a woman, she naturally could not use "the inheritance her parents left her" for "something as legitimate as an education"!

Less than half a year after Li Chao arrived in Beijing, her family was quarreling severely. Boyuan wrote to Li Chao on November 6:

. . . Chen Wenhong left Wuzhou for a few days after the Mid-Autumn Festival but had to return because of her illness. She left because she had quarreled with Jipu and they had stopped talking to each other. Their quarrels occurred first because of Jipu's concubine Yafeng, and second because of you. Yafeng was a bad woman, but the quarrels were all because of Chen Wenhong. Chen Wenhong wanted to get rid of Yafeng, but Jipu would not allow it because

Yafeng recently became pregnant and fell into his favor. Last month Fifth Uncle was sick, so Older Sister Jun returned to the village to mediate between Jipu, Chen Wenhong, and Yafeng. She failed to get them to resolve their problems, and left after three days. As she was leaving, Chen Wenhong kindly saw her off and told her not to worry because she would resolve things herself. As for Li Chao, she said, I will help her finish school even if I have to pawn all my jewels. Please write to her, but don't upset her. That night, Chen Wenhong tried to hang herself, though fortunately Sister Fu heard her choking and rescued her in time. . . .

Jipu is getting angrier and angrier at you for going to Beijing, so he won't send you one cent more. He said you can do whatever you want but he will have nothing more to do with you. He said you are always invoking your parents to support your arguments, but that, even if your parents were still alive, they would also chastise you for your behavior. Older Sister Jun told me to tell you never to mention your parents to Jipu again, since it only makes him angrier.

The first part of this letter said that Chen Wenhong had tried to hang herself on account of Li Chao, and the second part said that Jipu not only refused to send any money but also forbade her even to mention the word "parents" in her defense. Li Chao was furious when she received this letter. Soon after, she fell ill and started coughing up blood. By the spring of 1919, her illness had worsened, and the doctor diagnosed it as tuberculosis. By that time her illness was already terminal. She died in August.

While Li Chao was ill, her brother-in-law Ou Shousong wrote to her many times, telling her to stop worrying and to protect her health. In one letter, he wrote something that was sadly ironic. He wrote: "Your situation is similar to mine. The only difference is that I have to spend money even though I don't have it, while you have money but can't spend it." Li Chao had money but couldn't spend it, and went through countless hardships that caused her to fall ill and die—on whom, and on what system, should this be blamed?

After Li Chao died, all her funeral arrangements had to be made by two fellow villagers, Qu Hui and Chen Ying. Her brother and sister-in-law did not even bother to send a letter. Later it was still her kindly brother-in-law Mr. Ou who repaid her debts. Li Chao's coffin lies to this day in a dilapidated temple in Beijing. No one from her family has come to ask about it. Finally, a letter from her brother Jipu arrived, stating that Li Chao "died without regretting her actions, and thus deserved to die!"

Thus ends the biography of Li Chao. I have written a biography of this pitiful woman, this total stranger; indeed, it is a biography six to seven thousand characters long—it's a long one, as far as Chinese biographies go. Why did I expend so much time and effort to write her biography? It is because her unfortunate life is representative of the lives of countless Chinese women. Her biography can be used as material for research about the Chinese lineage system and the woman question in China. We can count her as a significant martyr in Chinese feminist history. In researching her life, we can at least raise these issues:

1. The clan-lineage system. "Fifth Uncle is the eldest man of the lineage, and Second Aunt is the eldest woman of the lineage. It would not be right for a maiden like you to go off to faraway Guangdong without asking their permission." What do you think of this?
2. The question of women's education. "Our ancestors have always been country folks and we all grew up in the village; not one of the women in our village or nearby villages has gone away for school. You would be the first. The villagers would be unhappy and blame you for it. They would criticize you for doing something unheard of." "But Jipu and Fifth Uncle Juting think that a few characters are all the education women need." What do you think of this?
3. Women's inheritance rights. "And this is the inheritance my parents left me. The men of the family can spend the family money at will, so why can't I use it on something as legitimate as an education? It is truly unfair to say that I am using too much money." What do you think of this?
4. The question of women not being counted as descendants. This is the issue at the heart of Li Chao's biography. The ancients practiced ancestor worship, the essence of the clan law social system. Henceforce, whenever a man has no son, regardless of how many daughters he has, it is as if he has no heir. Thus, even with a good daughter like Li Chao, Li Chao's parents were still deemed to have no heir, and thus had to adopt someone else's son—a "heartless" nephew—as their heir. Having read this biography, what should we think of this system?

Notes

1. The original text only mentioned the given names of most of the people in Li Chao's family, since all of them were surnamed Li. Full names are given only for women who had married into Li Chao's patriline, such as Li Chao's sister-in-law Chen Wenhong, since in China women traditionally kept their own surnames after marriage.

2. This name was omitted in Hu Shi's essay.

3. This kinship term refers to Li Chao's father's younger brother's son, to be exact.

4. In accordance with Chinese conventions, the writers of the original letters used kinship terms to refer to everyone, including themselves. To avoid confusion, we translated most of these kinship terms into names and personal pronouns.

5. Weijun was Li Chao's older sister.

6. Li Chao wrote these letters on Weijun's behalf, possibly because Weijun was illiterate.

7. Fujie was Li Chao's stepmother, the concubine of her deceased father.

8. This implies that Li Chao is living a promiscuous life, perhaps working as a prostitute, instead of studying as she claimed.

9. Hu Shi specifies here that the date is from the traditional Chinese lunar calendar, rather than from the Western (Gregorian) calendar. The Chinese lunar year consists of 12 months of alternately 29 and 30 days, equal to 354 days. Intercalary months are inserted to keep the calendar year in step with the solar year of about 365 days. Months are referred to by number within a year.

10. The kinship term refers to Li Chao's older sister's husband.

11. The kinship term refers to Li Chao's younger male cousin.

12. The kinship term refers to Li Chao's older female cousin.

13. The kinship term refers to Li Chao's older female cousin.

14. Fifth Uncle Juting is the eldest man of the lineage, whom Jipu mentioned in an earlier letter.

15. A *jin* is a Chinese unit of currency larger than the *yuan*.

16. Pinyuan is the name of the place where Ou Shousong works.

19
Words Spoken at Miss Li Chao's Memorial Service

Cai Yuanpei (February 13, 1919)

First published in *Beijing University Daily*, no. 506, under the name Cai Jiemin.

Today, at this memorial service for Miss Li Chao, we should certainly mourn for her, as her life was very sad indeed. But I think that countless others face the same circumstances she did, and many men as well as women have also come to this kind of tragic end. We should avail ourselves of this opportunity to pay tribute to all of them.

The speech Mr. Hu Shi just made and the biography he wrote for Miss Li not only memorialized her but also spoke of a way to resolve an unfortunate problem. I approve of this, but I think his emphasis is too much on women alone. I think that men as well as women suffer from the same problem, so we have to come up with a total solution.

First, there is the economic problem. The rights and lives of countless young people have been sacrificed to the unequal distribution of wealth and the monopolization of property rights. Li Chao was just one of these. If we change the present economic structure to one that follows the principle of "from each according to ability, to each according to need," wouldn't the obstacles to those seeking education be removed?

Second, moving back a step, we can try to solve it just as a question of education. Today, at the level of elementary school education, various nations give everyone the opportunity to acquire an education, regardless of whether or not they have money. But if we transform the educational system so that high school and college education are also free, what could stop good students like Li Chao from pursuing their education?

Third, moving back another step, there is a partial solution that could be implemented within the field of education. In other countries, wealthy people often donate money to set up a foundation that will pay for the tuition of poor students. This year, Beijing University created Chenmei Scholarship Society. Though it did not have a lot of money, it did help several poor students. If every school had this kind of organization, those like Li Chao whose families refuse to pay for their education could turn to a scholarship organization. Wouldn't the obstacles be removed then?

Miss Li is already dead, so we can only mourn for her. We have to come up with a solution to prevent a similar end from coming to countless others, resulting in countless more memorial services. We must raise consciousness about this.

20
The Incident of Miss Xi Shangzhen's Suicide at the Office of the Commercial Press

Chen Wangdao (September 20, 1922)

Originally published in the *Women's Critic* supplement to the *Republican Daily*, September 20, 1922.

On the seventh of this month, around seven o'clock, Miss Xi Shangzhen, a secretary of the Commercial Press, hanged herself in the office. This incident has become a hot issue in the public forums of Shanghai. She hanged herself using the wire of an electric teakettle. Newspapers speculate that she committed suicide because Mr. Tang Jiezhi, the general manager of Commercial Press, had borrowed five thousand *yuan* from her and refused to return it to her. Yet rumors have insinuated a different and very unsavory interpretation, one made possible by the evil side of Chinese national character. We should certainly not accept it without evidence.

Miss Xi, a native of Dongtingshan in Wu County, graduated from Shanghai East District Women's School. She was only twenty-four years old. Originally, she lived at 4 Tang Family Lane, Shanghai. When Commercial Press was first founded, her cousin Wang Boheng recommended her for the position of mail sorter at the Commercial Press. She shared an office with Mr. Tang Jiezhi. Her job was to open the incoming mail, show it to Mr. Tang, and then deliver it to various departments. Her monthly salary was twenty *yuan*.

Ms. Xi-Fang,[1] the victim's mother, told the coroner's office that Xi Shangzhen committed suicide because "Mr. Tang never returned her the money he borrowed last May." As Xi Shangzhen's sister, Ms. Wang-Xi, said,

Last May 3, Mr. Tang Jiezhi, general manager of Commercial Press, told my sister of the advantages of buying stocks and acquired 5,000 *yuan* from her. But the stocks did not increase in value, so my sister asked Tang to return her money. To her surprise, Mr. Tang told her that he had mortgaged the stocks. Up until mid-May this year, there was still no sign of his returning the money. My sister took an overdose of sleep medication; but she was saved by the doctor Tang got for her. She did not come home until daybreak. She was sent back home in a horse carriage by Commercial Press—it was claimed that she "had an acute disease." But my sister sat in the carriage and refused to get off, saying that she "would rather die right at work." So she was taken back and sent directly to Tongren Hospital. When I went to see her, she told me that "it was not because of an acute illness that I took the overdose. It was because Tang would not return my money and also said, 'You belong to me. Why don't you have some faith in me in terms of the money? Why don't you simply marry me?' " My sister said, "You have a wife; how can I be your concubine?" Tang had a written agreement with my sister, in which he promised to return the money in three installments. But he never kept his promise, which led to my sister's tragic suicide.

Nevertheless, Tang Jiezhi's statement completely denied the part about his proposition to Miss Xi. According to newspaper reports, he stated: "As for my asking her to become my concubine, that is an absolute lie. But even if it were true, why should she have committed suicide?" It is indeed exceptionally smart of Mr. Tang to have used words like "even if" and "why should she!" The urgent statement by Mr. Tang Jiezhi that was carried in various newspapers and checked and approved by his lawyer makes it sound as if his whole story were true. The following is his entire statement:

Regarding the suicide of Miss Xi Shangzhen, I feel obligated to issue the following statement to the public and friends. In order to buy stocks, the deceased had borrowed money from other parties and then asked me to purchase them. But when we were going to buy the stocks, I was under the assumption that all the money belonged to her. She intended to buy a large number of shares; but I believed that it was too risky and did not want to do it for her. Later, she raised a mortgage on her stocks from Shangbao Bank. When all her plans and efforts, unfortunately, fell through, she became very depressed and repeatedly asked me to help her out. She told me that she was under a lot of pressure and was getting reprimands from her debtors. She tried to commit suicide twice. Because she had been a great asset to me and the Press as a clerk, I, out of good will, had tried my best to assist her. On August 19, I gave her a written agreement in which I promised to pay back the 5,000 *yuan* in installments. It was stated in the agreement that, beginning from that date, I would pay 1,500 *yuan* in twelve months, then another 1,500 *yuan* in another twelve months and finally 2,000 *yuan* after the total thirty-six months. This contract was given to her prior to her suicide and is now in the hands of her family. Her family showed it to the authorities right at the coroner's. To this day, her family still has the contract. Apart from that contract, I cannot be held responsible for anything. I assert that I did all this entirely out of sympathy and with the intention of helping her out of her predicament. Not surprisingly, she was quite delighted when I gave her my written agreement. I, for one, am still very puzzled why she would have committed suicide after receiving the contract. Therefore, I have written this public statement, which has been approved by my lawyer.

After Miss Xi's suicide, the news media in Shanghai carried many commentaries. I think the most representative are Mr. Zha's article in the "Women and Family" column of *China New Tribune* and Miss Huang's special report on Xi Shangzhen in the "Bright Light" column of *Current Affairs*. They represent two opposite positions. Please refer to the following:

The Shortcomings of Women's Education:
Thoughts on Miss Xi Shangzhen's Suicide

Zha Mengci

From various points of view, the recent suicide of Miss Xi Shangzhen can be considered a big social problem. As an outsider who does not know the details, I don't want to comment too much; but I cannot help but feel great sympathy for such a young woman who had a good new-style education and yet was killed by society as soon as she entered it. I think her untimely death has taught our society—especially the society of the new woman—a good lesson, warning us not to let such tragedies happen again and not to take risks with women's education. That is the only way for us to show our sympathy for and commemoration of the deceased.

However, at the same time, I have to say that "there exists a big problem in China's education for women." Why is that? Aren't we who actively advocate women's education also advocating for women's independence? For their participation in society and for their economic independence? If so, we need to provide the appropriate preparation and training. Those who educate women need to give their students this kind of preparation and training. The lack of this kind of preparation and training is a reason for Miss Xi's tragedy.

First, we must teach women to get rid of vanity, to reduce their materialistic desire, and to foster a serious and honest outlook. Of course, this should be required for both sexes; yet it is more urgent for women, for they are less resistant to such desire. Take Miss Xi for example. From what we gather from both sides, it was she herself who wanted to buy the stocks. This tragedy was caused by a moment of mistaken thinking. According to her family members, even if she did get all the stocks she purchased back, they would have been gobbled up by last year's stock market collapse anyway. How can the little pin money gathered by several women not be taken away by those wicked stock-mongers? Last year when the stock market was in its upswing, even many old moralists were tempted, never mind a young woman like her. But China's women's schools generally do not teach how to guard against vanity. Miss Xi's ignorance was certainly no wonder.

Second, contemporary Chinese society is very depraved, thus making service to society an arduous task even for men, not to mention women. Consequently, those who educate women should train and prepare their students well. In other words, rather than merely learn how to sing and dance, students should be equipped with social skills and necessary knowledge about the world. Although the whole truth is not yet out, the suicide of Miss Xi can still be attributed to her lack of social experience. Otherwise, she could have thought of a solution or some other way out of the situation. Though a promising young woman, Miss Xi committed suicide. This is a really tragic incident, but it should also serve as a really good lesson for educators.

Third, for a woman to be independent, it is necessary for her to be strong. This also means that she should be able to establish herself in society and solve all sorts of problems. As the Chinese saying goes, "Be able to cope with a predicament," or as the Western saying says, "Be able to tackle the problem head-on." In such an evil society as ours, one needs a lot of patience; if one tries to solve any problem one encounters simply by ending one's own life, one has a very capricious attitude that has nothing to do with what we call independence. Traditionally, Chinese women have been inclined to commit suicide when confronted by a problem or when insulted and humiliated. This is all because they lack rigorous training and sufficient experience to deal with social pressure. We really feel sad and sorry for Miss Xi, who ended her life for merely

5,000 *yuan*. According to the information we have, both parties had already agreed to settle the issue by paying the debt in installments. If there were no other major problems, perhaps the tragedy was caused by a severe nervous breakdown. Understandably, a nervous and unstable person simply cannot take any mental duress. But at any rate, even though the death might have been triggered by a biological factor, educators should also bear some responsibility.

Now please bear with me as I make some wild remarks. What do I mean by the shortcomings of women's education? It is my belief that women's education as it currently exists is not suitable for training independent women.

At present, our women's schools teach only a smattering knowledge of science, technology, or arts, and are, in various degrees, cosmetic, decorative, and recreational. The living standard is above average, and not tough enough to train and temper people. To a certain degree, it is meant to produce cultured homemakers for so-called civilized families and not to train independent career women for society.

Chinese women's schools have just started to develop; their students are primarily from upper-middle-class families. From the start, women from those families are usually pampered and not supposed to be concerned with social responsibilities or familiar with worldly affairs. Additionally, our women's schools do not teach their students the knowledge and skills necessary for dealing with society, and do not foster in them the courage to be self-reliant. Given all that, how could we expect women to be successful in society?

There are many highly respectable women in traditional families in China's hinterland. They are humble and content with their modest means; they are full of tireless, self-effacing spirit in their assistance to their husbands and in their education of their children; they possess the virtue of diligence and frugality in the day-to-day running of their family businesses and boast an admirably appropriate character in dealing with society and people. In terms of teaching literary knowledge, new-style education is far better than traditional education; however, when it comes to the above virtues and qualities, the newly trained students are actually inferior to those peasant women in the hinterland. Here, I would like to call the attention of our specialists in women's education to the fact that Chinese society is really evil and that law cannot correct the evils of our society. Law is only a formality. A lot of evil can occur despite the presence of legal formalities.

That is why we still see endless crime in Western societies that are ruled by tight, strict laws. If a Chinese woman wants to be independent and serve society, she needs to rely on her own strength in her struggle. To be precise, she has to rely on her observational skills, strong character, wealth of common sense, and inflexible integrity in her struggle against traditional society. I believe that contemporary women's schools must overcome their shortcomings and make greater efforts to build the character of students. They must add, on top of the new scientific education, the self-effacing spirit and virtues of those hinterland peasant women, who are industrious, humble, and content. This last point is particularly important for women's schools in Shanghai.

Miss Xi's lot is really pitiable; one can only wish that such a tragedy will never happen again. The evil society that caused the death of Miss Xi, I think, will eventually be reformed by public opinion. For now, I only hope that our specialists in women's education will remember the untimely death of such a young woman and try to draw a lesson from this tragedy.

What Does *China New Tribune* Want to Say?

Miss Huang Qinghua

The "Women's Forum" of *China New Tribune* recently carried a commentary titled "The Shortcomings of Women's Education," making arguments that are totally wrong. One paragraph in it goes likes this:

> Take Miss Xi for example. From what we gather from both sides, it was she herself who wanted to buy the stocks. This tragedy was caused by a moment of mistaken thinking. According to her family members, even if she did get all the stocks she purchased back, they would have been gobbled up by last year's stock market collapse anyway.

This commentary was authored by "Mengci." We should point out Mengci's errors, as well as criticize the editor of the Women's Forum in *China New Tribune*. If an author commits an error, it is the editor's responsibility to correct it; otherwise, the editor should bear the consequences.

We should, first of all, make it clear who tempted Miss Xi to buy the stocks. Who talked her into this? And who actually bought the stocks for her? Now, as all the news media reported, it is Tang Jiezhi who tempted her, persuaded her, and eventually bought the stocks on her behalf. This was a man's mistake in judgment, not just a woman's; therefore, it is absolutely wrong to put the blame on Miss Xi herself for the tragedy. How the tragedy occurred has been reported by the media; yesterday's *Xiao Shen Newspaper* carried a particularly detailed report. *Current Affairs* also has a special column devoted to letters to the editor on this issue. So far, most people hold the view that the tragedy was caused by the fact that Tang Jiezhi refused to return Xi Shangzhen the 5,000 *yuan* and, on top of that, tried to force her to become his concubine. But it was Tang Jiezhi who beguiled her into buying stocks in the first place!

China New Tribune's essay also argued:

> In such an evil society as ours, one needs a lot of patience; if one tries to solve any problem one encounters simply by ending one's own life, one has a very capricious attitude that has nothing to do with what we call independence. . . . We really feel sad and sorry for Miss Xi, who ended her life for merely 5,000 *yuan*. According to the information we have, both parties had already agreed to settle the issue by paying the debt in installments. If there were no other major problems, perhaps the tragedy was caused by a severe nervous breakdown.

The above is once again absolutely wrong. How could one commit suicide except as a last resort? Suicide is indeed a cowardly act. But how many people are there in today's society who would give a woman true assistance? Judging from what we have seen, even if Miss Xi had chosen to fight rather than to commit suicide, she might have very likely failed as well. Now she is dead, and anybody who still has a conscience should stand up for her, and at least say a few words in fairness. But instead, unfortunately, people like Mengci and the editor of *China New Tribune* have chosen to attack a dead woman who has been wronged. This attack should be viewed as a mistake, if not completely unconscionable. In my opinion, Miss Xi's suicide was partly because of the 5,000 *yuan* and partly because of the fact that she felt deeply insulted by Tang Jiezhi's disreputable proposition. Chastity is an important matter in China; even though nowadays some people want to abolish it, it is, after all, a good thing if a woman still respects it and tries to keep it. Miss Xi was one of those women and felt so insulted and ashamed by Tang's indecent proposition, compounded with the 5,000 *yuan* debt, that she ended her own life in uncontrollable rage. *China New Tribune* certainly took a very cavalier attitude in blaming her for killing herself simply because of 5,000 *yuan*. As for the contract in which Tang agreed to pay the debt in installments, Miss Xi knew that it was only a piece of blank paper, given the fact that Tang had repeatedly failed to keep his word. Therefore, when further insulted by Tang's proposition, she just ended her own life in protest. If an educated woman like Miss Xi was driven to suicide, a traditional Chinese woman would perhaps have killed herself even sooner. It is ridiculous to assert that the suicide was due to a nervous breakdown. Perhaps the one who made this remark was himself suffering from a nervous breakdown. Almost all the presses now favor the deceased; *China New Tribune* alone attacked the deceased—indirectly playing down the crime of Tang Jiezhi. Why? Where is their conscience?

The above are two opposing views. The reader can easily discern which is the stronger argument. Can Xi Shangzhen's suicide be attributed, as Cha Mengci claimed, to the shortcomings in her education; or is the suicide, as Huang Qinghua stated, because she had "no way out?" I believe that we should all judge from explicit facts rather than pure imagination. Right now, we are trying to gather all the evidence and will make a final conclusion on who is right and who is wrong.

P.S.: Due to the fact that Mr. Tang Jiezhi is the general manager of Commercial Press, the media in Shanghai are divided in their attitudes toward him—some with goodwill and others with ill intentions. Therefore, we need to be especially careful in making our judgment. The decision over whether to cover up for him or to attack him is itself a story taking place behind the dark curtain of the Chinese press. Witnessing the situation as inexperienced readers, we can perhaps do nothing but heave a sigh.[2]

Notes

1. Traditionally, a Chinese woman's official name after marriage usually consisted of a combination of her husband's surname and her own surname, with the husband's name before her own. Thus, Xi Shangzhen's mother is called "Miss Xi-Fang" because her maiden name is Fang and she married Mr. Xi. Xi Shangzhen's sister was married to Mr. Wang and was therefore officially called "Miss Wang-Xi."

2. According to Professor Bryna Goodman, who did a thorough investigation into

the matter, the basic elements of Xi's suicide are spelled out in the newspaper clippings Chen cites in his essay and what happened afterward is that "Xi's family brought Tang to court, accusing him of defrauding Xi of money (they also accused him of responsibility for her suicide by pressuring her to be his concubine, but this charge was dropped by the court). Tang was convicted of fraud and sentenced to three years' imprisonment" (September 5, 1998).

21
In Memory of Miss Liu Hezhen

Lu Xun (April 1, 1926)

Originally published in *Yu Si*, no. 74, April 12, 1926.

I

On March 25, 1926, the National Beijing Women's Normal University held a memorial service for Miss Liu Hezhen[1] and Miss Yang Dequn,[2] who were killed right in front of the government house of Duan Qirui. While I was pacing by myself outside the auditorium, Miss Cheng[3] came up and asked me, "Have you written something for Liu Hezhen, sir?" I answered, "Not yet." Then she said eagerly: "I am afraid that you'd better do, sir; she was always so fond of your articles."

That I certainly knew. All the magazines and journals I have edited so far have had a bad circulation, possibly because of their often sudden disappearances. Despite the hard times, however, she stood out as the sole reader who subscribed to *The Wilderness*[4] for an entire year. I have all along felt the urge to write something. Even though I knew that this would not have any effect on the dead, it seems to be the right thing to do on the part of the living. If I could truly have faith in the afterlife, that would give a good relief—yet, as it is, that is perhaps all I can do.

However, I really do not know what to say; I only feel that the world we are in is not human. The blood of more than forty young people has swarmed [over] me and makes it hard for me to see, hear, or breathe. What can I say? One can start to feel the pain and to have a good cry only after the first shock was over. What saddened me even more was the vicious comments by several so-called scholars and men of letters. Yet, I have gone beyond rage and anger. What remains for me to do is to relieve my pain and sorrow by relentlessly revealing the darkness of this inhuman society. That is the least I, as a survivor, could offer to the dead.

II

A real hero should dare to face the tragedy of life and look un-waveringly at bloodshed. It is at once sorrowful and joyful! But the Creator has determined for the sake of the ordinary people to let time heal all the wounds and to leave behind only slight traces of blood and sorrow. It is in these traces of blood and sorrow that people get a humble life and manage to keep this woeful world going. When shall we see the light at the end of such a tunnel, I do not know!

III

Among the more than forty victims, Miss Liu Hezhen was a student of mine. At least, I used to think of her as one; but now I hesitate to call her my student, for it is I who should present her my sorrow and respect. She, as a young Chinese woman who has dedicated her life to the nation, is no longer a student of a person like me, who still lingers on superfluously in this world.

I first got to know her name last summer, when Miss Yang Yinyu, the president of the Women's Normal University, expelled six members of the students' union.[5] Miss Liu Hezhen was one of the six; but I did not know her yet. It was perhaps only after Liu Baizhao led his men and women to virtually drag the students out of the campus and when a student pointed out to me who she was, did I begin to match the person with the name. I also began to wonder, as I had always imagined that any student who dared stand up to the authorities and oppose a powerful president and her people must be a sharp and thorny person. But she struck me as a gentle young lady with a constant smile on her face. Only after we settled down and resumed classes at Zongmao Hutong[6] did she start to attend my lectures. Then, I got to see her more often and was always delighted by her sweet smile and gentle demeanor. When the school was resumed[7] and some former faculty and staff felt that they had fulfilled their duty and were ready to retreat, I noticed that she was so worried about the future of the school that she was in tears. After that, I never had a chance to see her again. In fact, that was, in my memory, the last time I ever saw her.

IV

On the morning of the eighteenth I got to know that there was a demonstration in front of the government house; and in the afternoon, I heard the terrible news that the guards had actually opened fire at the demonstrators, causing several hundred casualties, among whom was Miss Liu Hezhen. I was reluctant to believe the reports, although I am one of those Chinese who would think the worst of their compatriots. But how could I have expected such baseness and barbarism? How could such a smiling, innocent young woman like Liu have been slaughtered right in front of the government house?

But the day witnessed such a sad truth, with her body as the evidence. Yet there was one more body—Miss Yang Dequn's. Besides, it was not just murder, but extremely barbarous murder, for the victims' bodies bore many marks of clubs.

The Duan government issued a decree, stating that the students were "insurgents." That was followed by rumors that they were used by certain people. It is hard enough to face the massacre, but it is even harder to listen to those rumors about the victims What else can one utter? I have come to see why a declining nation remains silent. Silence, silence! One either bursts out or dies in silence!

V

Nonetheless, I need to say more.

I did not see it with my own eyes, yet I did hear that she—Liu Hezhen—went forward full of hope and zeal. Of course, it was only a petition; and whoever has any conscience would not ever have anticipated such a tragic ending. She was shot from behind, right in front of the government house; the bullet pieced her heart and lung; she was fatally injured yet did not die immediately. Zhang Jingshu,[8] who went with her, tried to lift her up and was shot four times—once by a handgun—and fell. Then Yang Dequn, who was also there, went to the rescue but was shot as well. The bullet went through her left shoulder and came out of her chest; she, too, fell. She struggled to sit up but was instantly killed by a soldier who hit her brutally on the head and chest with his club.

That is how Liu Hezhen—this smiling, gentle young lady—died. It is absolutely true; her body bears the evidence. Yang Dequn, a brave and loyal friend, also laid down her life. Her body bears the evidence. Only Miss Zhang Jingshu is still in the hospital, moaning and groaning from pain. However, just imagine what a magnificent, heart-rending scene it was when these three women fell so fearlessly under the firing of guns—weapons invented by civilized men. It is almost unfortunate that the valor of Chinese military men slaughtering women and children and the success of the Eight-Allied troops[9] suppressing Chinese students could have been paled by the bloodshed of these female students.

But those Chinese and foreign murderers still have the nerve to hold their heads high, refusing to admit the bloodstains on their faces. . . .

VI

Time goes by; now the streets are back to normalcy. Merely a few lives lost—nothing in China. At most, it would serve as a topic for after-dinner talks for certain good people, or give the material for "rumors" to certain hateful people. Other than that, I do not see much of deeper significance. It was merely a peaceful petition. It seems to me that the sanguineous history of human wars resembles the formation of coal, which took large quantities of wood to produce a small amount of coal. Yet, petitions are even less productive, not to mention peaceful ones.

The bloodshed of these students is a sad truth; naturally it will make its impact felt and will imbue the hearts of their families, relatives, teachers, friends, and beloved ones. Although, with the elapse of time, the bloodstains will fade, the image of a smiling, gentle young lady will continue to exist in our sorrow, however vague and light it might be. Tao Qian once wrote:[10]

> My relatives may still be mourning,
> While others are already singing.
> Now I have ceased to live—my body
> buried in the mountains—
> What more is there to say?

If this could be accepted, that would be enough.

VII

As I have said earlier, I have always been inclined to think the worst of my compatriots. But this time, several things were utterly out of my expectation. One is that the authorities could have taken such a brutal action; one is that the rumor-mongers could have degraded so low; still another is that these Chinese women could have confronted death so bravely.

It was last year that I started to notice that some Chinese women, albeit still a small number, have begun to join the workforce in society. But, I have been, for many times, deeply impressed by their great ability, strong will, and undaunted spirit. This time the immense courage these young women demonstrated in trying to rescue each other amid a hail of bullets is testimony to the fact that Chinese women, although having been discriminated against and suppressed for thousands of years, are still admirably brave and tenacious. That is where, I believe, the significance of these deaths lies.

Those who linger on to live a superfluous life will see a vague hope in the fading bloodstains, whereas real fighters will march forward with even greater courage and determination.

Alas, that is all that I can say for now, all that is in memory of Miss Liu Hezhen.

Notes

1. Liu Hezhen (1904–1926) was born in Nanchang, Jiangxi, a student of the National Beijing Women's Normal University, majoring in English.
2. Yang Dequn (1902–1926), born in Xiangyin, Hunan, a student of the National Beijing Women's University, majoring in education.
3. Miss Cheng refers to Cheng Yizhi, a native of Xiaogan, Hubei, a student of the National Beijing Normal University, majoring in education.
4. *The Wilderness*, a literary journal, was founded by Lu Xun in 1925. It started as a monthly and became a biweekly in 1926. Published by Weiming Publisher.
5. In May 1925, Yang Yinyu, the president of the National Beijing Normal University, gained a large measure of unpopularity because of her involvement in the decision to expel the six radical members of the students' union, also among whom was Xu Guangping, who later became Lu Xun's wife.
6. The oppositional students expelled by President Yang Yinyu rented some housing at Zongmao Hutong as classrooms and started school on September 21, 1925. Lu Xun and some sympathetic faculty members volunteered to give lectures there as moral support to those students.
7. After more than a year's fight, and with the support from progressive social

forces, the student rebels moved their school back to the original address at Xuangwumen.

8. Zhang Jingshu (1902–1978), a native of Changsha, Hunan.

9. In 1900, Great Britain, the United States, Germany, France, Russia, Japan, Italy, and Austria jointly invaded Beijing.

10. Tao Qian (365–427), the Jing dynasty poet, alias Tao Yuanming. The poem cited is from his "Elegy" (*waige*).

Part Three

Women's Education

Editors' Introduction

As these essays suggest, education was closely connected to women's ability to participate in social activism, which was dominated by intellectuals during the May Fourth era. But educated men were the leaders and the numerical majority in all May Fourth movements, and the women's emancipation movement was no exception. In Republican China, as in Imperial China, the authority, power, ability, and duty to lead society and engage in political activism rested primarily with intellectuals. Because women had far fewer opportunities to become educated, most intellectuals were men. In fact, most women were too restricted by patriarchal norms to participate in any kind of political activity, and only the most elite, resourceful, and rebellious women managed to participate in the public sphere. Women's education was still the exception rather than the rule, even in well-to-do families, and women's schools were often substandard compared to men's schools, as Deng Enming, Wang Jingwei, and Shao Lizi pointed out. There were very few women's colleges and coeducational colleges, and even these often had requirements that were difficult for women to fulfill, such as the requirement for previous training in a foreign language, which was usually not taught in high schools for girls (Gilmartin 1995). The barriers to women's education help account for why most spokespersons for the intellectual-dominated "women's movement" were men.

The Qing government abolished the Imperial examination system[1] in 1905 as part of its belated effort to introduce "modernizing" reforms. Meanwhile, schools emphasizing Western knowledge, instead of the Confucian canon, proliferated throughout China. Some of these schools were run by Westerners (especially Christian missionaries), and many more were run by Chinese reformers who saw Western knowledge as essential to the building of a new, stronger China. Schools were built for girls, and some schools became coeducational. A few all-female and all-male schools merged, as Bing Xin ambivalently reports in her account of the celebration of Union Women's College merger with Yanjing University. Some daughters as well as sons of elite families started studying abroad, especially in France, Britain, the United States, Russia, and Japan. Elite women had new opportunities to get educated, work, and become politically active in the public sphere.

May Fourth era Chinese intellectuals considered access to education a key to women's emancipation. The essays in this section describe the relationship between women's education and women's emancipation and explain some of the obstacles facing women who sought education. Xiang Jingyu's spirited letter to Tao Yi (whose essay, 16, appears in this collection), exemplifies the rhetoric and tactics of women activists struggling to improve women's access to education. The political, financial, and organizational difficulties alluded to in Xiang Jingyu's letter and Deng Chunlan's essay suggest that the effort to improve educational opportunities for women was an uphill struggle, even for women as talented and resourceful as Xiang Jingyu, Tao Yi, and Deng Chunlan. Deng Enming attempts to understand why women of his area have trouble getting a good education, and his lament that "there is really no way we can ask female students to write about this" highlights the difficulty of recruiting sufficient female leaders for the women's emancipation movement.

Much of the discussion of women's education in the May Fourth era focused on what kind of women's schools should be created and what kind of graduates they should produce. Wang Jingwei's essay exemplifies the ambivalent attitude many male activists held toward women's emancipation: on the one hand, he hoped that they would "fight fearlessly against traditional society," but on the other hand, he wanted them to preserve the "self-sacrificial spirit of Chinese women." This ambivalence, which was also apparent in the essay by Zha Mengci that

Chen Wangdao quoted in essay 20 in this collection, accounts for the inability of the kind of radical, individualistic feminism exemplified by Ding Ling's early writings to gain widespread acceptance in organized political movements. Even iconoclastic May Fourth activists favored a collectivist ethic—especially for women, whose traditional role of self-sacrificing supporter was too valuable to the movement (and, probably, to male activists themselves, as Shao Lizi emphasized in his praise of Wang Jingwei's wife) to be cast aside in the interest of promoting women's individualism.

Note

1. The Imperial examination system recruited and promoted government officials on the basis of examinations that tested knowledge of the Confucian canon and statecraft. This system began under the Han dynasty (202 B.C. to A.D. 220) and became fully institutionalized under the Song dynasty (960–1279). Highly prestigious and intensely competitive, the examination system encouraged the sons of elite families to spend most of their lives studying for and trying to pass the examinations. A good number of the few who were successful became scholar-officials and the respected elites responsible for running the Chinese government, while many degree holders never became officials. The far larger number of unsuccessful candidates constituted a supportive pool of local elites who knew the Confucian canon and accepted its hegemony. Ostensibly open to everyone regardless of social or regional background, the examination system helped maintain the hegemony of the Confucian order throughout the Chinese state's vast territory.

22

My Plan for Women's Emancipation and My Plan for Self-Improvement

Deng Chunlan (October 1919)

Originally published in *Young China*, vol. 1, no. 4.

Last month I published in the newspapers of Beijing and Shanghai a letter on behalf of all the advanced female elementary and middle school graduates of the nation, demanding that universities address the question of women's exclusion from higher education. I think those who pay attention to the woman question have seen this letter, but I still have not received a single reply. My family lives in Lanzhou, over four thousand *li*[1] away from Beijing. The distance is just about ten thousand *li* if you go by raft on the Yellow River, which takes you on a roundabout route through Inner Mongolia. I got to Beijing just in time to see our great president, the great commander exuding power and prestige, deploying military troops to suppress a group of men and women at Xinhua Gate.[2] This poured some cold water on my demand that universities address the question of women's exclusion from higher education! This was probably also the reason no one replied to the letter I wrote last month. But can we just let it end like this? In my view, it certainly cannot end. I am very happy we women have worked hard in all the patriotic movements that have followed May Fourth, and have not let anyone get in our way. I only regret that I have come too late to this endeavor, and have not fulfilled my duty to the utmost. But I also think that, while the patriotic movement is certainly urgent, our women's movement to emancipate ourselves is even more urgent. I say this for two reasons. First, passively speaking: because women have not been given the political rights of the day, our complicity cannot even be assessed when it comes to the wrongful deeds that have devastated the nation. Second, actively speaking: if a group is to have the right to lead others in discussions of "democracy," its members must have a "democratic" spirit at home. Thus, when America advocates a "democratic" League of Nations, people believe it, while people would be suspicious if Japan were to do this. Therefore, if we women are to struggle to bring a truly "democratic" spirit to the Chinese people, we must first struggle to bring a truly "democratic" spirit to the women of China. Only then can we win people's trust. As for the sequential order of the issues we address within the project of women's emancipation, I think we should first deal with education, then deal with employment, and then deal with political rights. After we have accomplished our goals in the area of political rights, the abolition of concubinage and the system of prostitution and the reform of the marriage system will be right within our grasp. As for my plan for this emancipation movement, I think we can organize a women's association in Beijing, with branches outside Beijing as well. The aim of the society would be to build a superb emancipation movement. Its work would proceed along two tracks, one focusing on making preparations and the other focusing on advocacy. Its preparatory work would include the creation of a school specifically for the purpose of preparing women to enroll in men's colleges. Its advocacy work would include producing publications and sending out speakers. When I arrived in Beijing I read in the *Weekly Review*[3] an essay written by Bang Shijun arguing that women's emancipation and the transformation of the family must proceed simultaneously. But I beg to differ. The division of labor is one thing, and women's emancipation is another; we cannot mix the two together when we talk. During the period of barbarism,[4] men had to cut firewood as soon as they finished tilling the fields, and fire up the kiln as soon as they finished cutting firewood. Likewise, women of that period had to be nursemaids, tailors, and cooks all at once. It was inefficient for each person to have so many different kinds of work with no specialty to speak of. Things are better now that there is already a division of labor emerging in the big cities. Look at what is happening to what is said to be women's work—cooking, sewing, and washing. There are now professional tailors and cobblers to make clothes and shoes, and we can pay others to make meals for a few *yuan*[5] a month. Indeed, these kinds of professions have been appropriated by men. Today, the only work that we women do which is not subject to a division of labor is the work of the nursemaid who takes care of children. But that is work that belongs to us women; why should it be an issue implicated in the emancipation of women and the transformation of the family? I think that the obligation to take care of small children is the only physiologically imposed handicap we have. And if prenatal education and kindergartens are put in place, women will only be held back twenty months to two years when they have a child. Moreover, we women have inherited a relatively kindly nature; we cannot become cutthroat grunts. These two issues aside, I do not think we women have any other handicaps. And there are those who say that the emancipation of women will be as difficult as the emancipation of black slaves in the United States, the emancipation of serfs in Russia, and the recent Chinese revolution against the Manchus. Again I beg to differ. The emancipation of black slaves in the United States naturally encountered resistance from the white masters who were to be dispossessed; the emancipation of serfs in Russia naturally encountered resistance from landlords who were to be dispossessed; the anti-Manchu revolution[6] in our own country naturally encountered resistance from the Manchus who were fighting with everything they had. But the 200 million of us Chinese who are women are in fact the mothers, daughters, sisters, aunts, wives, and daughters-in-law of the 200 million of us Chinese who are men, and those 200 million men are also the fathers, sons, brothers, uncles, husbands, and sons-in-law of those 200 million of us who are women. Of course they cannot say that they have anything to lose by emancipating us women, so what would be the difficulty? And as difficult as our revolution against the Manchus was, we were still able to thoroughly accomplish our goals because people of Sun Yat-sen's[7] caliber emerged to lead us. Sun Yat-sen wrote in *The Teachings of Sun Yat-sen* that he suffered ten failures before he led his revolutionary movement to victory.[8] I myself was born in the frontier area of Gansu. I was able to get some education thanks to my father. But there was a shortage of educators in our area, so I had to end my own education and become an elementary school teacher early on. Thus, I never did manage to get up to a high school graduate's level of education in English, math, etc., and I had even less opportunity to cultivate my social skills and public speaking skills. So now my own plan for self-improvement is, on the one hand, to get my education up to speed by taking classes at the Advanced Normal School for Women, and, on the other hand, to get in touch with like-minded comrades to work for self-improvement. If there is someone in the women's circles comparable to Sun Yat-sen and Cai Jiemin[9] of the men's circles, I beseech her to be my teacher.

Notes

1. A *li* is a Chinese unit of measurement equal to half a kilometer.

2. Here Deng Chunlan refers to the incident that touched off the May Fourth Movement. On May 4, 1919, when a student demonstration marched through Beijing to protest the Republican Chinese government's concession of Shandong rights to Japan at the signing of the Versailles treaty, President Li Yuanhong deployed military police reinforcements against the students (Schwarcz 1986, 12–23; Spence 1990, 311).

3. The *Weekly Critic* was an influential journal that started publishing on December 22, 1918 and was suppressed after August 31, 1919. It was edited by Chen Duxiu until June 1919, when Chen was arrested and Hu Shi took over (Chow 1963, 40).

4. The "period of barbarism" refers to the evolutionary stage that follows the stage of savagery and precedes the stage of civilization in the unilinear evolutionary scheme proposed by Louis Henry Morgan (1818–1881) in *Ancient Society* (first published in 1884) and interpreted along Marxist lines by Friedrich Engels (1820–1895) in *Origin of the Family, Private Property, and the State in Connection with the Researches of Lewis H. Morgan* (first published in 1884). In Morgan's scheme, the "savage" stage (the beginning of the human race) is characterized by fishing, hunting, and gathering; the "barbaric" stage is characterized by pottery, horticulture, agriculture, and iron; and the "civilized" stage is characterized by the use of writing. This evolutionary scheme was adopted by many Marxists worldwide as the proper frame of reference for the archeology and history of human societies.

5. A *yuan* is a Chinese unit of currency. During the May Fourth era, the term *yuan* usually referred to a tael of silver. Until 1933, when China established a national currency, Chinese money consisted of a combination of foreign currencies, ingots or coins of silver, and bank notes and checks, many of which were based on the *yuan*, or tael. Taels varied considerably in weight over China, depending on the scales used in a particular region or locality. The most important currency tael was the Shanghai tael, equivalent to 518 grains of fine silver. The Shanghai tael's exchange value fluctuated with the price of silver in London and New York City (*Encyclopaedia Britannica* 1996).

6. The revolution against the Manchus refers to the nationalist, anti-Qing revolution of 1911.

7. Sun Yat-sen (1866–1925) was the leader of the anti-Qing revolutionary movement and the founder of Republican China. Born in Guangdong, he went to Hawaii at the age of thirteen and attended a British missionary school. He attended colleges in Hawaii and Hong Kong and graduated from the College of Medicine for Chinese in Hong Kong in 1892. Beginning in 1894, Sun built up a vast but loosely organized international network of anti-Qing revolutionary groups and secret societies. He campaigned for support throughout Europe, North America, Japan, Hong Kong, and Vietnam, and maintained his revolutionary network despite suffering repeated failures. He was elected provisional president of the Chinese Republic after the revolution succeeded in 1911, but conceded the position to the powerful Qing court minister Yuan Shikai in 1912. He spent the rest of his life leading the Nationalist Party and struggling to unite various revolutionary factions and warlords under his control. He published many works of political theory and propaganda elucidating his Three Principles of the People (nationalism, democracy, and people's livelihood) and his Plan for

National Reconstruction. His ideology was strongly influenced by the Soviet Union toward the end of his life, though he maintained that Communism was not a suitable system for China. He died of cancer in 1925 (*Encyclopaedia Britannica* 1996; Schwarcz 1986, 28, 35, 46, 236; Spence 1990, 227–228, 240, 262, 294–296, 305, 323, 335–339; Sun 1931).

8. Sun Yat-sen wrote in *The Teachings of Sun Yat-sen*, a book about his political philosophy and revolutionary struggles, that his attempts to organize revolts against the Qing government failed ten times before 1911, when the anti-Qing revolution succeeded and the Chinese Republic was founded. *The Teachings of Sun Yat-sen* (also translated as *The Cult of Dr. Sun* and as *To Do Is Easier Than to Know*) became part of the Chinese Nationalist canon (Sun 1931).

9. Cai Jiemin is another name of Cai Yuanpei, a leading anti-Qing intellectual who served as president of Beijing University from 1917 to 1926.

23
A Plan for Women's Development

Letter from Xiang Jingyu to Tao Yi (December 20, 1919)

Originally published in *Collected Letters of the New People's Study Society*, vol. 2.

Dear Sister Yi,

The letter I wrote you yesterday should be arriving soon. Tonight, because of a conversation I had with Hesen,[1] it has suddenly occurred to me to tell you two of my greatest hopes.

First, I hope you will join the public association[2] at Beijing University.

Second, I hope you will urge the junior high school graduates, normal school students,[3] and high school students of our province to get together and ask that Beijing University establish a coeducational high school class.

Sister Yi! This year, a new current of thought began sweeping over a small number of people in our country. Because we believe that the well-being of humanity cannot be achieved without equity in social development, we want to raise the benighted half of the population who are women out of their hellish existence. Thus, the cries for "Women's emancipation! Women's emancipation!" grow louder every day. Yet, when we think about it carefully, we see that it all has to do with learning. This is apparent to everyone, so in the final analysis we must always return to the issue of education. Coeducation is the best way to improve women's education and to hasten the spread of social progress. You of all people should understand these reasons for coeducation, so I need not elaborate on them. On behalf of a well-grounded movement for coeducation, thirty women comrades who live in Tianjin requested that Beijing University become coeducational. This is truly unprecedented! In this era of grueling pioneer work, incisive, talented people willing to undergo hardships are essential. The more of this kind there are, the greater the accomplishments. Sister Yi! You have to take care of your mother, so you can't go abroad to study.[4] So why not use this opportunity to stand up for our promising plan? There are so many advantages to studying at Beijing University. It goes without saying that you would further your education. Don't we often think about fundamental change, Sister Yi? Beijing University just happens to be the hub of our country's thought about social transformation. The first advantage would be that, with the addition of sound thinkers like you, this center of transformational thinking would of course enjoy greater transformational power. And most women in our country are so muddle-headed and ignorant. If there is a group of sound thinkers in the university to lead the nation, talk about practicalities, and advance side by side, this group will naturally be able to transform women. This would be the second advantage. Though our knowledge is incomplete, we are certain that our minds are pure, our thinking is thorough, and that we should be the ones to fulfill the great responsibility of fundamentally transforming the world. We need great preparation to embark upon a great cause, and we must begin our preparation now. Our most important goal is to spread the seeds of change. We comrades should spread ourselves throughout all the important institutions. I am already too far away to help with things in Beijing, so I really hope that you will go and raise women's consciousness. With your enthusiasm, anything can be accomplished! This is the third advantage. Because of all these advantages, I very much hope you will go. Are you concerned about your academic qualifications? Anyone who has graduated from a normal school or high school can take their advanced preparation class. If you work hard to prepare, you will be able to take regular college courses next year. You may be concerned about your economic situation, but if there are problems, you can organize a work-study group or ask the Chenmei Scholarship Society for a loan. Work-study in China should be the same as work-study abroad; it just depends on your own ability to struggle. I hope that you will make up your mind as soon as you get this letter and join the movement to make Beijing University coeducational as soon as possible. Supported by activism on all sides, we shall certainly achieve our goal.

My second hope is even more ambitious than my first. The first is just about joining what already exists, but the second is about creating something new, so it is somewhat more difficult and ambitious. But I think it is the most important step toward gender equality in education. Mr. Hu Shi wrote in an article about opening the schools to women: "Even when colleges are coeducational, women cannot take [regular college courses] because they are not academically prepared for them. What causes this? It certainly would not be the case if high schools were coeducational. Therefore, while we should ask for coeducation in colleges, it is even more important that we ask for high school coeducation." This is what we already fervently believe; it is unfortunate, however, that neither public nor private schools have this kind of courageous and knowledgeable teacher to resolutely work for coeducation. Therefore I fervently hope that the university will set up a coeducational high school class to serve as a model for the entire nation, participate in a practical cultural movement, smash the obsolete views of the family and the society. This would be the most wonderful, glorious, and promising accomplishment. So I hope you will be a trailblazer of this movement and organize a group of about thirty to forty male and female junior high graduates and students currently in their first or second year of high school or normal school to go to Beijing University and Beijing's Ministry of Education to ask for a coeducational high school class. If there are people willing to do this, there will certainly be results. Why do I think so?

1. A bill for coeducation is being considered by the Shanxi educational association.
2. Beijing University already has plans to build another high school.
3. The president and faculty of Beijing University are all full of new ideas, so they will help rather than hinder you.
4. Beijing University is already coeducational.[5]
5. Due to the destruction wrought by Mr. Zhang,[6] Hunan has become a bastion of illiteracy.

Clearly, we can be confident of the validity of the above five reasons. If male and female students of our province go to ask for a coeducational high school class, they will not only gain good educations for themselves but also build a glorious path for womankind and a bridge to prosperity for all humankind. But these poor students have never experienced an education of the spirit. They lack a fighting spirit, so they need capable people to inspire and motivate them to take action. My students here at Shupu[7] want very much to develop a real force of their own to go to Beijing and become activists. You can also raise this issue with students in the Daotian preparatory course, second-year students in the Normal School, and first- and second-year students in Zhounan High School and encourage them to get together and go to Beijing to make their demands. As for the male students, Hesen said that Chen Qimin and He Shuheng[8] can exhort them to do the same. All of Xiao Zisheng's[9] students at Chuyi Junior High School are extremely ambitious and well trained. They will certainly be able to get together and ask for high school coeducation. We would only need about thirty people; the more the better, though. I think this is an issue of the utmost importance, and we cannot let this great opportunity pass by. Even if this will require the students to sacrifice some of their study time, what is there to study in Changsha? Even if they can study, what is the use of this perfunctory studying? And we are constantly advocating women's emancipation and communal living for humankind. Where are we going to begin working toward these goals? Are we going to do it or not? And when we do it, is it better to do it earnestly or casually? I really hope that you will work hard to promote ordinary women's self-motivation, Sister Yi. Perhaps you should even write to Wei, Lao, and Zhou[10] and ask them to come to Beijing. Urge them not to shut themselves up at home and let time slip by. If they want to eventually study in America, they should start preparing in Beijing this year. Regardless of how busy you are, Sister Yi, you will have to write to them and encourage them to come and ask that the university create a coeducational high school class. This would be the most promising, most spirited, and most memorable thing you could do. Do you have the determination to do this, Sister Yi? I originally planned to return to Hunan myself, but there is really not enough time (I am leaving on the twenty-fifth). I cannot spare the time from my work. You can discuss this with Qimin and Shuheng. I hope that you will take my advice, Sister Yi, and throw yourself into the movement!

This issue is so important that I could not sleep until I wrote this letter. I will propose that my Shupu girls' school start accepting boys as well, and this proposal will probably go through. But the two things I hope you will accomplish, if successful, would make things happen a lot faster and a lot more easily. As for traveling expenses, take out a loan if possible; sell your clothes if you have to! Once you get to Beijing, if you find yourself in economic difficulty, try to find work; just don't stop until your goal is accomplished, and you will surely succeed. At this stage of our development, we won't succeed if we are not willing to sacrifice or fight even a little! We will see whether all the students from my Shupu school who have sought educations in this province will have the daring to do this, to march forward and meet every obstacle with further resolve as Jinqiu and the rest did. It is late and my hand grows tired.

Give my best regards to Shuheng, Qimin, and Chu Shengzhu.

Jingyu
December 20

Notes

1. Hesen is the given name of Cai Hesen, who at the time was Xiang Jingyu's husband. Cai Hesen (1890–1931) was a leading activist in the early Chinese Communist Party and a close friend of Mao Zedong (Klein and Clark 1971, 851–853).
2. The term "public association" implies an association open to both men and women in this essay.
3. Many normal schools were designed for students at the high school level in Republican China.
4. Tao Yi, Xiang Jingyu, and some others spent the fall of 1919 organizing a group to prepare female students to go to France for a work-study program, but Tao Yi herself could not go because of family responsibilities (Zhonghua Quanguo Funu Lianhehui 1989, 89, 109).
5. Beijing University leaders resolved to make the university coeducational soon after May 4, 1919, and the university admitted its first female students in 1920 (Spence 1990, 311).
6. Zhang Jingyao was then the corrupt ruling warlord of Hunan (Li Jui 1977; Snow 1938).
7. Xupu is the town where the school founded by Xiang Jingyu was located.
8. He Shuheng (1874–1935), a native of Hunan, was the oldest of the original members of the New People's Study Society and the Chinese Communist Party. He was a friend of Mao Zedong and Cai Hesen and led the New People's Study Society in their absence. (Boorman and Howard 1971, 73).

9. Xiao Zisheng was also known as Xiao Xudong and Xiao-yu. Xiao and Cai Hesen were Mao's closest at Hunan's First Normal School, where the three of them called themselves "the three heroes." Xiao graduated in June 1915 and studied in France from 1919 to 1920 and from 1923 to 1924. He and Mao later became bitter enemies after their political paths diverged (Schram 1992, 19, 71, 610).

10. Wei Bi, Lao Junzhan, and Zhou Dunxiang were widely recognized as the three leading girls' school activists of the May Fourth Movement in Zhounan, according to the editor's note in the original anthology.

24
Report on Yanjing University's Ceremony to Celebrate the Beginning of Coeducation

Bing Xin (March 15, 1920)

The original Chinese essay was published in *Selected Works by Bing Xin*, Vol. 6, Shanghai Art and Literature Publishing House, 1993.

On March 15, 1920, I went to school as usual. When I got to the school gate, I happened to raise my head and see new signboards hanging on the top and two sides of the gate. Written on blackboard covers in golden characters, they looked magnificent. The board in the middle was covered with yellow paper and read "Yanjing University,"[1] while the two vertical boards on the sides read "Women's Liberal Arts" in both English and Chinese. All of a sudden, it dawned upon me that this was the day of Yanjing University's ceremony to celebrate the beginning of coeducation. We were certainly very intrigued and delighted by the boards and were full of cheerful hope. But the signboard of "Union Women's College"—what we had cherished most—was no longer there; there was not a single trace of it. Of course, we should not cling to the old when times are changing and resist the new when it is inevitably going to replace the old. However, we, as former students of the former Union Women's College, could not help but feel sorry for and nostalgic about the much-cherished old signboard.

It was such a nice, warm day—the weather seemed to favor that big event. American, British, and Chinese flags were hanging on the gates and walls of both schools, and the paths were flanked with potted flowers. It was a truly spectacular scene. The auditorium was decorated with lots of potted plants, and "Yanjing University" banners were hung up high. The banners and pendants, some rectangular, some triangular, all looked so very beautiful, adding life and atmosphere to the event. However, I could not help but think of our school flag, which used to fly triumphantly over every school event. At that moment, I heard a classmate say: "From today on, our school banner and school flag will be seen no more; neither will our school anthem be heard." Dean Mai said to us that "the changes our college is going through are just like when a child going to school has to change a pet name into a new official name. . Although giving up our pet name means that we have grown, we still feel a bit sad." I, too, nodded my head. So all of us were saddened by the change. Gong Ding'an's[2] poem reads: "No snowstorm today, yet my tears are just like snow. Don't blame me for shedding such snow-like tears—even at my age, I am thinking of my childhood." It is so true!

At 1:30 P.M., students of the all-male college started to arrive in groups and gathered on the right side of the auditorium—in the hallway of theory classes. All the faculty members stood in the courtyard, holding guest lists in their hands, welcoming the guests, and chatting with each other. Then alumni from both schools and their Chinese and foreign invited guests came. At about 2:30, all the male and female students entered the hall to the beautiful accompaniment of organ music and occupied the seats on both sides.

The speeches given by faculty, staff, and other representatives were indeed marvelous. The following are some excerpts:

After President Leighton Stuart's opening speech welcoming Dr. Mai and all the female students, Professor Cheng Guanyi gave an account of the history of the women's college. She herself graduated from Union Women's College and later studied education for several years in England before returning to teach at Union Women's College. The gist of her speech is:

The predecessor of Union Women's College was Beiman Girl's Middle School. Afterward, thanks to the joint efforts of many organizations, Union Women's College was founded in 1905 and gradually developed into a women's college that boasts a full four-year curriculum with departments such as physics, chemistry, education, and childcare. This owes a lot to the great work of Director Mai. . . . The most important component of a school is of course its student body. The school started

out with only four students, but now it has more than eighty. . . . Most
college affairs are run by the students themselves. For instance,
1. "part-time schooling" was designed to teach basic lessons to the poor
children who lived nearby, with all the fees and expenses covered by
students themselves. 2. A kindergarten was set up to engage the nearby
poor children in healthy games. 3. A "school for teaching the national
phonetic alphabet" was set up to teach illiterate women to acquire daily
knowledge through reading books and magazines. The students also collaborated with other social organizations and cofounded Local Service with
YMCA and "Popular Vocational School" with other female students in
Beijing. And these are just what was done by the students on campus;
needless to day, what our alumni have contributed to society and public
education is universally acknowledged.

Following Ms. Cheng's speech was Mr. Bo Chenguang's report on
the history of the men's school, in which he said:

> We are now standing on a bank looking out at the merging of two tributar-
> ies; yet one of the tributaries was also the result of the slow merging of
> several rivulets. . . . That is how Tongzhou Union College and Beijing
> Huiwen College merged; now we are again merging with Union Women's
> College. Facing this big river, we ought to have lots of hope!

After the women's choir sang, Director Mai stood up to give a talk
on American reactions to the merging of the two schools:

> Earlier, some Americans had some doubts about the merging of Union
> Women's College and Yanjing University. Isn't China a conservative
> nation? Have the Chinese students reached the necessary standards? In
> my view, China has witnessed a great enhancement of morale since the
> May Fourth Movement last year. China has proved that it is not a
> conservative nation and that its students are full of enthusiasm and
> courage, willing to serve and sacrifice for their country. The high spirits
> of the Chinese students are extremely surprising and touching. There-
> fore, it seems to me that our American friends are no longer in doubt
> and are, on the contrary, very supportive of the merge. . . . I think our
> achievements will surpass our expectations.

Speaking about the future prospects of Yanjing University, President Stuart said:

> First, I hope that our female students will from now on receive the same
> education as our male students, and grow and serve society in the future

just as their male counterparts have done. Second, the current residential buildings for both the men and the women are far too small. We shall build a larger university.... When the mid-twentieth century comes around and the Chinese nation is flourishing, a highly developed university will be what people expect; we simply need to have new buildings and dorms. Third, I hope that our young men and women will unite and raise their moral standards as they face a bright future.... Fourth, I hope that our students will become the salt of the earth after their graduation and use their knowledge to transform China. I do hope that these hopes will not turn out to be illusions.

Then, after the men's choir sang, Mr. Deng Zhiyuan of the Ministry of Education made a congratulatory speech, the gist of which goes:

I have served as an educator for more than a decade and have deeply felt that China needs coeducational schools.... Just last year, the National Education Association passed a bill supporting coeducation; however, it cannot be forced upon all the provinces.... Now your university has become the first to practice coeducation, thus solving a most urgent social problem. It is indeed an admirable and honorable event, which I believe will serve as a model for many other schools in the near future. Therefore, let me extend my heartfelt congratulations on the realization of your ideal and my best wishes for the bright future of your university.

Mrs. Mao, the representative of the women's academic associations in Beijing, made an excellent speech. She said:

There have been three great people in the world who have advocated and practiced the spirit of fraternity and unity. They are: Jesus Christ, the Siddartha Gautama, and Confucius.... The reason that China is so weak and poor is all due to the fact that most of our politicians are only interested in power and lack the spirit of unity and fraternity. Fortunately, many institutions and organizations in China have begun to get united.... The co-ed merge of Yanjing University symbolizes the spirit of fraternity and unity and should indeed be admired and congratulated.

When Mr. Cai Jiemin,[3] the well-known figure serving as the representative of men's academic associations, appeared on the platform, he instantly drew the attention of the entire audience. In his speech, he said:

I have received letters from people asking me "if Beijing University is forbidden to women"; in my reply to them, I usually said that Beijing

University was meant for both sexes, since both men and women should enjoy the same education; however, due to the fact that no women had applied so far, we have not had any female students. . . . At present, we have several female auditors and yet there are still some restrictions. . . . In the future, if there are female applicants, they will be tested and accepted just like male students.

I am deeply sorry that I could not record what he said after that, because my seat was too far from the platform.

Father Liu Fang, who represented all the Christian organizations in Beijing, said in his speech:

The old Chinese saying goes, "If one wants to succeed in doing something, one needs to first sharpen one's tools." If we want to teach young men and women to realize their full potential, we need to first have good schools. Young people are supposed to bring happiness to our society; our schools need to train them to be "true to themselves" as "real human beings." The faculty and staff members in your university are all devout Christians. You not only guide the students academically but also teach them to be "true to themselves" as "real human beings." As a coeducational institution of higher learning, you have set an excellent example for the nation. The nation has become the direct beneficiary and the Church the indirect one.

Unfortunately, Dr. Dewey, the long-awaited distinguished guest, was unable to come to the meeting. When President Stuart apologized on his behalf, we all could not help but feel disappointed.

Speeches by student representatives followed. Mr. Yu Zhenzhou, the male representative, and Ms. Qian Zhonghui, the female representative, gave two marvelous speeches in which they expressed their happiness about the occasion and their best wishes for the future of the university. In the end, the university choir sang the school anthem—with a melodious Chinese tune and lyrics written by Mr. Yang Wenzhou, a student. After the anthem, President Stuart asked the guests to leave some words behind. Mr. Chen Songhua from the Ministry of Education said: "As a matter of fact, coeducation should not have to be celebrated. This should have been a very normal thing. This merger has become an epoch-making event only because men and women have been strictly segregated for the past several thousand years in China. . . . Christianity has advocated that one can strengthen oneself by learning from the strengths of others. . . .

When Christianity spreads its roots throughout China, China will have hope."

Our music teacher Ms. Su played the organ. Afterward, President Stuart thanked all the guests for coming and then announced the conclusion of the event. All the guests, faculty, and staff members and all the students withdrew from the auditorium to attend the reception. After the group photos, this big event came to a close.

I have written a report on the celebration of the beginning of coeducation at Yanjing University, which is indeed a red-letter day for Yanjing. I have recorded it with nostalgic feelings toward the former "Union Women's College" and with my best wishes for the new Yanjing University. Long live Yanjing University!

Notes

1. Yanjing University was first founded in 1919 in Beijing by American missionaries, when Union College at North Tongzhou (Tong County) and Huiwen College in Beijing merged, and was joined in 1920 by North China Union Female College. Like many colleges and universities during World War II, Yenching University was moved in 1942 to Chengdu, Sichuan, and moved back to Beijing in 1946. American missianary Leighton Stuart served as its president for many years and later became American ambassador to China under Chang Kai-shek's Nationalist government. In 1951, Yenching University, together with many other missionary schools in China, was taken over by the Chinese Communist government (*Ci Hai* 1979, 1243).

2. Gong Zizhen, alias Gong Ding'an, (1792–1841), a native of Renhe, Zhejiang (Hangzhou), was a thinker, scholar, and poet (*Ci Hai* 1979, 1661).

3. Cai Jiemin was also known as Cai Yuanpei. His speech appears as essay 19 in this book.

25
The Condition of Female Education in Jinan

Deng Enming (January 15, 1921)

Originally published in *Promote the New*, vol. 1, no. 3.

When it comes to female education, China ranks lowest of all nations in the world, and Shandong ranks lowest in all of China. Ever since the new tide of thought swept over China, the woman question has received a great deal of attention everywhere, and all kinds of publications concerning the condition of female education have come out. How is female education in Jinan, the cultural center of Shandong? It is truly surprising that, up till today, no one has written about this. This kind of essay should normally be written by female students themselves. But Shandong does not have the kind of female education other places do, so there is really no way we can ask female students to write about this. Therefore, I have to be the one to make a haphazard attempt at writing about this. But I am a male student, and I am likely to get some things wrong. I hope that someone from a girls'[1] school will emerge to correct me or to make an even more detailed investigation; that would be much better.

Female education is not very well developed in Shandong. Though Jinan is the cultural center of Shandong, Jinan's relatively good schools for female education consist only of a normal school, a vocational school, a sericulture school, and four elementary schools. There are fewer than a thousand people in these schools. When education is available to so few girls even in a city as big as Jinan, it is clear that Shandong's female education is flawed indeed.

With over three hundred students, the Girls' Normal School is Jinan's most populous girls' school. Next is Jingjin Elementary School. The vocational school, the sericulture school, the Chongshi Elementary School, and the Shangbu elementary school each has about the same number of students. Even though the Girls' Normal School is the best in Shandong, it has very few high-quality students. So after graduation, few can go on to higher education. Nor are there many who can become teachers. Most of the rest have to go on to a hellish life. I think they are unable to get higher educations primarily because of bad grades, the low quality of their work, and restrictions placed on them by their families.[2]

Yet these problems must also be attributed to the teachers in charge of female education. If one were to ask these teachers why girls should be educated, or what the purpose of girls' education is, it seems they would not have an answer. I am not being sarcastic; this is just how it is. For instance, in three pieces of female education news recently published in *Democracy Newspaper*, the author wrote about a teacher who did not approve of doing away with the idea that girls should continue to be educated to become virtuous wives and good mothers. In response, a letter from the autonomous student government refuted this teacher, and Ms. Zhou, a lecturer, also wrote a letter to challenge this teacher. Judging from this, we would think that the Girls' Normal School is not too bad. But how is it in reality? It is just the opposite. Why? I think it is because of problems in the curriculum (which I detail in section B) and problems in the schoolwork. Aren't these problems the fault of the teachers in charge of female education?

The Normal School's Auxiliary Elementary School and Jingjin, Chongshi, and Shangbu elementary schools are all public schools. Jingjin has over three hundred students, and the other schools have a hundred students each. These schools are run fairly well, so many of their graduates can advance to the normal school or the sericulture school. Some graduates also go on to normal schools and vocational schools in other places.

The administrators of the recently established sericulture school are not very dedicated, and it can be said that society has not benefited from them at all.

The vocational school admits anyone who can read a few characters. They do this because the training of very advanced personnel is not their goal. However, the principal said that, in general, none of this school's graduates have been unable to live independently in society. Though the principal was exaggerating, the school is actually pretty good.

I have limned the general conditions of these famous schools. Now I will discuss these schools more specifically, from several perspectives.

A. The School

1. Faculty

The school should be like a big family, with parents and children.[3] The students should be like the children, and the faculty should be like the parents. They should live in harmony and support each other. Yet this is not true in Shandong schools, especially in girls' schools. Here, the faculty are faculty and the students are students; they don't care about each other at all. This is exacerbated by gender segregation rules. Some say that "teachers are there for the salary, and students are there for the diploma." This saying may sound a bit too sarcastic, but close examination reveals that there is some truth to it. Teachers do not care about students, so they are either totally laissez-faire or despotically coercive when they look at students' work. They do not care about students' work; all they care about is getting a few dozen *yuan* each month. And no matter how poor a student's work is, she will remain baffled because no one will inquire about her work or try to supervise her. After going through a few years of muddle-headed schooling, she graduates without having learned a thing. What is the reason for this? We cannot avoid blaming the teachers. Teachers fancy themselves untouchable sages. Students are both angered and intimidated by them and certainly do not dare to ask questions. Even if they do ask questions, the teacher is not very patient. Thus, the more intimidated students are, the more formidable teachers feel. But do students really fear teachers? Even though students do not dare to say anything in front of their teachers, they curse their teachers to no end behind their backs. In light of these conditions, should we say that Shandong's lack of development in female education is the fault of the teachers? What attitude should female students have toward their teachers? What should be our attitude toward those teachers? What attitude should the teachers themselves have?

2. Curriculum

On the surface, the curricula of postelementary Jinan schools such as the normal school and the sericulture school appear very complete. But actually they are just as bad. Today, every school claims to promote academics, moral cultivation, and physical education. But what do these schools really do? When it comes to academics, very few students are good at Chinese. Those who are relatively good at English can only compose a few very simple sentences, and the rest only know a few letters. To be frank, some students graduate without knowing anything about arithmetic, algebra, geometry, trigonometry, etc. As for moral cultivation, I will save that discussion for my section on "students." And then we have physical education. Every school has physical education classes, but students do not get enough extracurricular exercise. A few hours of calisthenics really cannot produce good results. At this point, I would like to address the teachers who run girls' schools. Students come to school to learn. When a school has this kind of curriculum, it is incumbent on the teachers to teach sincerely. If not, their schools end up with a fame that belies their lack of substance. Such schools might as well close down, to avoid wasting other people's valuable time and money.

3. Administration

Just about all Jinan girls' schools use despotic methods to control their students. Thus, a female student's freedom is completely under her school's control. She has to get her school's permission for every single move she makes. No matter how close a man's relationship with a female student is, he must first get through the demeaning paperwork and the despotic bureaucracy to get the principal's approval before he can visit her. I have never tried to do this, but I hear from others that it is really difficult for a man to see a female student. It's even more difficult than it is for subordinates to see the emperor! I will give another example. The examination of female students' mail is of course a means to "nip things in the bud." But I think this is truly demeaning to female students. How so? Well, if boys and girls are the same as persons, with equal status, then why is it that boys' schools do not examine students' mail, while girls' schools do? If boys' schools examined students' mail, I believe their students would certainly rise up in opposition. Therefore, I hope that Jinan's female students will see the examination of their mail as a gross insult, and rise up to oppose it. If they adopt the spirit of "Give me liberty or give me death," I think that they will eventually accomplish their goal. I also think that teachers themselves should think about why it is that boys' mail need not be examined, while girls' mail must be examined, even though girls, like boys, are persons. Teachers must ask their own consciences about how unequal and unfree this is!

B. Students

Even though Jinan has over a thousand female students, it seems that very few of them understand why they are getting an education, or what the purpose of an education is. Even if they were sent by their parents to get an education, they still do not understand what the purpose of an education is. The best of these kinds of girls can go on to Beijing Women's College, but they still do not realize why they are getting educated or what the purpose of an education is. Because of this and because of their oppressive environment and the restrictions placed on them by their families, none of them contributes anything to society even after they graduate. Can this be called receiving an education?

We should examine the article on "The Characteristics of the Female Student" published by W.P. in the *Democratic Daily*.

C. Female Students and Social Movements

The political activities of male and female Chinese students seem to have begun only after last year's May Fourth Movement. In other places, most of the female students started their movements together with male students. Only in Jinan is this not the case; here, female students have not dared to unite with male students to engage in movements for any issue. Those who worry that Jinan is lagging behind others organized a women's federation. But, not long afterward, it disappeared without a trace. At this point, I am starting to wonder why female students are like this. Could it be that they really cannot participate in social movements? I think that it can only be due to the following reasons:

1. Bad education
2. The injustice of society
3. An oppressive environment
4. Their inability to help each other

Because of the above reasons, we have the situation I have described. But we really cannot blame them; we can only pity them. We should think of how we can help them gain victory over all kinds of demons.

D. Female Students and the New Tide of Thought

Jinan's girls' schools are based on high-handed control. As long as female students bow their heads in study by a window, and spend their lives from morning till night in a pile of musty old books, their teachers are very happy. No matter how the new tide of thought surges forward outside, these students will not hear of it. Even if a few students want to go get a taste of this new tide of thought, they will arouse the indignant condemnation of teachers and administrators. If their family finds out, it will say that she has committed the greatest outrage. Her classmates will mock and scorn her behind her back, and some will even curse her to her face. Alas! You teachers who run girls' schools, you do not mind when students read base novels, but you come down like a scourge on the new tide of thought. I think that if you students can read base novels, you can certainly read the newest publications; but why do you not read them? If you want to know about all kinds of things such as women's equality and women's emancipation, it is up to you to work for them; who in society will help you? Who will be your allies? You cannot just hope that others will help you. I have to put it bluntly: Most people in our society want to oppress and toy with you. So you must arise, quickly arise!

Notes:

1. The original *nüxiao* could be translated either as "girls' school" or as "women's school", since *nü* just means "female" and does not specify age. Throughout this essay, we translate *nü* as "female" whenever possible. In sentences like this, where it is not possible to use the age-neutral "female," we use "girl" because the subjects of the essay seem to be children and adolescents.

2. In the early 1920s, women's colleges were even scarcer than girls' schools, and coeducation at any level was extremely rare. Thus, only a few of the most outstanding girls' school graduates could get a higher education (Gilmartin 1995, 54).

3. A more literal translation of *you fuxiong, you zidi* would be "with fathers and older brothers, with sons and younger brothers."

26
Thoughts on Women

Wang Jingwei (January 1924).

Originally published in *Women's Magazine*, vol. 10, no.1, in January 1924. Originally delivered as a speech at Jingxian Women's Middle School in Songjiang, a town near Shanghai, and transcribed by Gao Erbo.

It is most delightful for me to have the opportunity to join you today. I particularly admire all of you, teachers and students alike, for your fighting spirit.

Having been bound, on the one hand, by thousands of years of traditional education and old morality and influenced, on the other hand, by new thought from the West, Chinese women are now in a transitional period. They have come to realize that old morals and habits are incongruous with the spirit of the new age and should be smashed. During this process, conflicts between the old and the new tend to occur. While society and the family shelter old, conservative ideas, modern schools create new trends and ideas. Thus, it may be said that conflicts between old and new are also conflicts between schools and the institutions of society and the family.

Modern schools were originally created to meet the needs of social development. However, because of the nature of the transitional period during which the new replaces the old, modern schools should no longer take their cues from society. For instance, where society tries to retain conservative habits, schools should not follow suit. Instead, schools should serve as a catalyst to transform all the bad habits and old morals that exist in society. Only when our schools can play such a role will our society make progress and survive in this conflict-ridden world. Otherwise, our schools will always trail behind society and succumb to its old habits. If this happens, our society will never evolve or be competitive with other nations in the world.

Since modern schools should be the pillar and control the center of society, what should be the duty of our students during the period of social transformation? Is it enough for students to merely acquire the knowledge society demands they acquire?

Students go to school to gain knowledge. But often the knowledge acquired at school runs counter to the needs of society. In that regard, there are only two possible paths to take: (1) use our knowledge and insights to shatter the evil habits of society and the family, maintain our individuality, and fight fearlessly against traditional society; or (2) succumb to the demands of society and the family and accept their total control. As we know, society has a great deal of power to control people. If one does not have a fighting spirit, one will be easily devoured by one's society. Which path should we take? Of course, the first one—we should use the knowledge acquired at school to transform society, and never be assimilated by society.

When it comes to this, our schools for men are better off than our schools for women, because women's schools offer little that can be applied to the family and society, let alone knowledge that can be used to transform society and resist social assimilation. Women are certainly very important in society; society can never make progress if women are deprived of the knowledge and the spirit necessary to social improvement. However, this kind of new thought and spirit can only be attained and nurtured at school. In that sense, the current corruption of our women's schools is the biggest obstacle to social progress. Therefore, we should do our best to advocate women schools and imbue all our women students with the ability to transform society.

Now let me turn to the issue of how students should study. In my view, we should learn analytical methods and learn what is to be included and what is to be excluded in our curriculum. Our women's schools teach many bad things, but there is at least one outstanding thing about them: that any woman who has received a traditional education does not seek personal happiness and comfort and is totally self-sacrificing. Before marriage, she is willing to sacrifice herself for her parents' happiness and comfort; after marriage, for her husband; and in old age, for her son. It is important to know that this kind of blind self-denial is imposed on her by society. She should guard against letting society take advantage of her strong sense of personal responsibility. Nonetheless, it is indeed worthwhile if one sacrifices for true love; after all, this kind of willingness to sacrifice oneself is admirable—it is the root of all morality. The "loyalty and magnanimity" advocated by Confucius and Mencius, the "benevolence and mercy" advocated by Buddhism, and the "universal love" advocated by Christianity all share this kind of spirit, without which all morality would disappear. Even in the current transitional period, it is still necessary to preserve this kind of self-sacrificing spirit; we still need the spirit that is akin to that of traditional Chinese women. But every sacrifice should be worthwhile and done for the sake of Truth.

In recent years, people have advocated all kinds of freedom at our schools, which is by all accounts a very good thing. However, I do hope that our students will be able to think from a larger perspective when talking about freedom and try to put the freedom of the general public above, and when necessary at the expense of, their individual freedom. It is not genuine freedom unless it is based on the concept of "sacrificing one's individual freedom for the freedom of the general public." In my opinion, the self-sacrificial spirit of Chinese women is truly applicable here. On the one hand, it may maintain part of the essence of thousands of years of Chinese tradition; on the other hand, it can be used to serve as part of the foundation for modern ideas of emancipation. I hope that all women students at school nowadays will be able to live up to this expectation.

In conclusion, it is my hope that our women students will foster and maintain the self-sacrificing spirit embodied in our traditional education, and learn to endure personal suffering and hardships and not to seek personal happiness and comfort. I also hope that our women students will apply what they have learned at school to social transformation, break all the old habits, keep in mind the needs of the majority of women, and offer them help so that they will also be emancipated and live a decent life. The most important thing is to pursue the freedom of the general public and sacrifice one's personal happiness when necessary. It is indeed my sincere wish that all women students in China will be able to possess this spirit, particularly those who are now here attending Jingxian Women's Middle School. But you may well have already acquired this spirit.

Thank you.

27
A Few Words of Encouragement

Shao Lizi (January 1924)

Originally published in *Women's Magazine*, vol. 10, no. 1, in January 1924. Originally delivered as a speech at Jingxian Women's Middle School in Songjiang, a town near Shanghai, and transcribed by Gao Erbo.

Dear Students,

Mr. Wang Jingwei has just said that "we should use the knowledge acquired at school to transform society, and never be assimilated by society." This remark, it seems, is applicable here at Jingxian Women's Middle School. Why? We should teach students the correct ideas and then ask them to go to transform society after they leave school. Without the right ideas, they would certainly be unable to resist the influence of society. There are many schools in Shanghai and other places where the administrators have very wrong ideas—even superstitious ones. It is not surprising that their students also have the wrong ideas.

When I was in Shanghai, I had some contact with several women's schools. Yet, because my ability is limited, I was unable to change their very wrong ideas. One can imagine how the students might be led down the wrong path under the erroneous guidance of the administrators. How can we expect these students to be able to transform society and to resist the influence of society after they graduate? However, it is my belief that the educators at Jingxian Women's School, with their correct thinking, will not lead the students down the wrong path.

It has been more than two decades since China opened its first women's school. Unfortunately, women's schools have had zero success. For the male students, the most important thing is to get a diploma they can use to wangle a job from society. Female students only want to get some schooling so they can secure a better deal in marriage. Certainly, these two kinds of thinking are equally wrong. When a woman has this kind of thinking, she tends to be satisfied with having some elementary school education. Regardless of her potential, she would discontinue her study because her parents believe that elementary schooling is sufficient for her to attain a good marriage. Of course, her parents' idea is ridiculous. But she herself is also to blame, since she lacks vision and a fighting spirit. She should give up her dowry and ask her parents to use the dowry money for her school tuition. However, many young women also believe that an elementary school education is sufficient to qualify them for a decent marriage. They do not study for knowledge, for society, or to become a better person—their purpose in going to school is solely to qualify for a better marriage. Thus, just like those men who go to school merely to secure a job, these women contribute nothing to society. Of course, this is due both to the wrongful guidance of their school administrators and their own lack of the correct worldview and fighting spirit. But I can see that here at Jingxian Women's School, no such problem exists.

Now allow me to mention a role model for you—Ms. Chen Bijun, Madame Wang Jingwei. Ms. Chen went to school with the desire to improve society, and she is full of fighting spirit and self-sacrifice. During the time of the late Qing, she went to study in Japan and joined Mr. Wang Jingwei there. Later, when Mr. Wang went to Beijing to assassinate the Regent Prince, Ms. Chen accompanied him to fulfill this important mission. They did it with a lofty, self-sacrificial spirit, utterly without the expectation of surviving their task.

Mr. Wang's success is due to his own effort and talent; however, one can hardly deny the help and contribution of Madame Wang. If a wife, seeking only vanity and pleasure in life, does not try to assist her husband's just cause, the husband will not be able to succeed and the family will not achieve the ideal of happiness. One should not put all the blame on women, but, in all fairness, women should have their fair share of responsibility.

Thank you.

Part Four

Women's Emancipation

Editors' Introduction

The essays in this part discuss the means and ends of "women's emancipation." They address the condition of Chinese women, how this condition came to be, and how it could be transformed through education and employment.

The problematic nature of a women's emancipation movement led by men did not go unnoticed. In "The Great Inappropriateness of Women's Emancipation," Zhang Shenfu expresses his view of men who talked about emancipating women. He considers such talk condescending and argues that women should emancipate themselves instead of relying on men. His argument resonates with that of many women activists, including Lu Yin and Zhang Ruoming (essay 38 in this collection), though he is less specific about how women might emancipate themselves. Lu Yin's essay "The Women's Improvement Society's Hopes for Women" also criticizes the idea that women can rely on men to emancipate them. But Lu Yin also recognizes that most women have a long way to go before they are at the economic and educational stage where they can emancipate themselves. Until they attain such a position, she concedes, women need all the help they can get. Thus, she approves of organizations like the "Women's Improvement Society" that assist women in achieving emancipation.

In the process of trying to transform China by borrowing from the West, Chinese intellectuals constructed new concepts of womanhood and women's proper roles. They argued that women should assume not only the role of wife and mother but also the role of the "citizen" who would join in the project of making China strong in "modern," Western terms. May Fourth activists believed that Chinese women were far less emancipated than Western women, and took this as evidence of China's backwardness. They feared that Confucian patriarchy paralyzed half of China's population, thus making China an embarrassment in a world of modern nations. As Zhou Zuoren laments in "Women of the 'Advanced Country,' " Chinese women were no better off, and possibly worse off, than Japanese women. The emancipation of Chinese women was essential to the project of "modernizing" China.

Ye Shengtao, Wang Huiwu, and T.C. Chu view an oppressive marriage and family system as the main barrier to women's emancipation. Ye Shengtao argues that that system stifles women's character (*ren'ge*) by treating women like machines, confining them to the home, and depriving them of the right to make their own choices. His solution is to end the oppressive aspects of the marriage system and create a new one in which "the fact that a woman marries a man is a most natural thing and should be viewed as the same as a man marrying a woman." Wang Huiwu likewise attacks the marriage and family system, denouncing it as an insidious "trap," one that coerces poor women into being sold as commodities and tempts rich women into becoming "the pets and playthings of men." She presents an Engelsian narrative of how women first fell into the trap during the rise of civilization, when men used women's weakness during childbirth as an excuse to confine them to the home. After this happened, women's ability to participate in public life gradually atrophied. Her solution is for women to return to public life through education and employment, and encourage other women to do the same: "We should take on the responsibility of educating and enlightening those uneducated women and try to enable our 200 million female compatriots to gain economic independence." T.C. Chu also denounces the oppressive aspects of marriage and the family system for stifling women and adds that another obstacle to women's emancipation through employment is that "for a girl of moderate means with average ability, there seems to be no suitable occupation; she dislikes being ranked as a wage earner and is afraid to let it be known that her family circumstances force her to do work." Part of her solution is for women to put aside their pride and work outside the home.

Yet finding work outside the home was not easy for most ordinary women. Lu Xun is most concerned with women finding paid work that does not involve prostitution. In his talk on "What Happens after Nora Leaves Home?" Lu Xun points out that women who leave home have few options and that the most important thing women need is economic rights. Yang Zhihua observes that, even when they find employment, "women tend to lack confidence in their own strength and fear competition with men." She advocates that women learn "not to depend on men" and "help each other and never fall into the trap of jealousy."

Male and female activists alike recognized that most women were not in a position to emancipate themselves and needed help to attain the opportunity and the personal character necessary for emancipation. Despite their widely divergent perspectives and political affiliations, activists who wrote on women's emancipation tended to agree that an oppressive marriage and family system is the main barrier to women's emancipation, and that education and employment are the first steps on the road to emancipation.

28
The Question of Women's Character

Ye Shengtao (February 1919)

Originally published in *New Tide*, vol. 1, no. 2, February 1919.

Nothing in human history is free of the laws of time and space, and there is nothing that does not have a beginning and an end. But a historical fact is not necessarily the truth, and someone who can understand the causes and effects of a historical fact and make critical judgments is one who has embarked upon the path of progress. Those who mistakenly believe that all historical facts are truths because they are steeped in old traditions are anachronistic obstacles to social progress.

Chinese people are always full of inertia and have chosen the path of "nonevolution." Instead of using universally valid logic and reasoning, they resort to the time-honored method of "following the old tradition." They are taking the tradition that has been passed down over generations as the eternal, unchanging truth. Today I am raising the issue of "women's character," which they may not bother to recognize as an issue. I anticipate that they will say: "There is no need to talk about women's character because there is none, as has been indicated by history. This issue was resolved by history long ago." I would not have much more to say to them, but I have pondered the issue and I have been moved by the speeches of several progressive people I recently read. My conscience would bother me if I did not write about this issue. The following are some of my thoughts.

To discuss this issue, one has to first define "character"; which means to me "the kind of spirit that distinguishes one from others." In other words, "a spirit of integrity and independence even when one is part of a group." In order to be independent, one has to develop one's abilities fully; in order to have integrity, one has to love truth and never follow others blindly—these are the preconditions of character. Due to differences of age and status, the "magnitude" of character also differs; but people of the same era and the same status should have the same kind of character because we are all part of the same society.

Now that we have the definition of "character," our discussion proceeds.

First, are women entitled to character? The answer is definitely "Yes, they are, because they are human beings."

Second, do women currently have character? Up until recent years, there have been only a small number of independent women. Most women did not have true, firm worldviews, as they were confined to the home and relied on others, and their lives were neither complete nor independent. It is no exaggeration to say that these women had incomplete character or had almost no "character."

Third, let's talk about the reasons for women's misfortune. It is utterly unfair to say that the incompleteness of women's character is due to their own sins. At the time when labor was being divided, women had the misfortune of being assigned to bear children and then were forced to stay at home to raise children and to do other household chores. As human intelligence improved, human society became more and more developed, and all kinds of productive activities emerged. As a result, the worry-free men were the ones who had direct contact with society, while women were unable to produce social wealth because they were restricted by household chores. Even for those women who were involved in some productive activity at home, they were still subordinate to men and could not serve society directly without being represented by men. Such a social division of labor went on from generation to generation and caused women to gradually lose their independence and the ability to be self-reliant.

Confined to the home, women could do only trivial, low, and tedious housework. How could bound and exhausted women have the time and opportunity to gain access to events and ideas of the outside world and pursue serious study? Passed on from generation to generation, wrongs became rights and eventually social customs. It appeared that only men could engage in serious studies and moral pursuits. Gradually, women lost their real, firm worldviews, and their natural inclination for truth atrophied and disappeared.

The above is about women's misfortune; but it does not stop there. Owing to men's influence, women themselves, unfortunately, fully accepted the assumption that "women are essentially different from men" and, therefore, tended to take their own character lightly, either by not wanting to actualize it or by simply discarding it.

There are two kinds of "isms"[1] men hold toward women: one is "temptationism," which involves tempting women with all sorts of honors into discarding their own character; the other is "male chauvinism,"[2] which involves putting women down and refusing to treat them as equals.

Especially tempting are the "appellations." The "Three Cardinal Principles and Five Constant Virtues"[3] and "Three Obediences and Four Virtues"[4] are all powerful instruments used against women. These appellations are derived from "traditions lacking in truth." Taking for granted that "tradition is truth," the broad masses of people have blindly accepted these "principles" as "the relationship between husband and wife is just like that between the king and the subject" and "the ruler guides the subject, and the husband guides the wife." Since the Han dynasty, those who could really speak up have been mainly the followers of Confucius; and yet Confucius was the most spineless—he only wanted to serve as the loyal subject of one single ruler. It is no wonder that he, taking himself as the role model, made those insidious rules and codes of conduct. Human beings are often unclear in their thinking, and tend to be self-centered. Women, being the weaker sex, are often oppressed by men, who, in an attempt to gain certain benefits, made all those unjust rules. Someone put it well that "if it had been the wife of the Lord of Zhou[5] who made all the rules, they would certainly have been better and more balanced." As we can see, these rules and codes of conduct are the end products of men's selfishness.

"To be a good mother and virtuous wife" is another big admonition women have to follow. In recent years, women's schools have been founded; but to use this admonition as the founding principle is ridiculous; how can you expect a woman simply to be somebody's wife and somebody's mother? A woman is expected to be a good mother, simply raising children for her man, and to be a virtuous wife who helps her man to be successful in his career. If a woman as a person is reduced to being responsible only for individuals, doesn't it mean that her life differs not much from that of a dog or a cat?[6] If she has nothing to do with the big collective, doesn't it mean that she has become a dispensable tumor?

One can also look at it from the opposite point of view: if a woman is supposed to be "a good mother and virtuous wife," then a man ought to be "a good father and virtuous husband." Why are men allowed to monopolize scholarship when they can't commit themselves to being "good fathers and virtuous husbands"? It seems that any person with a complete personality is not interested in being one who belongs to others; he or she wants to be a whole, independent element in society. Unfortunately, women who have to be " mothers" and "wives" have been too easily deprived of their character.

There are other kinds of strong temptation, such as "chastity" and "martyrdom." This means that when a woman is married to a certain man—even if in name alone—she is never allowed to leave him, just like an indentured slave. If an unmarried woman is facing rape, she must protect her chastity in order to gain social approval. She might be praised not for refusing to succumb to violence, not for keeping herself unharmed, but for keeping her "chastity." It is as if once a woman is married or betrothed to a man, she has obligations toward her man alone, as a subject to a ruler, and hence should be content and reconciled. In fact, such things should not be an issue, since the most important thing between a married couple is love. If one must define "chastity," I would define it in terms of love. Love should be on both sides; if one party is no longer in love, it will not work, and the couple should separate. If people practice this, there will not be any problems regarding chastity. If a couple is deeply in love, they are certainly devoted to each other and would not have to concern themselves about infidelity or "chastity." In that case, love is chastity. Hence, the most essential concern of a couple should be about love. When two people are in love, active and free, they feel blessed and spiritually blissful, so much so that they might be willing to devote anything to each other, even perhaps their own lives. Needless to say, this kind of love and devotion is not what one would call "slavishness"; it should not be used as a yoke imposed on women. In reality, however, there are couples who are not in love and yet still remain together. Out of their selfishness, men created many rules and regulations to control women and to maintain the relationship—the concept and "title" of "chastity" being one of those. In fact, this kind of honor and praise is even crueler than those admonitions. Even some sensible women would be prone to vanity and thus pursue relentlessly those titles and honors, regardless of reality and truth; as for those who are uneducated and insentient, they simply follow suit inadvertently. Here, not intending to talk big, I simply hope that these women would tell me honestly whether they are truly willing or not. It is my belief that except for a few men and women who are truly in pursuit of lofty love, the rest are only doing things for an ulterior motive. If a person does not really treasure life and does not pursue true happiness, is his or her personality complete? Yet, all this has already been accepted by the world as Divine actuality and Heavenly Principle—no one would challenge its unfairness and unjustness. Thus, women are deceived and victimized.

One can detect male chauvinism whenever and wherever one looks. For instance, I have heard that a woman is just like a machine: (a) as long as a woman is paid for, she can be selected and can be moved into the house; (b) after being obtained, she can be used by her man at his will and at any time; (c) a woman can provide products—children—and the more, the better; (d) women like machines can be purchased and stored—you can never have too many; (e) if she is like a machine that is not satisfactory or cannot produce, the woman can be discarded and replaced. As we know, machines are dead things without free will and feelings; so this is an abominable analogy that flatly denies women their humanity.

Ever since Confucius said that "women and petty people are difficult to deal with," men have joined this misogynist chorus. Consequently, sayings like "never indulge in sex with women" and "never deal with women" have become men's sacred mottoes. To those men, "sex" is the only connection between men and women, and women are akin to "poisonous snakes and wild beasts"—absolutely unapproachable. One can deduce from it that "being a woman is evil"; a woman is considered evil not because of her ideas or behavior but simply because of her physical difference from men.

There were some capable and ambitious women in the past who did something worthwhile, though not necessarily significant. Then some men would start to make comments or write their biographies, using compliments like "women warriors" and "putting the men to shame." On the one hand, it is commendable for them to do that to "set up moral standards" and to "encourage the men." On the other hand, it does sound like they are saying that "all the lofty causes and virtuous deeds should be patent to men; yet, now that some women have done such things, we men, the noble stock, should try to catch up." In other words, women are not qualified to be engaged in some causes. Although the so-called democracy adamantly advocates that "all men are born equal," it does not recognize women's rights to participate in government and politics. While we can further discuss whether participation in politics is good or bad; we do see here that the so-called "human rights," in these people's eyes, were meant to be "men's rights."

We can look at the so-called "civilized wedding." The most civil part involves having the bridegroom say: "Yes, I will protect my wife" and for the bride to say: "Yes, I will respect and take good care of my husband." "To protect" normally means to take care of children or the vulnerable, which in essence deprives the protected of their rights. Why should a woman's rights be taken away by a man? And why should a woman be obligated to take good care of a man? One day when I had quite a few friends over at my place, one of them said: "So-and-so fell ill; but his wife really took good care of him, giving up sleep and pleasure but never complaining." When the rest of my friends heard it, every one of them praised her highly—not so much for the deep love between them as for the way she performed her "sacred duty." To be able to wait on men! Why? That same day, another friend there said: "So-and-so recently lost his wife, and is feeling extremely sad and lonely. When she was alive, the two were such a handsome and happy couple who often walked hand in hand." Upon hearing that, the crowd laughed and one of them even went so far as to say: "Mr. So-and-so is indeed a filial husband."[7] From all this, I figured out the psychology of men. When a woman dies, she is not even worthy of being remembered. Where is love? Mr. So-and-so went against the common psychology of men, and was thus ridiculed by other men. From this, we can see all the praises we heard from them before were fake.

Women get married because they are supposed to wait on men and then be protected; but after marriage, they even lose their maiden names and are called "Mrs. So-and-so." If we try to go against this tradition by addressing a man as "the husband of So-and-so," the man would certainly not be happy. It is because he believes that "women are only subordinates and enjoy no social status whatsoever."

These are the causes of women's misfortune. To sum it up briefly, we can come to the conclusion that, due to oppressive social realities, women have gradually lost their own identity and reasoning ability. Because of their selfish motives and beliefs, men have been taking advantage of that fact and trying to lure women with all sorts of honors and titles and at the same to repress women with their male chauvinism. More or less conditioned by this kind of repression, women have come to accept the status quo; and other people have also taken this for granted and live under the delusion that "this is reality!" This goes on like a vicious circle, during which women have lost their character.

Women's misfortune is a fact, one that is caused by thoughts and situations based on the wrong notion of "tradition is truth." To rectify the situation and arrive at a satisfactory, happy solution, a woman needs to have a certain degree of consciousness. She ought to know that she is a "human individual" and try to develop her ability to its full extent and achieve as an individual human being. She should also know that, while adhering to truth, she should discard and destroy those erroneous "appellations" and "pseudo morals." She differs from men in physiology alone, which is natural and nothing to be ashamed of, and has nothing to do with good or evil, superiority or inferiority. Women's ability to bear children is not for men alone but also for society; and it is a sacred cause. Importantly, when a woman cannot be independent and self-reliant because of her duty as a mother, society has the duty to reward her. Therefore, we need a fundamental socio-economic reform, one that is unprecedented in history and yet will be certainly achieved in the not too distant future. The fact that a woman marries a man is a most natural thing and should be viewed as the same as a man marrying a woman. A married woman should not be the property and slave of her man; she should not be reduced to helping him manage family affairs and making the property grow.

At the same time, men should know that one who does not respect other people's dignity is also damaging one's own dignity. Men's superstition that "tradition is truth" and their selfish prejudices have already ruined numerous women since ancient times and have hindered human progress for numerous generations. If we as a society want to get onto the road of progress quickly, we need to get rid of "temptationism" and "male chauvinism" completely.

Men and women should be united as "human beings." Each and every one of us is part of the collective effort for social progress. Each and every one of us should endeavor to be independent, and each and every one of us should enjoy happiness, light, respect, and freedom.

Notes:

1. Along with the influx of Western thoughts and ideas, after the May Fourth Movement, "isms" (*zhuyi*) became popular among young Chinese intellectuals during the May Fourth era.

2. The original text is *shili zhuyi*; literally, it means "snobbery."

3. The Three Cardinal Guides are that the ruler guides subject, father guides son, husband guides wife; and the Five Constant Virtues are benevolence, righteousness, propriety, wisdom, and fidelity.

4. The Three Obediences are that a woman should obey her father before marriage, obey her husband when married, and obey her son after her husband's death; and the Four Virtues for women are morality, proper speech, modest manner, and diligent work.

5. The original saying goes "The Lord of Zhou made the rules and rituals." (*Zhou Gong zhi li*); the version here is "The wife of the Lord of Zhou" (*Zhou Po zhi li*).

6. The original text uses "Ah Hei" and "Ah Huang"—common names for dogs and cats in China.

7. Normally, the term is "filial son" *xiaozi*; "filial husband" is used here as a contemptuous joke.

29
The Woman Question in China: Emancipation from a Trap

Wang Huiwu (October 1919)

Originally published in *Young China*, vol. 1, no. 4, October 1919.

For thousands of years, it has been a time-honored practice in China to claim that "the husband is the ruler of his wife," "the male is superior to the female," "the husband is comparable to heaven," and "women should be submissive, meek, and humble." These claims, along with the "Three Obediences and Four Virtues," are the admonitions imposed on Chinese women by their parents and teachers. The moralists tend to preach that "these are the principles of Heaven, which women must obey." But actually they are nothing but tricks used to fool women and traps used to bind them!

The majority of our female compatriots are honestly willing to carry out the most important obligation known to humankind: the bearing of children. Those from middle- and lower-middle-class families work very hard at housework, and those who are very capable can even support the entire family. Yet women have been unfairly denied the right to participate in state affairs or become officials. Of course, the bright side of this is that none of those imbecile congressmen, treasonous bureaucrats, and other kinds of traitors can be a woman. We women only resent the fact that society has been appallingly ungrateful to us despite the important contributions we have made. We 200 million Chinese women have received nothing in return besides the entrapping notions that have poisoned our minds and controlled our lives for thousands of years. We have been completely deprived of a correct worldview and independent character. This has happened to women all across society, ranging from wives and daughters of the rich and famous to sluts and prostitutes. I do not mean to be sensational, but I do want to give my female compatriots a wake-up call to enable them to escape the trap that society has created for them.

Many of the daughters of the rich and famous in China have traditionally received a good education and hence are reasonably progressive in their thinking. But they are still tightly bound by "saintly" admonitions, such as the "Three Obediences and Four Virtues," and other codes of conduct. Often, they follow in the footsteps of their female kin, footsteps that lead right into slavery. Nefarious warnings like "women should be locked inside the inner chambers" and "women should be hidden in a golden house" have become a trap that prevents women from entering society. Thus, many of our promising young women gradually became the pets and playthings of men. Their only compensation consists of silk, jewelry, fancy foods, and smart servants, all of which are there at least partly for the enjoyment of the men themselves. Deprived of the opportunity to receive a good, thorough education, many women lose their willpower and almost willingly fall prey to the gilded cage. They no longer want to resist and, on the contrary, become arrogant mistresses, bullying and bossing the servants around. Subject to the combined forces of sexual desire and external pressure, these women often end up being the "shame of the inner chambers" and "the scandal of Mulberry Patch."[1] You poor women are the victims of an evil society!

Times have changed, and people are more open-minded now. Unfortunately, however, these poor women have only a smattering of education and are still bound by the shackles of those old rules and archaic codes of conduct. Words like "obedience" and "submissiveness" are still flying around our schools. Influenced by society, many women still seek an extravagant lifestyle characterized by diamonds, imported fabrics, cars, gardens, and amusement centers. They often force their husbands to overwork, lose their jobs, or even fall into bankruptcy. This is again the fault of an evil society of traps!

The above describes upper- and middle-class families. Now let us look at the impoverished, who compose the majority of Chinese society. They work extremely hard but have a very limited income. Once a girl is born into a poor family, she is destined to be traded for money. In accordance with old customs, the marriage and wedding ceremony are nothing short of business transactions. A woman's father and brothers are her bosses at home; after marriage, her husband becomes her boss. If the husband's family is impoverished, she is sold to another family. Poor woman, you have sacrificed so much to perpetuate the existence of humankind, only to be sold as a commodity. You can work to support yourself; why should you be willing to accept such a fate? Of course, it is worse if you have a wicked father or an evil husband who would sell you to a brothel for the sake of earning more money. Either because they are manipulated by their social environment or because they are tempted by the fancy food and clothing, some women fall into the trap and become sex machines, concubines, or performers, trampled and violated by men. Although they satisfy their vanity and desire with fancy clothing, delicacies, cars, and servants, and appear to be proud and enviable, they are actually pitiful! I hear that there are thousands of young women in Beijing who admire and envy the lifestyle of some famous female performers and are willing to bring themselves so low as to start learning operas![2] Alas, what an evil society of traps! We women, young and old, rich and poor, are all compelled to walk on a pitch-dark road, without any light to guide us!

We bear the most essential responsibility known to humankind, and yet we have fallen so low. Some say this is because "women lack their own philosophy of life and therefore cannot claim to have any personal character." How ridiculous! It is, after all, the trap selfishly created by men that has robbed women of their own philosophy of life. We women have been trapped for so long that it looks as if we put the trap on ourselves. Saddest of all, sometimes even women themselves see men as the source of divine guidance and heavenly principles. Worse still, this evil society has indeed forced some of us women to engage in disgraceful affairs. We women, chained and shackled, are tumbling along a dark road, with evil old social customs constantly surrounding us, beating us, and luring us! We are driven forward, unable to escape our trap! Oh, we women are most unfortunate, chained and driven!

We women should find a way to get away from those evil external forces, as well as from the trap that we have internalized. Both of these result from our economic dependence on men. Men have used their economic power to cheat and oppress us to an extreme. The word "economy" is our Achilles' heel, the origin of our trap and the evil forces that work against us. Why have we women fallen into this trap? There was no such economic relationship between people in those ancient times before fire was discovered, when people were drinking animal blood and eating raw meat. After civil society developed, there were marriages. Weakened by childbirth, women were forced to rely on men for their support. Of course, it was absolutely reasonable for women to be supported by men right after giving birth. This was irrefutably an obligation of men, an obligation necessary to a fair relationship between the sexes. However, what is despicable is that men, ignoring our rights and their obligations, asserted that "women are brought up by men." They cheated and oppressed us and created notions about "heaven and earth," "yin and yang," and "noble and base," openly advocated that "men, being superior, should rule over women," and thus totally negated women's character. Then, fearing that women would resist, men used the carrot-and-stick approach to lure and bind women with food and clothing. Not surprisingly, women had no choice and gradually allowed men to take things for granted and force "saintliness," "morality," and various codes of conduct upon women. As time went by, women got used to these devious devices and also internalized and accepted that pernicious morality. Then, fearing that women would break their trap by working hard outside the home and gaining economic independence, men compelled women to do all the household chores—cooking, sewing, and everything else—and ruined their opportunity to earn money and be independent. At best, women were allowed to raise silkworms and weave cloth, but even then they were still confined to the home. In those days, the land was still rather undercultivated and the population was small, so one man's work was enough to support a whole family, and even produce a surplus. Men became the breadwinners, while women's talents were wasted and allowed to atrophy. Gradually, women were no longer fit for the important jobs in society.

Men's selfishness knows no bounds. In order to prevent women from becoming an important social force, they created devices such as "morality," "saintliness," and "social codes of conduct" to curb women's desire for power. Out of jealousy, men set up barriers between themselves and women, and barred women from any social contact, forcing women to fall eternally into an unbreakable trap.

Although there are now loud cries for women's emancipation, female education specialists and their publications still stick to those clichés. I once studied at Jianxing Women's Normal School, where old sermons about the "Three Obediences and Four Virtues," "filial piety," and "being a good mother and virtuous wife" constantly reminded me of this dismal reality. Women's magazines published by the Commercial Press are no exception. The *Everyday Encyclopedia*, published this past summer, even carries *Cao's Admonitions for Women* with an additional comment that "It is absolutely and eternally necessary for women to bear in mind: 'Annihilate conceit and sloth before they bud, and strengthen rules and restrictions to prevent degradation.'" But do they know that "conceit and sloth" is also the result of keeping women trapped and, furthermore, is caused by the debauchery and decadence of society? Instead of getting rid of the root cause, namely, the traps and evils of society, these moralists coined those senseless maxims to fool and coerce women. Little did I expect that there would be new publications with such antiquated rubbish in this new age, a time when the praises of women's emancipation are being sung. Men's cruelty is so obvious; but I did not realize until recently that women's bamboo trap has turned to iron!

It is said that "the woman question should be resolved by women themselves." Now that we know about this trap, we should break away and depart from this bleak social reality in order to achieve our own independence. First, we should gain our economic independence. United in sisterhood, we should get our own lives and our own jobs. Once we have these, we will never again fear men's oppression. However, the sad but true fact is that the overwhelming majority of Chinese women lack education and are still living in a dream, utterly unaware that they are trapped. As for those few educated women, they are still tempted by wealth, fame, scholarship, and power, and remain unable, or perhaps unwilling, to escape their trap. Not long ago, I met several female students who had returned from studying abroad. Their philosophy in life turned out to be none other than "once abroad, it is easy to find a rich, famous, and influential husband." Oh, iron trap, you are indeed so sharp and tough that even those women who have received higher education cannot free themselves!

Now that we know about the devious devices employed by society, we should do our utmost to spread our beliefs and ideas in order to awaken our sisters. We should take on the responsibility of educating and enlightening those uneducated women and try to enable our 200 million female compatriots to gain economic independence. Only then can we truly gain our own independence! But that iron trap, the evil social environment, and all kinds of knots and cords have bound us tightly. We should struggle with all our strength! Break the iron trap and struggle against this evil society and those cruel men! We have passed the point of no return, and we are all mobilized! As vanguard women on the front line of the battlefield, we should regard our educated but unawakened sisters as comrades-in-arms from the same headquarters. At present, we are certain that a great many more of our countrywomen are getting ready to join us; at the same time, we are aware that there are magazines like *Young China* that take a neutral position.

The enemy is approaching! Cannons are heard nearby but only serve to enhance our spirits. We should all awaken and dash forward to the front line, and encourage the masses, our fellow soldiers in reserve, to get ready for the fight. At the same time, we also demand that those who have taken a neutral position form an alliance with us. Furthermore, we should reorganize and improve our internal finances, so that we will not be economically troubled and sabotaged by our enemy. In front of us, high above, there flies a large flag with "Emancipation" written on it; step by step and arm in arm, we march forward. Guns, cannons, and military bands are heard all around us. Heroic, solemn, wrathful, firm, and dauntless, we march forward, shouting at the top of our lungs: "Emancipation, emancipation. . . !"

Author's Note

My essay is an answer to the question: Why has the situation of Chinese women become so bad? Quite unexpectedly, as I finished my essay, I heard and envisioned my 200 million fellow countrywomen shouting in unison: "We shall break the trap; we demand emancipation!" That is why I used those words in the title of my essay, though I was not sure about how to articulate my viewpoints and arguments. Having read the advertisement of *Young China* and having learned that the fourth issue of that magazine will be a special issue devoted to women, I am presenting my essay here in the hope that more and more enlightened women will join me in the study and discussion of women's emancipation in China.

Notes

1. According to Li Ji-Yue Ji (see *Ci Hai*, 1979, 497) Mulberry Patch (*Sangjian*) was a place by the Pu River in the ancient state of Wei. Men and women were said to have met for clandestine rendezvous at Mulberry Patch.

2. Opera singers were associated with social disgrace and immoral activities in late Imperial China, and their disrepute remained in the Republican period.

30
The Emancipation of Chinese Women

T.C. Chu (October 1919)

Originally published in English in *Chinese Recorder*, October 1919. *The Chinese Recorder* was published monthly at the American Presbyterian Mission Press in Shanghai, China.

China is an old country. Before the introduction of new influences, there were settled ideas and established customs for every phase of life. In the case of women, certain ideas and customs have been the guiding principle of conduct for several thousand years. They were regarded as sacred rites of womanhood, carefully recorded in the classics, and most faithfully observed by the best women of all ages. Some of the ideas and customs are good and should be preserved, while others are bad; it is from the latter that the Chinese women need to be emancipated.

Take, for example, the question of marriage. To the Chinese mind it was almost inconceivable how a woman could remain single and yet be counted an individual. According to the old concept, she had no separate existence, but lived the life of a dependent, first under the protection of the father, then by the support of the husband, finally in the care of the son. This is the well-known doctrine of three-fold subordination, against which no woman in the past dared rebel, and with which she secured the necessary subsistence of life. Besides the material support, a woman gained dignity through marriage; hitherto she was only a maid, but now a matron, a position much to be preferred, as it placed her on a higher plane.

Such a practice as mentioned above has still its influence among the Chinese people, and the effects are bad. First, it is generally believed that a respectable girl must get married, otherwise her life is incomplete. Thus marriage seems to be a necessity to her growth, and the recognition of her womanhood. Second, most parents prefer marriage for their daughters, as it gives them the surest guarantee of support and the best solution of a living. Some girls may be lazy and incapable, but will have no difficulty in getting through life, in regard to food and lodging, by this arrangement. Third, many girls are put in school only so long as required for fitting them for marriage, thus too often their studies are discontinued and their zeal for knowledge is cooled: it is most pathetic to see some talents which might be developed with wonderful results thus smothered. I have actually known girls who feel unhappy for many years after marriage, because their education was thus hindered. Others who are quite capable of rendering some years of service to the public are deprived of the opportunity on the same account. In short, this old-fashioned idea of marriage is a drawback to the progress of women, it lowers the standard of education and disheartens those who seek for an independent living.

How can this state of affairs be remedied ? Will the rise of industry and commerce give new openings to women? Do the men in China grudge sharing the professions with women? I should say that the hearts of this people have been brought low during these recent years of national weakness, and that Chinese men have no prejudice against Chinese women taking part in the doings of the world, if the same is already done in the West. Indeed, the few among us who have proven worthy in public undertakings are much respected by men and are given the needed help very generously. But there are other difficulties to be overcome: namely, the traditional wrong idea of labor and the suspicion of misconduct from the freer intercourse of men and women.

The Chinese have overexalted mental work; as a result they despise manual labor. They have given high value to name and fame, so anything that savors of the earning of money or the exchange of goods is not sought after by the genteel classes; alas, however, they dearly love to accumulate wealth and have often done so through corruption and graft! On the surface, however, they pretend not to take much interest in such affairs, and leave the development of industry and commerce to the less privileged classes. Only lately did they begin to respect businessmen and put them on the same level with scholars; yet their attitude is only changed towards the captains of industry and the big businessmen, and they still belittle the shop-keepers and the craftsmen; but it is exactly the latter positions which some of the modern Chinese young women might occupy. They are certainly not yet ready to be commercial and industrial leaders, not having the education, ability, or experience necessary. Yet to be stenographers in offices, clerks in stores, seamstresses, milliners, or the like is considered to be below the dignity of girls of well-to-do families. One who is skillful in teaching or writing may become a tutor or an author, and one of very poor origin may work in a mill or factory. But for a girl of moderate means with average ability, there seems to be no suitable occupation; she dislikes to be ranked as a wage earner and is afraid to let it be known that her family circumstances force her to do work.

Regarding business intercourse between men and women, the old custom forbids it. In respectable society, it is still felt inconvenient for the two sexes to mix, not that there is any actual misbehavior, but because of the dread of being talked about and criticized by others. This fear is not without foundation, for Chinese men and women are not accustomed to meet often; they seem to have lost faith in one another's morality and fear that some wrong might result. For this reason, it is extremely hard to induce young girls to do work outside of their homes. Those who are specially attractive are even kept from going to schools where there are men teachers. It also explains the stiff manner of men and women when they meet in public; old ideas necessitate extreme formality and fewness of words. In the interior, all women engaged in professional work are very simply dressed, and schoolgirls are usually in cotton uniforms. Thus one may easily realize the impracticability of Chinese women entering the business world just now: most of us who are anxious for their improvement do not dare to encourage it, so long as the old notions obtain.

To summarize what I have already stated, Chinese women still seem to be weak and incapable, depending upon marriage for support and for comfort. They are regarded not as equals of men but as a special class, whose charm and feminine qualities often trouble men instead of inspiring them. They prize themselves as ladies and are unwilling to mingle with wage earners. In other words, the concept of women of themselves is as bad as the attitude of others toward them. In my judgment the safest and only way of improving the situation is to give women enough of education, both the good old training and the new knowledge and learning; for this alone can reform the heart, strengthen the will, and stimulate ambition. Hitherto, they have served the nation in the position of subordinates and dependents; how much more good they would be able to do if they were free and independent in thought and action! Chinese women themselves must initiate the new day and start the right kind of living. Marriage is, of course, the career for most girls, but it is a sacred duty, not a means of winning men's favour, but an opportunity to live in a larger way. They must also be taught that to earn an honest living is much more honorable than to rely upon others; to work for dollars and pennies is better than to ask for help. A true lady is one who can defend herself both morally and physically; she is not a piece of precious jewelry that must be hidden in the house, but a light in the world to dispel darkness.

Such power and ability, faith and courage, can only come through education; some old Chinese teaching is still good for the development of character, the addition of new knowledge gives a more all-round training. Both public lectures and publications on activities of women, the value of their work, their influence upon the nation, will help to enlighten the people and change popular ideas about women, but only education can remake the women. After all, the trouble lies in the latter's inability and uselessness. Give them a chance to develop, and marvellous results will be seen. Chinese women did not show up very badly in the past; they were really as good as those of any other nation before the new era. Signs of improvement are already visible everywhere, in the work of schoolgirls, in the service some of the so-called new women render to the public, in the life of modern homes, in the training of children. If Chinese girls have the same educational advantages as those prevalent in the West, they will be as capable and useful to the world as their European and American sisters. At present, however, they are still under the influence of some bad old ideas and customs, and must be set free. I think only education can solve the fundamental problems of women.

31
The Great Inappropriateness of Women's Emancipation

Zhang Shenfu (October 1919)

Originally published in *Young China*, vol. 1, no. 4, October 1919, under the name Zhang Songnian.

The cry for "women's emancipation" rings out loud and clear nowadays. Some talk about "women's emancipation," and others talk about "emancipating women." Since "women's emancipation" is a nice-sounding catchphrase, one only needs to repeat it in a parrotlike fashion. Yet it is essentially a big but erroneous catchphrase expressing a big but erroneous idea.

We should ask whether men and women should enjoy the same status in society, and we should ask what has caused our contemporary social reality. Since ancient times, men, who accidentally became the "stronger sex" in society, have been taking advantage of women, have been wholeheartedly engaged in their indispensable work for society. Men bullied and oppressed women and at the same time created "morality" and "rules" to confine and condition women. Nothing in human history can be more brutal and inhumane than footbinding, which serves this dual purpose. Thousands of years have gone by, and still the men who have committed such wrongs have not awakened. They have not confessed or shown signs of repentance. They feel no pain, no embarrassment, and no shame; instead, they put on this holier-than-thou attitude, declaring arrogantly that "I am going to emancipate you all." Nothing is more brazen than this!

If the English respect the Irish and the Indians, they should help them achieve independence. If the Japanese respect the Koreans and Taiwanese, they should also help them achieve independence. And if the Chinese respect the Mongolians and Tibetans, they should also grant them independence. The same applies to men and women. If men really respect women, they should recognize from the bottom of their hearts that women have the same worth as men and should also enjoy independence. If one group coerced another group into slavery and later felt a bit remorseful and then started talking about emancipation, can they be trusted? Nowadays, men talk about emancipating women; but their words are often less than heartfelt. They show insincere sentimentality and seem interested in using such talk to gain prestige and superiority. We wonder whether enlightened laborers can be truly reconciled with those capitalists who talk about emancipating laborers.

Think about it. The word "emancipation" is rather contemptuous. Needless to say, the emancipator and the emancipated are not on an equal footing. When friends respect each other, one will never say to the other, "I am emancipating you." The butcher who lets one pig back into the sty may also claim to be the pig's emancipator. Those men who crow about women's emancipation may boast that "after being emancipated, women can share in the same kind of life that we men have." Doesn't that sound even stranger? If your life is like that of pigs and dogs (let's assume that the lives of pigs and dogs are no good), how can you impose the same kind of life on others? How can you assume that your life is better? Talk about emancipation is bad enough; it is even worse with this string attached.

Those who respect the worth of others do not speak condescendingly of emancipating them; those who are aware of their own worth are not willing to be emancipated by others. Someone with dignity and wisdom never seeks favors from others; someone who seeks favors from others will only be seen as weak, lazy, self-degrading, and, at best, overbearing. Someone strong and capable would shun and despise such behavior. Why can't one start from scratch? Why can't one rely on oneself? What one gets from begging is unreliable. The donated fruit lacks sweetness, and so does being emancipated by others. What happiness is there when one is let go after being molested? Right now, women are bound and enslaved; they should emancipate themselves from their fetters and obtain independence though their own efforts. It is useless and shameful to wait for emancipation by others.

It is only appropriate for one to talk about emancipation for oneself. What does self-emancipation truly mean? It means the breaking of all fetters, the smashing of all idols, and the elimination of all tyrannies and conventions. One should not be subject to bondage of any kind, visible or invisible. One should not be enslaved by the past or by the present. Anyone who has any independent thought should watch out for senseless parroting. Each and every individual has innate worth.

One ought to protect one's own worth and individuality, since without these one will cease to exist. Bear in mind that all laws and morals are fundamentally unnecessary (remember that all laws are man-made). Even customs and habits can be constructed from scratch. All these fetters and idols should be broken again and again. Don't imitate others, don't rely on others, don't sit on the fence, and don't follow trends. Whenever necessary, one needs to rely on one's own experience, observation, deliberation, and imagination. All of these should arise from one's own will; otherwise they are not one's own. One should not believe what big shots such as officials, degree holders, and professors say. A gullible person is a slave even worse than a conquered subject (even among conquered subjects there are distinctions). Today the vernacular is in vogue, but it should still be acceptable for one to write in the classical language. Today everyone is talking about democracy, but it should still be acceptable for one to discuss and even advocate aristocracy on appropriate occasions. Talk about the new is all the vogue today, but one can also believe in the old, if one is convinced that one is not merely sticking to archaic conventions and old prejudices. The worst thing one can do is follow the fads and fashions blindly. The world can do without another parrot! A self-conscious and self-confident belief in the old is much more desirable than any kind of muddle-headed parroting. Self-emancipation involves independent thinking. Unfortunately, this is not how it is with "women's emancipation."

An ideal human society is one that provides everyone with enough to eat, enough to wear, free education, and academic freedom, a world in which everyone has the freedom to work, knows no fear or sense of loss, and has no adversaries. In such a society, everyone would be friends. They would always smile at each other and appreciate each other from the bottom of their hearts. Unlike the profiteering, capitalistic society we see at present, an ideal society should be like this—boundless, fearless, free of traditional obstacles, and free of gender discrimination. Due to certain physiological differences between the sexes, there would still be certain things that could not be shared by men and women alike even in such a society, but that would not matter. It would be just like the difference between a mathematician and a writer, who may also be physiologically different and unable to do the same kind of work, and yet are equally valuable and enjoy the same status. Since we all want such an ideal society, we do not approve of the insipid old ideas expressed by certain men and will refrain from uttering condescending, high-sounding words about "emancipating women." Those who use such words may not have ill intentions, but these words are inappropriate and thus unwarranted. If one intends to accomplish such an important goal, one cannot afford to be so undiscriminating.

We believe that talk about "emancipating women" arises from improper ideas. If a man really respects women and believes that women have the same worth as men, he should not talk incessantly about how to emancipate women. Rather, he should give sincere and enthusiastic assistance to women as they pursue their own independence. In other words, we should talk about "women's independence" instead of "women's emancipation." Some may say, "Women's suffering was caused by men of the past; our current talk about emancipating women may be belated, but it is also a praiseworthy awakening." So it is, but trying to distance oneself from those men of the past is like saying that "other people's sins have nothing to do with me." You may claim to believe this, but you will still feel a pang of guilt from time to time.

32
The Women's Improvement Society's Hopes for Women

Lu Yin (February 19, 1920)

Originally published in Beijing's *Morning Post Supplement*, February 19, 1920.

A few days ago, I read Guo Mengliang's[1] essay "'Women's Emancipation': A Means of Saving the Nation" in the *Morning Post*. It recommended the organization of a "Women's Improvement Society" to help ordinary women who have consciousness but lack the means to emancipate themselves to achieve their goal of emancipation. As soon as I finished this essay, I had a question. Why do women need men to solve their problems for them? Why don't women recognize their own suffering? Women have brains, and also four limbs and five senses, so why don't they have feelings? Women need men's initiative and guidance in everything. This is truly unthinkable!

The cry for women's emancipation grows louder every day, but the reality of women's emancipation is mostly a failure. Why? The reason is that women themselves lack consciousness, so they cannot withstand hardship or solve their own problems. Another source of failure is women's desire to ask men, who have less of a personal stake in the issue, to solve it for them. There are indeed many men with consciousness these days, but a lot of them are lost in a pipe dream, or use the high-sounding term "women's emancipation" to further their own cunning schemes. If women themselves lack consciousness and blindly follow men, they will not only fail to achieve their goal of emancipation but also produce endless impediments to the future of women's emancipation. Thus, I believe that the issue of women's emancipation must be resolved by women themselves. But "emancipation" will just be an empty word unless we think of concrete measures that will transform emancipation theory into an emancipated reality. There are many such concrete measures, such as the creation of women's professional organizations, women's factories, work-study mutual aid teams. But these measures are all part of the second step; if women are to enter professions, they must first have professional skills; if women are to enter factories, they must have factory skills; even a work-study mutual aid team requires some ordinary skills. Without these kinds of knowledge, they cannot accomplish the above goals. So for now we must concentrate on getting these ordinary women with consciousness but no ability through the first stage. The ship that will take them through this stage is the "Women's Improvement Society" mentioned by Guo Mengliang. The more organizations of this kind the better, since they can provide the assistance that will enable our female compatriots to "climb out of the fire and take their place at the feast." This is very relevant to women. We should also respect our own character, and certainly not follow others blindly. So I look forward to the day when my beloved female compatriots will awaken and solve their own problems. I dearly hope that the "Women's Improvement Society" will take my sisters to that day!

Note

1. Guo Mengliang was a graduate of Beijing University's Philosophy Department. He was one of the leading activists of the May Fourth Movement. He married Lu Yin in 1923 but died of typhoid fever in 1925.

33
Women of the "Advanced Country"

Zhou Zuoren (October 14, 1922)

Originally published in the *Morning Post Supplement*, October 14, 1922, under the name Shi Fen.

I read a passage in one of the newspapers:

> Japan is supposedly an advanced, civilized country, and yet its women are still as much in the dark ages as ever. I have lived in Japan for years, and I have done thorough studies of Japanese politics and the woman question, and I am under the impression that the speed and development of women's emancipation in Japan is really not comparable to that in China. I fully concur with Japanese newspapers which have recently advocated that Chinese and Japanese women interact in public life. If women of China—an advanced country, in this regard—could cross the border and help improve the social status of oppressed Japanese women, it would be indeed an admirable and laudable contribution.

Here I am not going to elaborate on the present conditions of Japanese women, simply because I have not "done thorough studies" and don't want to make a fool of myself. However, I do have some doubts about whether women in China—a so-called "advanced country"—really enjoy a "heavenly" status. Frankly, due to China's current economic condition, even our men are still in the Dark Ages, not to mention our women. Numerous Chinese women are engaged in long- and short-term sexual transactions as mistresses, household managers, concubines, and secretaries. How could they help others? As the *The Book of Songs* says, "If I cannot even take care of myself, how could I worry about my children?" In reality, this saying appropriately describes the situation of Chinese women, which is quite similar to the situation of Japanese women and really nothing to boast about. Only China has one little extra: the bound feet of its women. I don't know what other people think, but I, for one, am very disturbed to see my female compatriots swaying and staggering painfully on their tiny bound feet. I cannot take pride in being a citizen of such an "advanced country," indeed, I may not even qualify as a citizen of a less advanced country. I may well be considered a keen patriot; but precisely because of that, the more I love China, the more I hope that its future will be bright; the more I hate its dark side, the more I want to attack it—that is quite natural. The reporter I quote at the beginning lived in Japan for years and may have forgotten the situation in his own country. This is not unusual. But I fear that people might see his view as another indication of China's chauvinism and superiority complex, so I have added a brief note here. I have also heard that a certain eminent expert often publishes in the *Journal of Geography* articles like the one I quoted. Although his doctor suspected that he might be suffering from an "obssessive love," I do not particularly agree. In my view, it is only because he had also been to Japan a couple of times and had completely forgotten the situation in his own country.

The most essential thing in life is to understand one's own weaknesses as well as the strengths of others. This is something one has to bear in mind, especially when one tries to criticize another country. Bertrand Russell's articles on Britain and China can serve as the best examples of how this could be done.

34
Women's Careers

Yang Zhihua (November 1922)

Originally published in the *Women's Critic Supplement* to the *Republican Daily*, November 1922.

"Women are more narrow-minded than men; women are more jealous than men." These two remarks are often on people's lips. When women hear these words, they will certainly retort: "We women can never accept these fallacies. Though there are some women who are narrow-minded and get jealous easily, aren't there also men like that? Probably, men are even more narrow-minded and jealous than women!" It might be right for women to say this, but do women's actions bear this out? If so, how often?

Traditionally, women's position in society is lower than that of men and their life is more boring than men's. This is because women cannot be independent and have to rely on men. The root cause of women's dependence on men is the fact that women, confined and conditioned by the social-historical forces, have accepted the fallacy that, because of differences in ability, it is men and not women who are entitled to freedom, knowledge, power, and careers. Upper-class women may appear happy and glorious; yet that is only an appearance. It is completely unnatural, for they are only parasites relying on their men and their wealth and power. At the same time, women from poor families are restricted by their parents since childhood, and are controlled by their husbands after marriage. If married to the wrong men, they end up being miserable slaves all their lives. Their life is truly tiresome and unhappy!

In recent years, many have advocated women's education and equality, and there are schools and institutions to educate women of bourgeois and middle-class background. Nowadays, there are also women who, thanks to their education, have acquired good jobs, such as working for banks, factories, and telephone and telegraph companies. Life for these women is much better than life for the average woman; but it is still questionable whether they can be entirely independent.

My observations suggest that women tend to lack confidence in their own strength and fear competition with men. This is because men, being the favored gender in history, have always monopolized the most powerful positions in all institutions, leaving women behind as mere assistants. There are nowadays many working women in our society. However, in order to keep their jobs, many of them have to kiss the asses of the men in power. If they cannot get close to those men, they try to win favors from those who are their bosses or who are close to the highest positions. In their relations with female colleagues, these women try all sorts of tricks to ridicule and put down others so that they themselves can monopolize all the power. Do you think this kind of woman can stand tall in society? Of course not! Their behavior clearly tells men that "we have no strength, cannot be independent, and have to rely on others; we are narrow-minded and prone to jealousy! In order to keep my job, I ought to resort to such means." Once their baneful behaviors are brought to light, they are disdained by their bosses and attacked by their peers and thus lose their careers. These women not only become dependent on others but are also despised and discarded by society. What difference is there between these women and those who have never had any schooling?

When we educated women receive good opportunities in society, we should think of those women who have been denied education and those who are mistreated by men. We should intensify our efforts whenever we think of their suffering. We have to rely on ourselves eventually and try not to depend on men. As for our fellow women, we should help each other and never fall into the trap of jealousy. We have to rely on our own strengths, for jealousy never helps us—it only harms our careers!

No matter what kind of position we occupy in society, we as women have to respect ourselves as well as others. Working women especially should bear this in mind. One has to rely on one's own strength; wouldn't it be good if we could openly compete with men in broad daylight?

35
What Happens after Nora Leaves Home?

Lu Xun (December 26, 1923)

Originally given as a talk at the Beijing Women's Normal College on December 26, 1923. This translation was published in *Silent China: Selected Writings of Lu Xun*, edited and translated by Gladys Yang, published by Oxford University Press, 1973, pp. 148–154. It is reprinted with permission from Oxford University Press.

My subject today is: What happens after Nora leaves home?

Ibsen was a Norwegian writer in the second half of the nineteenth century. All his works, apart from a few dozen poems, are dramas. Most of the dramas he wrote during one period deal with social problems and are known as social-problem plays. One of these is the play *Nora*.[1]

Another title for *Nora* is *Ein Puppenheim*, translated in Chinese as *A Puppet's House*. However, *puppen* are not only marionettes but also children's dolls; in a wider sense the term also includes people whose actions are controlled by others. Nora originally lives contentedly in a so-called happy home, but then she wakes up to the fact that she is simply a puppet of her husband's and her children are her puppets. So she leaves home—as the door is heard closing, the curtain falls. Since presumably you all know this play, there is no need to go into details.

What could keep Nora from leaving? Some say that Ibsen himself has supplied the answer in *The Lady from the Sea*. The heroine of this play is married but her former lover, who lives just across the sea, seeks her out suddenly to ask her to elope with him. She tells her husband that she wants to meet this man and finally her husband says, "I give you complete freedom. Choose for yourself (whether to go or not). On your own head be it." This changes everything and she decides not to go. It seems from this that if Nora were to be granted similar freedom she might perhaps stay at home.

But Nora still goes away. What becomes of her afterward Ibsen does not say, and now he is dead. Even if he were still living, he would not be obliged to give an answer. For Ibsen was writing poetry, not raising a problem for society and supplying the answer to it. This is like the golden oriole that sings because it wants to, not to amuse or benefit anyone else. Ibsen was rather lacking in worldly wisdom. It is said that when a number of women gave a banquet in his honour and their representative rose to thank him for writing *Nora*, which gave people a new insight into the social consciousness and emancipation of women, he rejoined, "I didn't write with any such ideas in mind. I was only writing poetry."

What happens after Nora leaves home? Others have also voiced their views on this. An Englishman has written a play about a modern woman who leaves home but finds no road open to her and therefore goes to the bad, ending up in a brothel. There is also a Chinese—How shall I describe him? A Shanghai man of letters, I suppose—who claims to have read a different version of the play in which Nora returns home in the end. Unfortunately no one else ever saw this edition, unless it was one sent him by Ibsen himself. But by logical deduction, Nora actually has two alternatives only: to go to the bad or to return to her husband. It is like the case of a caged bird: of course there is no freedom in the cage, but if it leaves the cage there are hawks, cats, and other hazards outside; while if imprisonment has atrophied its wings, or if it has forgotten how to fly, there certainly is nowhere it can go. Another alternative is to starve to death, but since that means departing this life it presents no problem and no solution either.

The most painful thing in life is to wake up from a dream and find no way out. Dreamers are fortunate people. If no way out can be seen, the important thing is not to awaken the sleepers. Look at the Tang dynasty poet Li He whose whole life was dogged by misfortune. When he lay dying he said to his mother, "'The Emperor of Heaven has built a palace of white jade, Mother, and summoned me there to write something to celebrate its completion." What was this if not a lie, a dream? But this made it possible for the young man who was dying to die happily, and for the old woman who lived on to set her heart at rest. At such times there is something great about lying and dreaming. To my mind, then, if we can find no way out, what we need are dreams.

However, it won't do to dream about the future. In one of his novels Artzybashev challenges those idealists who, in order to build a future golden world, call on many people here and now to suffer. "You promise their descendants a golden world, but what are you giving them themselves?" he demands. Something is given, of course—hope for the future. But the cost is exorbitant. For the sake of this hope, people are made more sensitive to the intensity of their misery, are awakened in spirit to see their own putrid corpses. At such times there is greatness only in lying and dreaming. To my mind, then, if we can find no way out, what we need are dreams; but not dreams of the future, just dreams of the present.

However, since Nora has awakened, it is hard for her to return to the dream world; hence all she can do is to leave. After leaving, though, she can hardly avoid going to the bad or returning. Otherwise the question arises: What has she taken away with her apart from her awakened heart? If she has nothing but a crimson woolen scarf of the kind you young ladies are wearing, even if two or three feet wide it will prove completely useless. She needs more than that, needs something in her purse. To put it bluntly, what she needs is money.

Dreams are fine; otherwise money is essential.

The word "money" has an ugly sound. Fine gentlemen may scoff at it, but I believe that men's views often vary, not only from day to day but from before a meal to after it. All who admit that food costs money yet call money filthy lucre will probably be found, on investigation, to have some fish or pork not yet completely digested in their stomachs. You should hear their views again after they have fasted for a day.

Thus the crucial thing for Nora is money or—to give it a more high-sounding name—economic resources. Of course money cannot buy freedom, but freedom can be sold for money. Human beings have one great drawback, which is that they often get hungry. To remedy this drawback and to avoid being puppets, the most important thing in society today seems to be economic rights. First, there must be a fair sharing out between men and women in the family; second, men and women must have equal rights in society.

Unfortunately I have no idea how we are to get hold of these rights; all I know is that we have to fight for them. We may even have to fight harder for these than for political rights.

The demand for economic rights is undoubtedly something very commonplace, yet it may involve more difficulties than the demand for noble political rights or for the grand emancipation of women. In this world countless small actions involve more difficulties than big actions do. In a winter like this, for instance, if we have only a single padded jacket we must choose between saving a poor man from freezing to death or sitting like Buddha under a bo tree to ponder ways of saving all mankind. The difference between saving all mankind and saving one individual is certainly vast. But given the choice I would not hesitate to sit down under the bo tree, for that would obviate the need to take off my only padded jacket and freeze to death myself. This is why, at home, if you demand political rights you will not meet with much opposition, whereas if you speak about the equal distribution of wealth you will probably find yourself up against enemies, and this of course will lead to bitter fighting. Fighting is not a good thing, and we can't ask everybody to be a fighter. In that case the peaceful method is best, that is using parental authority to liberate one's children in the future. Since in China parental authority is absolute, you can share out your property fairly among your children so that they enjoy equal economic rights in peace, free from conflict. They can then go to study, start a business, enjoy themselves, do something for society, or spend the lot just as they please, responsible to no one but themselves. Though this is also a rather distant dream, it is much closer than the dream of a golden age. But the first prerequisite is a good memory. A bad memory is an advantage to its owner but injurious to his descendants. The ability to forget the past enables people to free themselves gradually from the pain they once suffered; but it also often makes them repeat the mistakes of their predecessors. When a cruelly treated daughter-in-law becomes a mother-in-law, she may still treat her daughter-in-law cruelly; officials who detest students were often students who denounced officials; some parents who oppress their children now were probably rebels against their own families ten years ago. This perhaps has something to do with one's age and status; still bad memory is also a big factor here. The remedy for this is for everyone to buy a notebook and record his thoughts and actions from day to day, to serve as reference material in future when his age and status have changed. If you are annoyed with your child for wanting to go to the park, you can look through your notes and find an entry saying: "I want to go to the Central Park." This will at once mollify and calm you down. The same applies to other matters too.

There is a kind of hooliganism today, the essence of which is tenacity. It is said that after the Boxer Uprising some ruffians in Tianjin behaved quite lawlessly. For instance, if one were to carry luggage for you, he would demand two dollars. If you argued that it was a small piece of luggage, he would demand two dollars. If you argued that the distance was short, he would demand two dollars. If you said you didn't need him, he would still demand two dollars. Of course hooligans are not good models, yet that tenacity is most admirable. It is the same in demanding economic rights. If someone says this is old hat, tell him you want your economic rights. If he says this is too low, tell him you want your economic rights. If he says the economic system will soon be changing and there is no need to worry, tell him you want your economic rights.

Actually, today, if just one Nora left home she might not find herself in difficulties; because such a case, being so exceptional, would enlist a good deal of sympathy and certain people would help her out. To live on the sympathy of others already means having no freedom; but if a hundred Noras were to leave home, even that sympathy would diminish; while if a thousand or ten thousand were to leave, they would arouse disgust. So having economic power in your own hands is far more reliable.

Are you not a puppet then when you have economic freedom? No, you are still a puppet. But you will be less at the beck and call of others and able to control more puppets yourself. For in present-day society it is not just women who are often the puppets of men; men often control other men, and women other women, while men are often women's puppets too. This is not something which can be remedied by a few women's possession of economic rights. However, people with empty stomachs cannot wait quietly for the arrival of a golden age; they must at least husband their last breath just as a fish in a dry rut flounders about to find a little water. So we need this relatively attainable economic power before we can devise other measures.

Of course, if the economic system changes, then all this is empty talk.

In speaking as I have, however, I have assumed Nora to be an ordinary woman. If she is someone exceptional who prefers to dash off to sacrifice herself, that is a different matter. We have no right to urge people to sacrifice themselves, no right to stop them either. Besides, there are many people in the world who delight in self-sacrifice and suffering. In Europe there is a legend that when Jesus was on his way to be crucified he rested under the eaves of Ahasuerus's house, and because Ahasuerus turned Jesus away he became accursed, doomed to find no rest until the Day of Judgment. So since then Ahasuerus has been wandering, unable to rest, and he is still wandering now. Wandering is painful while resting is comfortable, so why doesn't he stop to rest? Because even if under a curse he must prefer wandering to resting; that is why he keeps up this frenzied wandering.

But this choice of sacrifice is a personal one that has nothing in common with the social commitment of revolutionaries. The masses, especially in China, are always spectators at a drama. If the victim on the stage acts heroically, they are watching a tragedy; if he shivers and shakes, they are watching a comedy. Before the mutton shops in Peking a few people often gather to gape, with evident enjoyment, at the skinning of the sheep. And this is all they get out of it if a man lays down his life. Moreover, after walking a few steps away from the scene, they forget even this modicum of enjoyment.

There is nothing you can do with such people; the only way to save them is to give them no drama to watch. Thus there is no need for spectacular sacrifices; it is better to have persistent, tenacious struggle.

Unfortunately China is very hard to change. Just to move a table or overhaul a stove probably involves shedding blood; and even so, the change may not get made. Unless some great whip lashes her on the back, China will never budge. Such a whip is bound to come, I think. Whether good or bad, this whipping is bound to come. But where it will come from or how it will come I do not know exactly.

And here my talk ends.

Note

1. Chinese title for *A Doll's House*.

Part Five

Women and Social Activism

Editors' Introduction

The essays in this part focus on the role of women as social activists, and the significance of the "woman question" in social movements. They address the means by which women can become socially active, as well as the kind of movement activist women should promote.

Many activists recognized the need for women leaders in the women's emancipation movement. Ming Hui argues that China cannot be a true Republic without women's suffrage, but laments that "we are partially at fault, because we lack a fighting spirit." She hopes "that we women will unite and fight side by side to get rid of the unequal system and win the right to vote through our own struggle." Zhang Ruoming envisions a woman well-educated or skilled in business, wholeheartedly devoted to the women's emancipation movement, and unwilling to marry for fear that family obligations would distract her from her activism. The difficulty of achieving a female-led women's emancipation movement is highlighted by the discrepancy between Zhang Ruoming's vision and the realities of the vast majority of women, who were poorly educated, unable to get paid jobs, and heavily restricted by a powerful patriarchal family system. Only a few elite women could aspire to Zhang Ruoming's vision. It is no wonder that Shen Yanbing would argue that the leadership of the Chinese women's movement must necessarily come from the intellectual class. Influenced by Marxist thought, however, Chen Wangdao and Wang

Jianhong argue that the Chinese women's movement should shift its focus to the lower class. Li Dazhao expresses great admiration for the achievement of women's suffrage, political activism, and employment in England, Russia, and the United States, but still concludes that class issues are more important than gender issues. He advocates a two-pronged approach: "on the one hand, consolidate the power of all women to smash the patriarchal system; on the other hand, we must still consolidate the power of proletarian women of the world, to smash that arbitrary social system of the capitalist class (including both men and women)."

In his speech before the Guangdong Federation of Women's Circles, Chen Duxiu emphasizes the similarity between the women's movement and socialism. Marxists were sympathetic to feminist ideas, both because women's emancipation from Confucian patriarchy was important to their goal of "modernizing" China and because feminism was an important component of Communist movements worldwide. Marxists saw Communism not only as the most important step toward women's emancipation but also as a panacea for women's problems. They imagined that gender inequality would disappear once a Communist system was established. Thus, they stressed that the fight for socioeconomic equality took priority over the fight for gender equality, that feminism should remain only a component of socialism, and that women revolutionaries should channel their energies into the Communist movement, rather than into movements that focused on the issues most relevant to middle-class women. Like Lu Xun's essay on "What Happens after Nora Leaves Home" (essay 35 in this collection), Chen Duxiu's speech warned that the goal of women's independence was no solution to women's problems in a society where independent women had no means of economic support.

Marxists probably looked askance at Ida Kahn, whose emphasis on Christianity as the key to the transformation of China contrasts sharply with the secular visions espoused by most other Chinese activists of the May Fourth era. Yet her vision also has much in common with theirs. Like them, Kahn sees the emancipation and social activism of women as a vital means of strengthening and transforming of the Chinese nation. Kahn's vision of the socially active Chinese woman is the mother who lays "the foundation of a more Christ-like character in the lives of children, and these little ones will become the pillars of state," the woman at the "patriotic meetings which are held in the home and in which men and women from the most influential ranks meet and formulate plans to serve their country," or the doctor who nurses a woman who attempts suicide back to life and brings her "to the hospital where she not only recovers but is converted and finds hope and comfort for life." This vision differs from that of the militant "Vanguard Women" advocated by Zhang Ruoming, but it resonates with the role imagined for socially active women by Zhang Weici (essay 4 in this collection).

Communists focused on the mobilization of peasant and proletarian women into the Communist movement. In the process of mobilizing these women, Communist activists helped emancipate them from many forms of patriarchal domination, such as footbinding and confinement to the home. But feminism still had a relatively low priority in the overall socialist agenda, which focused on fighting class inequality and not on fighting gender inequality. Marxists assumed that gender equality would automatically follow from class equality. History, however, has shown this assumption to be problematic at best. The Chinese Communist regime indeed brought unprecedented opportunities to Chinese women, but socialist policies were no panacea for problems of gender inequality, in China or anywhere else.

36
The Postwar Woman Question

Li Dazhao (February 15, 1919)

Originally published in *New Youth*, vol. 6, no. 2, February 15, 1919.

The spirit of modern democracy is intended to enable everyone who shares in the organization and lifestyle of a democratic community, regardless of race, gender, class, and regional background, to have equal opportunities in politics, society, economics, and education; to develop their personalities; and to exercise their rights. The movement for women's participation in politics is also inspired by this spirit. Though men and women have different genders, women's position in society should be just like men's, and women should have their own status, life goals, and legal rights. Why should women allow themselves to be trampled under men's feet? Even before the Great War,[1] the movement for women's suffrage had its own history of struggle. This movement was already in progress in many American states. But at the time there were many who opposed this kind of movement. They kept saying that women would not make good political leaders because they are weak in judgment and are easily moved by emotions. There were also some who were doubtful about women's abilities. We Orientals have an even stranger attitude toward this issue. We talk about "the propriety of ritual avoidance," and how "men and women should not get close to each other," meaning that women should be men's "helper inside the home," taking care of things relating to "the inner quarters." It was only when war came and men went one by one to the battlefield that women got the opportunity to set examples and show those men that women do have ability.[2] There were women who became police officers; there were women who did all kinds of labor; there were women who worked as nurses for the Red Cross; there were women who worked hard at military rear bases. These women accomplished all kinds of things, which did away with the old excuses that devalued women. Therefore, after the war ended, women's political rights were recognized in America, England, and Germany. In the Russian Bolshevik government there was a public welfare commissar named

Kollontay,[3] who was a woman. This was indeed a new era for women's political participation.

The women's suffrage movement up to today has finally gotten over one stage. The unsettled questions of the past half century at least have a hope of being resolved. At the time when America declared war on Germany, the state of Montana had a congresswoman named Jeannette Rankin,[4] who was America's first congresswoman. She faced a lot of criticism. This was so because, when called upon to vote on the resolution to declare war, she did not respond the first time or the second time she was asked, and when she was asked for the third time she responded, weeping, in a shaking voice, "No." Later, when interviewed by a reporter, she said that she felt it was necessary to punish Germany, but did she not approve of war. Then people said: when women decide something, they usually rely on emotions alone, and not on reason; therefore it is inappropriate for women to become political leaders. Yet we are truly suspicious of this kind of talk. Is the rationality of those political leaders the kind that turns its back on human emotions? Is this rationality that turns its back on human emotions completely good? Is it completely correct? Are these irresistible emotions completely wrong? Are they completely bad? We should all look deeply into our consciences before we speak any further about these points. For instance, in America there are many women with even more independent judgment and thought than the men who have the right to vote. In the western states of America, there are many places where women's political participation has been effectively carried out. Several years ago, there was a husband and a wife in Colorado, each of whom had one vote. The people they voted for just happened to be in opposing parties. The person whom the wife voted for lost, but the family's affections were not affected by this. Doesn't this example prove that women also have independent judgment abilities, and that women's participation in politics will not have a bad effect on their families and society? Even if women's judgment and knowledge were truly weaker and poorer than men's when it comes to understanding the sociocultural and educational systems and legal customs they share in common, what about women's particular interests, which have nothing at all to do with their fathers, brothers, and husbands? Isn't it far more appropriate to give women themselves opportunities to express their opinions than to have men completely monopolizing politics, rendering women a class excluded from politics? Again, some say most women are not interested in politics. This does not tell the whole story. For instance, in the American states of Colorado and Utah, women of all classes are generally rushing to take the opportunity to cast their votes, thus proving that the enfranchisement of women is appropriate. Another instance is the recent election in England, in which women rushed to take the opportunity to vote, stunning everyone. Because there is a demand for women's suffrage, society should establish the kind of system that will meet this demand. This is the only appropriate course to take.

I predict that after the war, women in European and American societies will face many problems that are difficult to resolve.

First, there is the issue of the unbalanced gender ratio. According to official censuses, Europe and America already had a higher proportion of women than men before the war. On top of that, many able-bodied men have died on the battlefield during the war. Many married women have became widows, women who had not married worry every day about how hard it is to marry, and the proportion of women to men grows more and more unbalanced, to the point where the problems of this situation have become noticeable. The society of our time will be full of tragic scenarios, with each day worse than the previous one. It will be difficult to marry, but divorce will increase. Each day there will be more prostitutes, abortions, and children born out of wedlock. If women are affected by these tragic scenarios, all of society will be greatly affected as well.

Second, there is the issue of women workers versus men workers. Working men have all gone to the battlefield. All factories would have had to close down if they did not use women workers to fill the labor shortages left by the men. Ever since the war started, the British government has allowed women to work on the condition that after the war everything will be returned to the way it was before the war. Most other nations have done the same. When European women suddenly got the opportunity to work, it was like opening up a new territory. Since women are paid less than men, the capitalists have been very willing to hire them. After the war, men who were sent to the battlefields will come home and see that their old jobs are now filled by women working for lower wages. Naturally, they will struggle against these women workers. Because they are struggling to survive, these women will certainly be unwilling to give up the territory they have already won. Nor will the capitalists be willing to fire women willing to work for low wages. In the past, the biggest shortcoming of women workers was their lack of job skills. This kind of shortcoming will no longer exist, since women underwent training during the war and have benefited from the expansion of job training. Offering cheap labor without the shortcoming of inexperience, women workers will be used by capitalists to manipulate men workers. To avoid having men workers compete with women workers and prevent manipulation by the capitalists, workers must try to get equal pay for equal work. But this is hard to do, since women's labor unions are not resolute and their force is weak. They cannot oppose capitalists alone, and it may well be that they will not be able to get paid as much as men. Some hope that, to resolve this problem, the government will pass a law guaranteeing that everyone will be on the same wage system. Some advocate trying to encourage men's and women's labor unions to unite. In any case, when there is a conflict between men and women workers, it will be a good opportunity for capitalists to take advantage of the situation. The results will be disadvantageous to all workers. If men and women workers unite, they will bring their power to a higher level in the class struggle. It is difficult to determine which path they will use as a way out in the future. Judging by the trend of torrential evolution in Russia and Germany and even by the general situation in Europe, it seems that England and France will also crumble sooner or later. I think men and women workers will most likely not fight each other, but rather support each other and raise the strength of their class struggle to a higher level.

The third issue is that of working-class mothers. During the war, able-bodied men left home to fight, leaving no one to take care of the old and the weak. Those people were pitiable. Therefore, some countries mandated a solution, giving the families of active soldiers a stipend. The amount of the stipend was not based on the soldier's wages before he went to war; instead, the amount was set in accordance with how many family members he needed to support. This kind of stipend brought security to working-class mothers, who had lived every day in suffering because their incomes were insufficient and insecure. It can be said that they enjoyed a bit of the good life during the war. But this good life ended with the war, and they will have to return to their temporarily forgotten lives of suffering. How they are going to abandon this short-lived good life and go back to enduring their old unwanted lives—this will truly be a problem. Many able-bodied men died in the war. As part of the plan to make up for population losses, special attention should be paid to the protection of mothers. That kind of pension and various other ways of protecting mothers cannot be left unresearched. Also, the war left England with two hundred children's shelters, with enough room for sixty thousand children. This kind of institution should be further expanded after the war because of the working mothers. If they work, they will not be able to take care of their children. This kind of institution is truly necessary. The shifting of children's upbringing and education from the family to society will truly be a new vision of social improvement.

Although we cannot say that there will be no result at all if we depend solely on the women's movement to resolve these issues, we must see that the women's movement also has a class nature. Ever since English women attained the right to vote, their political organizations set out the agenda of what English women should try to attain item by item:

1. Women being elected to parliament;
2. Women attending the postwar economic conferences;
3. British women who marry foreigners being allowed to keep their British citizenship;
4. Women becoming judicial officials and jurors;
5. Women becoming lawyers;
6. Women becoming high-ranking government officials;
7. Women becoming police officers;
8. Women teachers and men teachers having equal status;
9. Government pensions for widows and their children;
10. Equal rights for mothers as well as fathers;
11. The same standard of morality applying to both men and women.

These items are all relevant to middle-class women. But they have nothing to do with working-class women. Those middle-class women want to have equal rights as men within gentry society. Proletarian women own nothing in this wide world except their own bodies, so they would hardly wish for anything more than the improvement of their lives. Middle-class women want to rule over others; proletarian women want to raise their own lives out of the misery of poverty. The interests and the demands of the two classes are fundamentally different. Therefore, the women's rights movement and the labor movement are two completely separate things. If a proletarian woman is arrested for prostitution and taken into the courtroom, and the one who arrests her is a female police officer, the one who judges her is a female judge, and the one who prosecutes her is a female lawyer, then are the problems of this woman resolved? What difference does it make whether this prostitute is arrested and investigated by female officers rather than male officers? Even if there is a bit of difference in how light or heavy the sentence is, it is still just a minor issue. The basic issue, whether directly or indirectly, is the existence of a society organized in such a way that it forces women to resort to prostitution. How can we count the placing of one or two women in the ruling apparatus of such a society as representative of the interests of all women? The interests of middle-class women cannot be called the interests of all women; the expansion of middle-class women's rights cannot be called the emancipation of all women. I think that the way to resolve women's problems completely is, on the one hand, to consolidate the power of all women to smash the patriarchal system; on the other hand, we must still consolidate the power of proletarian women of the world, to smash that arbitrary social system of the capitalist class (including both men and women).

I cannot arbitrarily judge whether our Chinese women have any interest in the issues facing women of the world. But I hope very much that our country will not have this "half-paralyzed" society for much longer. I hope very much that the world civilization of this new century will not be a "half-paralyzed" civilization due to the existence of China in the world.

Notes

1. The Great War refers to World War I.

2. Here Li Dazhao is apparently referring, not to Chinese women, but to European and American women whose labor was mobilized during World War I.

3. Aleksandra Mikhaylovna Kollontay (1872–1952) was a Russian revolutionary who advocated radical changes in traditional social customs and institutions in Russia. She became commissar for public welfare in the Bolshevik government that assumed power after the October Revolution (1917) and used her position to remodel Russian society, advocating the practice of free love, the simplification of marriage and divorce procedures, the removal of the social and legal stigma attached to illegitimate children, and various improvements in the status of women. She later became a Soviet ambassador (*Encyclopaedia Britannica* 1996).

4. Jeannette Rankin (1880–1973) was a member of the U.S. House of Representa-

tives from 1917 to 1919 and from 1941 to 1943. She was a feminist, pacifist, and crusader for social and electoral reform. She became an outspoken isolationist and was one of forty-nine members of Congress to vote against declaring war on Germany in 1917. This unpopular stand cost her the 1918 election, but she again won election in 1940. She effectively terminated her political career when she became the only legislator to vote against the declaration of war on Japan after the Japanese raid on Pearl Harbor on December 7, 1941 (*Encyclopaedia Britannica* 1996).

37
The Place of Chinese Christian Women in the Development of China

Ida Kahn (October 1919)

Originally published in English in the *Chinese Recorder*, October 1919. The *Chinese Recorder* was published monthly at the American Presbyterian Mission Press in Shanghai, China.

World interest centers at present in the development of China, for like a giant she has awakened from the sleep of ages and is training to break the laws and customs that have bound her down for centuries. One-third of the human race has thrilled to life and is groping for the light. Shall the self-determination of its people be along the lines of progress and peace, or shall it be along the lines of reaction and war? What element will be the chief guiding factor in the race for development and self-expression? Let us say it with all due reverence and humility: Chinese Christian womanhood will be the most potent factor in the regeneration of China, for it will attain the strongest place in the fabric of Chinese society, and its function will be to lead other women in the march of progress. It will be their place to make or mar the history of the world, for the oldest, the most stable, and the most numerous of the human race cannot move in such a strong tide without making or marring history. Germany is down and out, and for generations at least she cannot dominate world politics. Russia is too inchoate and too incoherent to impress herself upon the world. Bolshevism is strangling the life out of her, and Christianity will have to fight for its very existence in that country.

There remains, then, the Anglo-Saxon race with its centuries of culture and Christianity, and the Mongolian race with its centuries of endurance and toil. What an oddly contrasting team! Yet a team destined to play with or against each other for generations to come. Shall the Mongolian race, led by the militant Japanese, strive to grip the world by militarism and guile, and thus swing it back toward paganism and vandalism? Or shall the Mongolian race led by the Christian women of China join hands with the Anglo-Saxon race and make the world safe for democracy and peace? This is the question before the world today.

It may sound as if we were unnecessarily alarmed, and yet it is nonetheless true, and thus it is important. A nation can never rise higher than its women, therefore the higher plane of development the women can attain, the better it will be for the country. It is beyond dispute that the Western nations owe their development and progress to Christianity, and thus the hope of China lies in the spread and growth of Christianity in this country. Who can promote this growth better than the Christian women of China? Theirs will be not only "the hand that rocks the cradle" but the mind to direct young China on its way, and the soul which shall enable adult China to cling to its way along the narrow path of righteousness and truth. China cannot develop without sweeping away all that is wrong and false, and who can do this clearing better than the Christian women? Theirs will be the hand to raise a high standard, theirs to demand a cleaner record, and a sterner probity in all strata of society. Theirs will be the voice to negate the debasing practice of concubinage, theirs to claim freedom from the subtle bondage of ancestral worship and the demoralizing vices of gambling and opium smoking. Ultimately theirs will be the vote to decide whether China shall be democratic in name or in truth. There is nothing boastful in these statements. All who are familiar with Chinese history know that compared with other heathen countries her women are held in higher esteem and consideration. Christianity alone can crown her and give her an equal share in the home and nation, and it is the Christian women who must come forward and assist in the development of the country.

Already in thousands of Christian homes they are laying the foundation of a more Christ-like character in the lives of children, and these little ones will become the pillars of state. Unlike the students of old, they are willing to work with their hands as well as with their minds, and the double toil will enable them so much the more, so that the results of their labor will be the production of a new race, not effeminate but strong and masterful, and capable of accomplishing all that is required of them whether in the home or state. Their spiritual welfare will be fostered also by these same Christian mothers. Thus grace of mind will be enhanced by the moral beauty of the soul. A true race of patriots will arise who will scorn self-seeking and by the integrity of their lives prove that Christianity has the power to save men whether white or yellow. Japan then will not be able to coerce China, when the Christian element will be strong enough to crush traitors. Already many of ,the recent reforms such as anti-footbinding and anti-opium smoking have been largely brought about by the Christian women of China, and their influence will become more patent as their circle enlarges.

In social service the Christian women will be able to mold those outside of their immediate home sphere. Already an army of Bible-women and day school teachers are scattered throughout the length and breadth of the land and are bringing light and life to thousands of homes which would be otherwise cut off from all means of advancement, intellectual as well as spiritual; nurses, doctors, and higher-grade teachers are also adding their quota of enlightenment, and you have a leaven of immeasurable value in the development of the country.

And now for a concrete example of what a handful of Chinese Christian women can do for their country, and you may multiply this instance by thousands differing only in degree and variety. About two decades ago a Chinese doctor was called to a large provincial center in the interior to attend a patient. While there with a foreign missionary she was stoned and driven into a house for refuge. The incident impressed upon her mind the need for Christian work in this large heathen city, so a few years later she came and started work with one nurse to help her and with no financial backing at that time from her Mission; only after she had made good in the undertaking did they come to her assistance. What are the results now even after so short a time of service? She has the finest property and hospital in her Mission in Central China, and not only that but the land was given to her almost entirely by the people of the city, and she has a yearly grant from them as well. And what work are they doing now? Let us take a few instances from this year's record. When the local Red Cross Hospital gets a cut-throat case from the police court which they dare not tackle, they send it over and in a short time the patient has recovered. The police courts also send their accident cases so that this year alone almost every variety of suicide case known has been treated in this Christian hospital.

When another woman from a good family in the country over forty *li* distant cuts her throat in a most ghastly fashion, the doctor is sent for and arrives on the sixth day with her nurses, after braving a winter sleet, in order to succour the sufferer. It is a bad case and the nurse has to stay in the country fifty-two days, and then eventually has to bring the woman to the hospital where she not only recovers but is converted and finds hope and comfort for life. Not only does the doctor go forty *li* into the country but she has been known to go over four hundred and fifty *li,* and patients come to her from a radius of over nine hundred *li.*

Again, when a child plays and falls over a bottle and cuts himself in the abdomen so that his intestines protrude in unsightly loops, the neighbors instantly rush mother and child off to the hospital, and there he is cleaned and operated upon and soon made whole.

Or an entire family gets burned down and all five members are carried to the hospital where four are healed. So the thing goes on. When a pupil in the State Normal School cuts her finger to prove her patriotism the doctor is called in too, and when epidemics of influenza sweep through the schools the doctors and her staff of nurses are put in full charge until everything is right. Again, if a tiny waif from the orphan asylum becomes fearfully diseased she is sent post haste to the hospital for treatment. Frightful carbuncle cases come from far and wide and from homes rich and poor, and return rejoicing in being made whole. Even when the governor himself is ailing, he too sends for the doctor! So the list goes on and when you realize that the annual number of visits to and from the hospital may run into the tens of thousands, you may get an idea of what one doctor and her nurses are doing. One must not forget to mention the patriotic meetings that are held in the home and in which men and women from the most influential ranks meet and formulate plans to serve their country. Thus this small group of Chinese women have made themselves vital factors in the life of their city and from this instance you may visualize what Chinese Christian women may accomplish in helping to develop their country. Thus it is that the place of Chinese Christian women in the development of China is one of no mean importance, and may well embrace every sphere of usefulness.

38
Vanguard Women

Zhang Ruoming (November 5, 1919)

First published in *Awakening*, no. 1, November 5, 1919.

I am filled with mixed feelings as I pick up my pen to write this essay. It is both hard and joyful to be a woman. For thousands of years, women have suffered because of evil traditions. Women have been seen as useless people without talent or knowledge, without hope of improvement, dependent on those around them, and unable to fend for themselves if others do not take care of them. Most families with knowledge and education only care about the education of boys, because girls' education is considered too much trouble and is carelessly tossed aside. A friend of mine once heard an official in charge of education say: "All women need to know is a few characters and a few household skills. Why do they need to attend a normal school? If women get higher education, it will just be harder to control them." Judging from the above statement, the idea that women can depend on others for guidance is just a fantasy. There is a lot of talk about "populism" nowadays, but it is only meant for men and never applied to women.

Although there are some people who talk about women's emancipation, they provide no concrete solutions. Women's emancipation should begin with women emancipating themselves; women simply cannot wait for other people to emancipate them. However, without higher education, without outside assistance, and with the burden of family duties, women themselves find it hard to move forward. That is where the hardship lies. On the other hand, the age we are in now demands vanguards and pioneers. During this transformational time, we women should carry out our "heavenly duty" and be pioneers for the women's emancipation movement, where our great joy lies. Even though, as we are aware, it is hard for women to make progress, women simply have to move ahead. Therefore, let us women fight for our own emancipation in the spirit of revolution.

The word "revolution" is the biggest taboo in China; whoever dares to advocate revolution will be damned by Heaven. However, I look at it differently; to me, revolution should be an ordinary thing, a spirit that everyone who seeks truth should have. Having suffered from misogynist oppression for thousands of years, women in China have more or less internalized all the old ideas and unequal systems and are particularly apprehensive of any kind of rebellion. The reasons for such apprehension are twofold: (1) blind faith in so-called moral standards; (2) job discrimination due to women's biological features. I think, at this transitional stage, women should replace such fears with the spirit of revolution.

First, we should get rid of blind faith in traditional moral standards.

During the recent student movement,[1] many parents advised their daughters that a strict line should be drawn between male and female students and that they should be on guard even if they have the purest intentions. Nowadays, there are people in society who advocate gender integration in work and education. But the old moralists are adamantly against it, claiming that "it is absolutely absurd for men and women to mix and those who advocate such promiscuity are not human beings." Based on their moralistic views, those traditionalists attack those who advocate equal rights between men and women. But we all know that if women want to make progress, it is essential for them to have equal opportunity in work and education. Since the state and society are financially strapped, there cannot be any higher learning institutions, factories, or companies specially created for women; it is necessary for women to break the formal moralistic tradition and stand side by side with men in work and education. Ethical codes should be spiritual and cannot be formally defined. Some moralists often talk about the so-called Three Cardinal Guides and Five Constant Virtues; but reality and practice are often at odds, and who wears a mask and only pays lip service to moral responsibilities can only be a laughingstock. True moral standards cannot really be established until formal and superficial moral standards are replaced by sincere and heartfelt ones and men and women are totally free from those restrictive social conventions. Superficial moral standards were set up by those who do not trust themselves. Those who reprimand other people's superficial moral standards trust neither themselves nor others. Therefore, I advise that we women should adhere to the moral standards of our own conscience rather than those superficial moral standards. Only then can women enjoy the opportunities society has to offer.

Second, we should eradicate erroneous notions about psychological and physical differences between men and women.

Educational inequality between men and women results from these notions. Many believe that just because women are born gentle, delicate, fragile, and unfit for rough, heavy work, they are not entitled to the same education as men. That is ridiculous!

The purpose of education is to maintain the strengths and overcome the weaknesses of humankind. Those people would not have uttered such nonsense if they had truly understood the function and significance of education. The proper way is to recognize women's physical limitations and try to do something to compensate for them. In the olden days, the deaf and mute were by and large abandoned, but nowadays, there are many ways to help them study. If one finds that women are weaker psychologically as well as physically, one should blame our undeveloped educational system rather than deny women the opportunity for education. We human beings are still in the process of evolution; if one of our organs is used often, it gets developed; otherwise, it degenerates. Since women traditionally received less education than men, it is only to be expected that men and women are somewhat different. But the blame should be placed solely on the old educational system. We should never try to restrict women's education, using the psychological and physical differences between men and women as an excuse. Furthermore, why can't women who are supposedly more psychologically sensitive and refined be engaged in research and higher learning? Never believe in those fallacies, my fellow women! We should eradicate them with our revolutionary spirit!

Third, end gender inequality at work.

Some people say that, since men are in charge of outside affairs and women are in charge of domestic affairs, women should be happy to be housewives all their lives and need not learn any particular vocational skills. This is an absurd catch-22. Men invented the so-called rule of "men take charge of the outside and women take charge of the inside" in order to control women. Obviously, this is designed to deprive women of their labor rights, economic rights, and independence. Then men can claim that women have no skills and are fit only for housework. If women had been in charge of outside affairs historically, I'll bet that the situation would have been totally reversed. It is said that in the rural areas of Guilin, Guangxi Province, it is the women who go to work in the fields and the men who do all the housework. So why should women do all the housework in most other places in China? Differences between men's and women's obligations should be reflected in reproduction alone; those who believe in gender inequality at work are too authoritarian for the modern world. We women should not be deceived by such a fallacy; when completely deprived of economic independence and subject to all kinds of maltreatment, it will be too late for regrets. Women's duty does not lie in reproduction alone; most jobs in human society should be accessible to women.

Anyone can engage in a "mental revolution" along the lines of what I described above. But the actual implementation requires courage and perseverance, and can only be accomplished by those who have extraordinary consciousness and are capable of fighting against the forces of darkness. These pioneers should not only seek their individual emancipation but also act as trailblazers for the masses. Any cause or major social change demands "a major battle," so to speak. And defeat and victory will most likely be determined during the preparation stage. All women should in theory be emancipated as they battle the forces of darkness, but emancipation is actually out of reach for most of them. Therefore, we need to have pioneers to lead the masses in the fight for emancipation. To do this, these pioneers need to first prepare themselves and then lead the masses.

I. Recruiting Comrades

Based on the experiences of the most recent student movement, we realize that a big group may not be as good as a small group. Big groups tend to create a lot of hot air without any substantial results, because they may suffer from complicated organizational problems and frictions. Women's emancipation is not easy; it will be unable to advance smoothly and may possibly end up being abortive if compromised by internal impurity and disunity. Therefore, in order to destroy the forces of darkness obstructing women's emancipation, we need to mobilize "vanguard comrades," whose qualifications should be demonstrated in the following three ways.

First, the vanguard should be wholeheartedly devoted to the cause.

For a woman to seek her own personal emancipation is a relatively simple matter; it is obtainable if she tries hard. But the emancipation of the women of the masses is no easy task. The first step should be to awaken the masses; the second step is to prepare them for emancipation. How can one achieve the fighting spirit necessary for such a difficult task without first having the intention of emancipating the masses? If one has certain personal motives, what one practices may well be in conflict with the interests of the masses. For example, there are many calls for public social contact between men and women these days, but many who are willing to "set examples by their own conduct" often do so for the sole purpose of finding a husband or a wife, thus endangering the future of "public social contact between men and women." Many young men and women may be victimized in the sense that they still cannot be free from the traditional type of family—their families will be old wine in new bottles. If this happens, "public social contact between men and women" will lose its true meaning for most. If that happens, who will be left to advocate women's emancipation? Even if there are some advocates, they will not have many followers. Consequently, the movement will be inadequate, tainted, and hindered for several more decades. Only those who are genuinely devoted to women's emancipation and willing to sacrifice everything and smash anything standing in the way of women's emancipation can be considered true comrades.

Second, the vanguard should have the spirit of self-sacrifice.

Advocacy of women's emancipation places us in conflict with the current social establishment, so of course we need to dedicate a lot of time and energy to it. It may even be at the expense of our reputation, because breaking the social barrier between men and women as I mentioned earlier conflicts with social convention. It is no exaggeration that one may be attacked for being "inhuman," "immoral," "scandalous," and "anti-traditional." One needs to possess the spirit of self-sacrifice to survive those attacks; otherwise, it would not take long at all before one loses heart and collapses. In addition, one also needs to sacrifice the love of one's family when necessary to the spirit of revolution; sometimes, one may even run the risk of losing one's life. A worthy comrade must possess the spirit of self-sacrifice.

Third, the vanguard should remain single.

Those who sincerely advocate women's emancipation have to be wholeheartedly involved in a lifelong cause. The cause of women's emancipation needs such people if it is to have a bright future. Women's emancipation cannot be successful without this spirit of devotion. In contemporary Chinese society, those who are willing to be the vanguard of women's emancipation would do best to stay single. I am sure that some people would challenge such a statement. Isn't "marriage" one of the important issues in the women's emancipation movement? Isn't freedom of marriage part of women's emancipation? Isn't a good free marriage good news for women's emancipation? Can't those who are happily married serve as role models for our society? I assume that these are the four main questions people might ask. But before I address these questions, I would like to make it clear that those who are willing to remain single for the sake of women's emancipation can be devoted to the cause and yet need not, and cannot, try to personally see the cause to completion. In fact, the work of women's emancipation never ends. As long as one is willing to devote one's whole life to the cause, one will be of great assistance. Besides, marriage is only one issue in the entire women's emancipation movement; and it does not mean that one cannot advocate and practice women's emancipation without being married first. Now allow me to address the above four questions.

"Marriage " is one of the issues in the women's emancipation movement; but it is not an essential one. The more important issues have to do with gaining proper education and economic independence. Once a good education and economic independence are achieved, the issue of "marriage" will automatically be solved.

Once equipped with the same education and economic independence that men enjoy, women will certainly be able to get rid of the old ideas about marriage and then enjoy truly happy marriages.

That women can enjoy happy marriages is certainly good news for women's emancipation, but it is not necessarily a premise for the cause.

Those who advocate women's emancipation should fight for the women of the masses and help them to smash all kinds of fetters and to seek true happiness. Of course, those who are happily married can serve as role models in the women's emancipation movement; but this does not mean that those who are unmarried cannot be effective leaders of the movement as well. As a matter of fact, the latter may very well win people's trust, and trust may even be more proper and powerful as a leading social force.

Having answered the above four questions, I would like to ask some questions in return:

1. It is still extremely difficult to advocate women's emancipation in China today. Issues of the highest priority, such as gaining a proper education and economic independence, cannot be solved overnight. Those who are willing to be part of the vanguard in this cause cannot

afford to allow their personal concerns about marriage to interfere with it, because that would further complicate the issue.

2. Those who intend to be the vanguard in women's emancipation are working for the women of the masses; if they try to solve their own personal problems first, they will not really be able to popularize women's emancipation.

3. To be in the vanguard of women's emancipation requires self-sacrifice. If one remains single, one will be able to dedicate oneself, heart and soul, to the cause.

4. Since marriage is one of the issues addressed by the women's emancipation movement, we should take it seriously and imbue it with a new social meaning that accords with its true significance. Those in the vanguard who advocate women's emancipation should devote their full attention to it and cannot afford the "leisure" of falling in love and solving what has been called "life's most important issue."[2]

5. In our society today, marriages that accord with life's true significance are rare. Can those so-called modern free marriages of some young men that we have seen so far be considered true model marriages? No, not by me! What passes for "love" is often an impulsive act, while the combination of feeling, thought, and personal desire is hard to come by in our society. It is not easy for a man and woman to get married, since it is very difficult to find "a perfectly compatible" partner from your circle of friends and gradually reach a perfect mutual understanding. Since a perfect marriage is so rare, we often see marriages that just make the best of an inadequate situation. Once a marriage is like this, it is no longer a marriage. In due course, the husband and wife become estranged and will cause each other a lot of frustration and agony. In that case, those who are unhappy in their own marriages will simply feel incongruous with the ideals of women's emancipation and be less powerful as a leading force for the cause.

Based on the above five points about the differences between single and married women, it should be clear which kind of woman is best suited for the vanguard of women's emancipation. However, we should avoid overgeneralization, since those who want to remain single do not necessarily share the same convictions. We should discuss the issues on a case-by-case basis.

Now, let us examine several kinds of women who remain single.

The first is the kind that believes that love should not be given to one person alone. Love should be cherished and protected, but it should be everlasting, ever-shining, and all-encompassing, and shine out on everyone like a bright star.

The second kind has faith in the Buddhist teaching that "if just one last being has to be left out of nirvana, I shall be that one."[3] We human beings should have this kind of conviction: one should give to all and remain single in order to save the world.

The third kind believes that they have seen the truth and realize that there is no such a thing as a perfect marriage, with a spiritual bond as well as mutual understanding, love, and desire, and would rather remain single all their lives.

The fourth kind aims too high and thus cannot find a spouse and has to remain single.

The fifth kind consists of natural loners who have a very jaded attitude toward marriage.

The sixth kind does not want to be burdened by family duties and household chores or is afraid of giving birth to babies and ends up being single.

The seventh kind may have suffered from heart-breaking experiences and is forced into being single.

The eighth kind views the family as a mechanism that restricts and hinders one's personal development. They choose to remain single so that they can devote themselves wholehearted to working for society.

Among these eight kinds of people, the first, second, third, and eighth are resolute supporters of women's emancipation. Meanwhile, the fourth and sixth are not so reliable and cannot be loyal to the cause because they may change their minds once they either find a good partner or overcome their fear of family duties and childbirth. The fifth kind may not change their minds so easily, but can they fully understand and be truly dedicated to women's emancipation? I don't know. Nor will the seventh kind be a strong, reliable force unless they become awakened and march along the correct path.

Now that we are trying to recruit "vanguard comrades" and have already adopted the policy of remaining single, we, as young people with strong consciousness, should do as we advocate. This is what we anxiously expect of our comrades.

II. Educational Preparation

To be a qualified comrade, one needs to be educated. Women's emancipation is more easily accepted by those who have had some education; but the pursuit of personal emancipation is more readily accepted than the struggle for the emancipation of the masses. In the field of education, we need women who are themselves educated to advocate women's education. The dearth of women is even more obvious in other professions. As women themselves know, women's lack of education cannot completely be attributed to unequal educational opportunities. We should first train a small number of comrades who seek higher learning for themselves and then try to popularize equal education, which ought to teach both academic knowledge and business skills.

1. Academic Training

Why do we need to raise issues specific to women when we are seeking to make women's education equal to that of men? The answer is that we are addressing those who are now in the process of creating the women's emancipation movement. Academic learning is the most valuable part of human knowledge, and the objective as well as the subjective goals of human evolution are defined primarily by academia. Those goals defined by men are suitable for men but not necessarily for women. Take the populist society advocated by men, for example. The so-called "education for the masses" is actually meant for men alone. Discussions about issues such as family reform, equal educational opportunity, and equal distribution of labor may not concern men at all, since they have never suffered because of these issues. Therefore, we can see that the goals and methods of women's emancipation will not work unless they are defined and designed by learned women themselves.

2. Business Training

Elementary school teaching is the only job besides working at home that is currently available to women. Women are barred from business jobs because they do not have any basic knowledge of or training in business management. Without economic independence, women are of course controlled by men at home. So, to seek emancipation, women need to be trained in business management; only when economically independent can women be free from suffering.

III. Economic Preparation

When a small number of people are themselves trained, they will be able to educate the majority. Equality should start with equal education for men and women; workplace equality does not necessarily mean that men and women should hold the same jobs. Women need to first be educated separately and then begin to realize that they are ready for coeducation and make it happen. During this transitional period, women should be allowed to work by themselves and then gradually move on to working side by side with men. And when women work separately, they will need organizers. But even what I have said thus far will be difficult to accomplish. Even with the right comrades and the right knowledge, it will be useless to organize workers or advocate equal education without the right economic preparation. All comrades who share the same spirit should practice a division of labor, with some making economic preparations and others making academic preparations. Only with this kind of cooperation can we achieve the goal of emancipating the masses of women.

My knowledge is limited, and I can only provide some preliminary suggestions here. Let me end this essay by saying to my female comrades: "We need revolutionary spirit to achieve emancipation; and we need a small number of pioneers to prepare for the ultimate emancipation of the masses."

Notes

1. This refers to the May Fourth student movement.
2. The term "life's most important issue" is a term for marriage in Chinese.
3. This is a teaching of Guanyin, the bodhisattva of mercy, who remains a bodhisattva in order to ameliorate the suffering of earthly beings, and refuses to attain nirvana until every other being has attained nirvana.

39
Women's Right to Vote

Ming Hui (December 5, 1919)

Originally published in *New Youth*, vol. 7, no. 3, March 1920.

Dear Reporter:

At present, women in most advanced countries in the world enjoy the right to vote. Why not women in China? Some say that "Chinese women have not yet reached that level." I simply don't know when those people think that time will come. If they allege that Chinese women have not yet done anything significant, we need to tell them that this is only because they have not been given the chance to serve society, so they are not to blame. Although we are endowed with ability and strength, we have not been given the opportunity to demonstrate them. This is truly detestable, but we are partially at fault because we lack a fighting spirit. I highly doubt that the right to vote will be placed in our idle hands if we do not rise up soon. I figure that everything is hard at the beginning and that we need not fear the difficulty. But for the revolution a few years back, we would have been still bound and oppressed by a despotic tradition.

Eight years have gone by since the Republic was founded; but, in reality, nothing substantial has been implemented. By definition, a republic should allow its nationals to express their individual opinions through voting. Men have already been granted this right, yet we women are still ignored and excluded just like in the old days. Personally, I don't believe that men can vote on behalf of us women. Some say that suffrage should be the privilege of men alone. They are again absolutely wrong! Just a few years ago, all the power was in the hands of a despotic emperor, depriving the ordinary people of their right to vote. Under such circumstances, people would have laughed if men had then demanded the right to vote, just the way some people are now laughing at women who demand the right to vote. Fortunately, there were men who did not fear such stupid ridicule and contributed to the founding of the Republic and the establishment of their right to vote. I, for one, truly admire and respect these men, but why should we not follow our own hearts? It is my sincere hope that we women will unite and fight side by side to get rid of the unequal system and win the right to vote thorough our own struggle. We cannot claim to be true citizens of the Republic as long as our goal remains unfulfilled. As long as that is the case, our Republic is not a republic in the true sense of the word.

Sincerely yours,

Ming Hui, December 5

40
How Do We Make the Women's Movement Truly Powerful?

Shen Yanbing (June 5, 1920)

First published in *Women's Magazine*, vol. 6, no. 6.

I.

How do we make the women's movement truly powerful? Everyone wants an answer to this question. Speaking more broadly, we could say that this question is related to the entire New Culture Movement. But this essay will only address the women's movement itself.

I think that we need to look at which class the bulk of the women's movement comes from in order to determine the strength of the women's movement. In other words, we need to determine which class of women are the women who have already developed consciousness.

II.

Observations of society suggest that there are, roughly speaking, three classes of women in every society, whether foreign or Chinese. They are present in societies that have never democratized, and inevitable in democratic societies.

In the past, when the class system was extremely strict, men and women alike were subject to strict bondage and could not break through the limits of their class. The four classes of old China, the aristocratic, priestly, and common classes of Greece and Rome, the landlord and serf classes of recent Russian history, etc., invariably exercised great power over all individuals and made upward mobility almost impossible for any individual. Even if an individual had the ability to be upwardly mobile, the social system still would not allow that individual to move up. Thus we have the ancient Chinese saying, "The son of a scholar is always a scholar, and the son of a peasant is always a peasant." The customs of medieval England and France did not allow upstart merchants to join the gentry class. These were the realities of class limitations on upward mobility.

But the so-called classes of a democratic society are not like this. These kinds of classes are not fixed in accordance with an individual's social status. Instead, they are fixed in accordance with each individual's economic situation. In ancient times, even someone who suddenly became wealthy could not squeeze into the upper class. Today, this is no longer the case; as long as one has money, "even a beggar is equal to a duke." Classes are completely defined by wealth. Such classes always precede the implementation of economic democracy.

Based on this, we can also discern the situation and character of the three classes of women in contemporary society.

III.

Roughly speaking, women in today's society can be divided into (1) wealthy wives and rich young ladies; (2) wives and young ladies of middle-class, scholarly families; (3) women of poor families, who depend on their own labor to make ends meet. These three classes of women are present not only in Chinese society but also in Western societies. Moreover, in Western societies the middle-class women are the most numerous.

Now that society truly has these three classes of women, we must pay special attention to the livelihood, education, mentality, and moral values of each class of women when we do research on how to develop the women's movement.

This essay intends to focus on the women's movement in China, particularly on the three classes of women in our society today.

IV.

Let's see! What kinds of lives do the wealthy wives and rich young ladies of China lead? What kind of education do they have? What do they think? What are their moral values? They are arrogant and accustomed to living in comfort and luxury! And they have certainly been imbued with the influence of their evil environment! Even if they have some education, they got it by being chauffeured to elite schools to receive elite educations. (Of course there are also a good number of exceptions and outstanding people among them, but statistically speaking, even though there may be many such exceptions, I don't know if they would add up to even one percent of the total!) They grow up amid reams of beautiful silk, never knowing about the suffering of their little sisters in the third class. Even if fighting for the right to suffrage ("What's the right to suffrage!") seems fun to them, I'm afraid they are not willing, able, or daring enough to go out and work with working-class women. On top of this, most of them hardly know or think about anything (and even if they do, it is nothing but corrupt thinking). We certainly won't get anything accomplished if we depend on them to form the center of the women's movement!

These upper-class women actually comprise only a small portion of Chinese society, but they are potentially very influential. Those who have the least power in society are actually the most numerous. Many of these are women of the lower class. These women suffer oppression in their daily lives. They are the ones who will be "left behind" in life. Unless they work their fingers to the bone, they cannot catch up with the other classes in this life. They have to struggle for survival every day and do not have the time or money to get educated. With such a bad environment, they hardly have the leisure to think about anything and can only act on impulse. Because they are always oppressed by their low social status and endure unbearable treatment, their moral level is also pretty low. Needless to say, it would also be very difficult to depend on this class of women to carry out the women's movement. They will not be able to accomplish anything until they get some guidance and good education.

V.

Since women of the upper class and women of the lower class cannot take on the important tasks of the women's movement, middle-class women—the wives and young ladies of middle-class families—are our only hope.

This class of women comprises about half of the women in our society. They don't have to worry about making a living, and they have access to education. Not yet imbued with arrogance, they are still industrious. They can think. They have a sense of morality and the courage to go out and do things. They can bear hardship. Obviously, this class of women must necessarily form the center of the women's movement. Only then can the women's movement truly accomplish something.

But I don't know whether or not this class is at the center of our country's nascent women's movement.

VI.

It is my hope that women of the middle class will quickly arise to breathe life into the women's movement! Arise! Do you suffer oppression in your lives? Do you not yet have opportunities to get educated? Do you feel that you have no freedom to think for yourselves? Do you suffer from moral double standards? These are not just your own concerns. They do not hurt women alone. Instead, these are issues that vex our whole society. Therefore, we should all arise and fight them together. Do you fear that we won't be able to march forward in unison? I say, have no fear; just start by uniting everyone in your own class! Do you fear that you are still weak, and that you do not dare to lead the charge against the old society? Have no fear; you have your little sisters of the lower class, and you can raise them up to fight together with you.

VII.

It is not China alone that depends on women of the middle class. Based on developments in the West, we see that it has always been the women with education but no property who were the first to rise up. The cries of the movement for women's suffrage sometimes originated with women of the upper class, but today the woman question is not just about women's suffrage. Nowadays, women's suffrage cannot address the entire woman question. Who has built the women's emancipation movement?

Chinese women of the middle class! You should understand your status and your responsibility. We have been talking about the woman question for over six months. But everyone has forgotten who the true bearers of the mission are. Today we say, it is you—you women of the middle class, who have knowledge but no property!

41
I Think

Chen Wangdao (November 15, 1920)

Originally published in *New Woman*, vol. 4, no. 4.

I've thought of something else.

I think there are two kinds of "women's movements." One is the women's movement of the third class; the other is the women's movement of the fourth class. The women's movement of the third class is the middle-class women's movement; the women's movement of the fourth class is the working-class women's movement.[1]

These two kinds of movements have very different aims and should definitely not be conflated. Briefly put, this is how it is: The goal of the third-class women's movement is to restore all the liberties and privileges that women have been deprived of "just because they are women"; the goal of the fourth-class women's movement is to eradicate all the unfairness and unreasonable treatment women have suffered "just because they are poor." Thus, the third-class women's movement is a human rights struggle between women and men, while the fourth-class women's movement is an economic struggle between the capitalists and the workers. The goals and demands of these two movements are very different.

The third-class women's movement demands equality between women and men. Therefore, it devotes itself above all to opposing differences between men and women. It seeks to destroy preferential treatment for men and to expose feudal restrictions on women. It demands coeducation, women's suffrage, free social interaction between men and women, and marriage based on freedom of choice and new definitions of chastity. This kind of movement seeks to eradicate all aspects of society that punish women just for the crime of being "women."

If I remember correctly, the penal code specifies punishments for all kinds of vices and crimes. It is written that officials can assign various kinds of penalties for those who commit crimes of murder or assault, and for those who steal or rob others' property.

Those laws are at least somewhat reasonable; however, this treatment of female gender as a crime punishable with all kinds of oppression seems truly unreasonable to those of us who do not believe in the "Old Testament."[2] It is quite proper for the women's movement to try to abolish these barbaric inequalities and restrictions.

But we need to remember that, even if this movement succeeds completely, we would only have equality between men and women of the capitalist class, not the "equality of all humankind."

To achieve the "equality of all humankind," we must still pay attention to the fourth-class women's movement, which is the struggle between workers and capitalists.

This kind of movement is necessary to the eradication of poverty. Women are not the only ones who are poor. Men and women should work together in this kind of movement. It is not like the third-class women's movement, in which women take aim at men.

In every country, the women's labor movement began after the men's labor movement. In contemporary China, even most men do not know what the labor movement is; fourth-class women are of course even more hopeless in this regard.

Yet we still cannot approve of devoting oneself solely to the third-class women's movement and viewing it as the entire women's movement.

Notes

1. Like Wang Jianhong, Chen Wangdao loosely borrows from the class terminology of the French Revolution, which classified society into the first, second, third, and fourth estates (Gilmartin 1995, 244).

2. Here Chen Wangdao refers to the Old Testament of the Christian Bible.

42
The Woman Question and Socialism

Chen Duxiu (January 30, 1921)

A speech delivered before the Guangdong Federation of Women's Circles, originally published in the *Guangdong Masses Newspaper* on January 30, 1921. This speech was also published in *Awakening*, a special supplement to the *Republican Daily*.

Today I will speak on the woman question and socialism. Many people have researched the woman question in recent years, but their efforts have been piecemeal and unsystematic. Therefore I will talk a bit today to delineate this question and try to make some sense out of those piecemeal efforts.

The so-called ethics of the present day can probably be divided into two kinds: one kind seeks to help the weak resist the strong; the other kind sacrifices the weak's resistance to the strong. Today's militarism is totally of the latter kind; indeed, it sacrifices the weak in order to help the strong. The opposite of this is socialism, which helps the weak resist the strong. The most important issues in socialism are labor issues. But what do labor issues have to do with the woman question? We need to understand that women and laborers are the most power-less members of society. Laborers are subject to the oppression of the capitalists, and women are subject to the oppression of men. We must help women resist the oppression of men as well as help laborers resist the oppression of capitalists. But today we are focusing especially on the woman question, so we should leave labor issues aside for the moment. Yet, though I will only be speaking about the woman ques-tion, this question is also related to labor issues. This is because labor is not just men's affair; women also have a lot to do with labor.

Because there are many conflicts between women and society, the woman question really cannot be separated from socialism. Our dis-cussion of women must first be related to socialism. The woman ques-tion will never be resolved if it becomes separated from socialism. Socialism has developed because the social system has created many inequalities, and because society has made people unequal and depen-dent. Naturally, the woman question has developed concomitantly. Though there are many woman questions, they are all at bottom due to a lack of economic independence. Lack of economic independence gives rise to a lack of personal independence, which in turn gives rise to countless instances of suffering.

Chinese women have to abide by the moral creed of the "Three Obediences": at home they must obey fathers, after marriage they must obey husbands, and when they are old they must obey sons. Because they have to obey their fathers at home, women must subject all their activities to their fathers' meddling. To be a woman is almost like being a vase on the table, set in one place and totally useless. Those who are fathers can sell their daughters, or give their daughters away. And if the father wants to flatter and curry favor with someone, he can give his daughter to him at will, as a wife or concubine. Even if the daughter does not want to marry this rich and powerful man, she cannot refuse. Of those Chinese women confronted with the issue of marriage, only one or two in a hundred want freedom in deciding whom to marry. The rest submit to their parents' will. And parents do not think solely of what is best for their daughters. Instead, they give their daughters away as wives in order to secure their alliances with powerful people. In the process of social climbing to achieve wealth and status, parents just use their daughters as steppingstones. It can be said that daughters who must obey their fathers have absolutely no dignity.[1] After marriage, women must obey their husbands. This means that when men tell women to do something, women cannot resist. If they resist, society will punish them. Not only can husbands order wives around, they can also sell their wives or give them away. We all know that there are many men who sell their wives or force their wives into prostitution to pay for opium. Someone has told me that in Guangdong there is a place—I'm not sure if this is true or not—where husbands can rent their wives out to others. This kind of thing happened a lot in the society of the past. Of course I don't believe that this kind of barbaric behavior still occurs in Guangdong. But even if it does not occur in the flesh, perhaps it does occur in spirit.

Today, when women marry, it is almost always because their parents covet wealth and status. Not only do parents destroy their own dignity by using their daughters this way, but many women also destroy their own dignity. I am not completely clear on the situation in Guangdong, but I know that the situation in Shanghai is very sad. There is a very famous girls' school in Shanghai where most of the students lack independent thought. Even though they know a lot, they only think about one thing: that they must wear expensive, fashionable clothes. If a student does not dress fashionably, everyone looks down on her, and she herself feels that she looks unseemly. All they think about is their desire to marry students who study abroad and will become high officials after they return to China. But where will their clothes and jewelry come from? They do not work, so they cannot get clothes by themselves. Therefore, they hope, and can only hope, that men will give them clothes. This kind of thinking naturally causes them to lose their dignity. Today there are many women who do not want independence, but only want to wear expensive clothes. They are, at the same time, losing their dignity.

Regardless of whether they are obeying fathers or husbands, Chinese women have no dignity. If they depend on their fathers for a living, then of course they have no dignity. If they depend on their husbands for a living, they also have no dignity. Therefore, women's loss of dignity is entirely an economic issue. If women can be economically independent, then they will no longer be subject to oppression by their fathers and husbands.

Under socialism, men and women will all work. Before they come of age, they will get a public education. After they come of age, they will work for their community and society. Thus, because socialism recognizes the dignity of all men and women, women will not suffer oppression from their families and husbands. Women will not be subsidiary to their fathers or husbands.

Now there is another issue. Many might say that women can be independent even without socialism; that even in the absence of socialism, women could avoid suffering from parental and male oppression. This statement seems very reasonable at first, but it is actually very wrong because society will not permit women to leave their lives of familial enslavement to seek independent lives. Let's think about it: If a woman leaves her home to live independently, where will she go to live? Where can she make a living? No matter where it is, it will be under the control of the capitalist system. In this system, some people hire others to work, while other people are hired workers. If a woman leaves home, will she be hiring or hired? If she wants to hire people, it will be taken as a joke; it certainly wouldn't happen. Because women cannot hire others, they must be the ones hired by others. They will certainly be subsidiary to capitalists. Thus, they will become slaves of the capitalists. Women were slaves of their families; once they leave their families, they will become slaves of the capitalists. No matter what, they are still slaves; the woman question is still unresolved.

It will not be like this under socialism. There will be no differences between workers and capitalists; everyone will have to work. Therefore, the woman question will be fundamentally resolved only when socialism arrives. Women will have independent dignity at home as well as in society.

Today I have spoken on the woman question and socialism because the woman question so far seems piecemeal and unresolvable. We cannot conclude this discussion without talking about socialism. At least nine out of ten instances of women's suffering are economic issues. Socialism will resolve all questions, not only the woman question. The principles we are talking about do not sacrifice the weak to help the strong, but rather help the weak resist the strong—this latter is socialism. Women and laborers are all weak. So, if we want to help the weak resist the strong, there is no other way besides socialism. I think that everyone, women and men alike, should research socialism. It would be good if women fight even harder than men. We cannot divide the woman question piecemeal, into issues of education, jobs, social interaction, etc., for our discussion. We must take socialism as our sole guide. This is not just something that concerns women; it is the same for men. Thus, I say today that men and women alike should work hard for socialism, and unite in the resistance of the weak against the strong.

Note

1. *Ren'ge*, which we translate here as "dignity," can also be translated as personality, character, personhood, individuality, human worth, or moral quality.

43
The Center of the Women's Rights Movement Should Move to the Fourth Class

Wang Jianhong (December 10, 1921)

First published in the first issue of *Women's Voice*, under the pen name Jian Hong.

The women's emancipation movement has clamored on from May Fourth to the present. Yet women have not accomplished much in terms of building a movement truly grounded in reality. Sure, we can find in any newspaper or magazine a shallow and superficial history of the women's emancipation movement. Yet none of these is untainted by elitist thinking biased toward the third class.[1] Everyone thinks that merely to gain for women the same political rights and inheritance rights that men have would be enough, and that these rights by themselves will put men and women on equal footing. They think that, once this is accomplished, it will not be necessary to go any further;

that it will be time to stop fighting. But would the attainment of these rights really mean that the women's emancipation movement has succeeded completely? Would it really mean that society has become completely humane?

I think that this kind of movement is slanted in one direction. It has deserted many poor compatriots; it has left them in the fiery pit and forgotten them. And this cannot truly be called a total awakening of consciousness.

Inequality between the two sexes does not lie merely in the political realm. The most important inequalities still lie in the educational and economic realms. Those lacking economic independence, education, and opportunities to get an education certainly cannot think about getting a foothold in the political realm. If the issue of food has not been resolved, can we ask them to participate in politics on an empty stomach? If they still lack sufficient knowledge, can we ask them to participate blindly in Congress?

Because humankind is governed by its material conditions, robbing and fighting are social realities. This gave rise to all kinds of classes. At the very beginning, when the male sex conquered the female sex, men were the oppressing class, and women were the oppressed class. At the same time, several classes formed within each sex. One class oppressed another, and the history of humankind became the history of class struggle.

As a result of the recent Industrial Revolution, the capitalist system has simplified the class system. Thus, society has been divided into two classes: a capitalist class and a proletarian class. We women have been laborers since ancient days; we were always the victims of plunder. The capitalist system has cleared away the obstacle of gender, and we have become members of the proletariat. Therefore our demands for emancipation arise out of the realities of this class struggle. The tactics we use to achieve emancipation must also be born of these realities. Now let's see if the consciousness of our class is up to it.

In male-centered society, women have no status to speak of. For women, marriage is a means for survival. Women's status depends completely on whether they make good or bad marriages. Whether a woman becomes an official's wife or a laborer's wife depends on the kinds of marriage opportunities she has. This social system relegates women to the status of slaves without the slightest consciousness. Thanks to the protection of their fathers and brothers, some women have the opportunity to make good marriages. They marry officials or capitalists, and then adopt the imposing air of officials' wives or capitalists' wives and oppress and abuse proletarian women. Thanks to the protection of their fathers and brothers, some women have the opportunity to get an education or study overseas. Once they have obtained good qualifications for marriage, they suddenly put on the haughty, holy airs of upper-class women and despise uneducated women. These educated women are sometimes exposed to the new tide of thought sweeping over the world and calling for action, and they have spoken out about the women's rights movement. Yet their motive is merely to raise their own status especially high in women's circles. The contemporary economic system has already separated male and female capitalists from male and female proletarians at a fundamental level. This women's movement is merely an expression of upper-class women's class thinking. They have forgotten the circumstances of their dependency and cannot develop a movement with an awakened consciousness. Therefore, on the one hand, we must feel sorry for them; on the other hand, we must raise a special warning about the future of the women's movement. The warning is this: the center of the women's movement must move to the proletarian class.

Recently, the struggle between the capitalist class and the proletarian class has gradually become more obvious. We women who have an awakened consciousness should organize a group, join the proletarian army at the front lines, and work hard to fight against all plunder and oppression. We must fundamentally transform society and construct a free and equal society in which men and women work harmoniously together. We must end this historical period of inhumane principles, disgrace, and unanswered demands for emancipation. Only then can we say that our goals have been accomplished!

Note

1. Like Chen Wangdao, Wang Jianhong uses the term "fourth class" to refer to the working class, and the term "third class" to refer to the middle class. Their terminology is loosely borrowed from the language of the French Revolution, which classified society into the first, second, third, and fourth estates (Gilmartin 1995, 244).

Works Cited

Barlow, Tani E. 1989. "Introduction." In *I Myself Am a Woman: Selected Writings of Ding Ling*, ed. T.E. Barlow and G.J. Bjorge. Boston: Beacon Press.

Boorman, Howard L., and Richard C. Howard, eds. 1971. *Biographical Dictionary of Republican China*. 4 vols. New York: Columbia University Press.

Brown, Felida. 1977. "No Way Out." *New Scientist March* 153: 34.

Cai Kaisong, and Yu Xinfeng. 1991. *Ershi Shiji Zhongguo Mingren Zidian* (Dictionary of Famous Chinese People of the Twentieth-Century). Shenyang: Liaoning Renmin Chubanshe (Liaoning People's Press).

Cavanaugh, Jerome, ed. 1982. *Who's Who in China, 1918–1950*. 3 vols. Hong Kong: Chinese Materials Center.

Che Chengyuan. 1991. *Zhongguo Funu Renming Cidian* (Dictionary of Chinese Women). Shijiazhuang, Hebei: Hebei Kexue Jishu Chubanshe (Hebei Scientific and Technical Publishers).

Chen Yutang. 1993. Zhongguo *Jinxiandai Renwu Minghao Da Cidian* (Dictionary of Figures in Modern Chinese History). Zhejiang: Zhejiang guji chubanshe (Zhejiang Antiquarian Books Publisher).

The China Weekly Review. 1936. *Who's Who in China*. Shanghai: *The China Weekly Review*.

Chinese Recorder. 1919. Shanghai: American Presbyterian Mission Press, October.

Chow, Tse-tsung. 1960. *The May Fourth Movement*. Cambridge: Harvard University Press.

———. 1963. *Research Guide to the May Fourth Movement: Intellectual Revolution in Modern China 1915–1924*. Cambridge: Harvard University Press.

Ci Hai bianji weiyuan hui. 1979 *Ci Hai Dictionary*. Shanghai: Shanghai Dictionaries Press.

Dirlik, Arif. 1989. *The Origins of Chinese Communism*. New York: Oxford University Press.

Ding Ling, and W.J.F. Jenner. 1985. *Miss Sophie's Diary and Other Stories*. 1st ed. Panda Books. Beijing: Chinese Literature. Distributed by China International Book Trading Corp.

Dooling, Amy D., and Kristina M. Torgeson, eds. 1998. *Writing Women in Modern China: An Anthology of Women's Literature from the Early Twentieth Century*. New York: Columbia University Press.

Encyclopaedia Britannica. 1996. *Britannica Online (computer file)*. Chicago: Encyclopaedia Britannica.

Feigon, Lee. 1983. *Chen Duxiu, Founder of the Chinese Communist Party*. Princeton: Princeton University Press.

Feng Xuefeng. 1980. "Lu Xun: His Life and Works." In *Lu Xun, Selected Works*, ed. Yang Xianyi and Gladys Yang, 1, 9–31. Beijing: Foreign Languages Press.

Fowler, Robert Booth. 1986. *Carrie Catt, Feminist Politician*. Boston: Northeastern University Press.

Gilmartin, Christina. 1993. "Gender in the Formation of a Communist Body Politic." *Modern China* 19 (January 1): 299–329.

———. 1995. *Engendering the Chinese Revolution: Radical Women, Communist Politics, and Mass Movements in the 1920s.* Berkeley: University of California Press.

Grieder, Jerome B. 1970. *Hu Shih and the Chinese Renaissance; Liberalism in the Chinese Revolution, 1917–1937.* Cambridge: Harvard University Press.

Gu Shu Diangu Cidian (Dictionary of Classical Allusions). 1984. Jiangxi: People's Publishing House.

He Dong, Yang Xiangcai, and Wang Shunsheng, eds. 1991. *Zhongguo Geming Shi Renwu Cidian* (Dictionary of Personages in Chinese Revolutionary History). Beijing: Beijing Chubanshe (Beijing Publishing).

Huang, Sung-K'ang. 1965. *Li Ta-Chao and the Impact of Marxism on Modern Chinese Thinking.* Paris: Mouton.

Hung, Eva. *May Fourth Women Writers.* Hong Kong: The Research Centre for Translation at the Chinese University of Hong Kong.

Klein, Donald W., and Anne B. Clark. 1971. *Biographic Dictionary of Chinese Communism, 1921–1965.* 2 vols. Cambridge: Harvard University Press.

Kuo, Thomas C. 1975. *Ch'en Tu-Hsiu (1879–1942) and the Chinese Communist Movement.* South Orange, N.J.: Seton Hall University Press.

Levine, Marilyn Avra. 1990. "Transcending the Barriers: Zhang Ruoming and Andre Gide." *Chinese Studies in History* 23, no. 3.

Li, Jui. 1977. *The Early Revolutionary Activities of Comrade Mao Tse-tung.* White Plains, N.Y.: M.E. Sharpe.

Merriam-Webster. 1995. *Merriam-Webster's Encyclopedia of Literature.* Springfield, Mass.: Merriam-Webster.

Perleberg, Max. 1954. *Who's Who in Modern China.* Hong Kong: Ye Olde Printerie.

Reetz, Dorothea. 1987. *Clara Zetkin as a Socialist Speaker.* New York: International Publishers.

Richmond, Mayo-Smith. 1896–1899. *Science of Statistics.* New York: Macmillan.

Rosenblum, Charles Eric. "The Last Lienü, the First Feminist: Miss Zhao's Use as an Icon during the May Fourth Period: An Analysis of the Nature of Female Suicide in China." Senior Honors Thesis, Harvard College, 1992.

Schram, Stuart, ed. 1992. *Mao's Road to Power: Revolutionary Writings 1912–1949.* Vol. 1. Armonk, N.Y.: M.E. Sharpe.

Schwarcz, Vera. 1986. *The Chinese Enlightenment: Intellectuals and the Legacy of the May Fourth Movement of 1919.* Berkeley: University of California Press.

Snow, Edgar. 1938. *Red Star Over China.* New York: Random House.

Spence, Jonathan. 1990. *The Search for Modern China.* New York: Norton.

Sun Yat-sen, and Wei Yung. 1931. *The Cult of Dr. Sun.* Shanghai: *The Independent Weekly.*

Van Voris, Jacqueline. 1987. *Carrie Chapman Catt: A Public Life.* New York: The Feminist Press.

Witke, Roxanne, 1967. *Mao Tse-tung, Women and Suicide in the May Fourth Era.* China series reprint, no. C–1. Berkeley, Calif.: Center for Chinese Studies.

Wolf, Margery, 1975. "Women and Suicide in China." *Women in Chinese Society.* Stanford: Stanford University Press.

Xue Weiwei. 1988. *Zhongguo Funu Mingren Lu* (Records of Famous Chinese Women). Xi'an: Shaanxi renming chubanshe (Shaanxi People's Publisher).

Yap, Pow-meng. 1958. *Suicide in Hong Kong, with Special Reference to Attempted Suicide*. Hong Kong: Hong Kong University Press.

Zhonghua Quanguo Funu Lianhehui (All-China Women's Federation). 1989. *Zhongguo Funu Yundongshi* (History of the Chinese Women's Movement). Beijing: Chunqiu chubanshe (Spring and Autumn Publisher).

Glossary

This glossary is of proper names that are either historically important or relevant to the texts, and includes well-established foreign names in Chinese, such as John Dewey, Leighten Stuart, Henrik Ibsen and Bernard Shaw.

Awakening	《覺悟》《民國日報》副刊
Beacon of Learning	《學燈》《時事新報》副刊
Bing Xin (Xie Wanying)	冰心(謝婉瑩)
Cai Hesen	蔡和森
Cai Yuanpei(Jiemin)	蔡元培(孑民)
China New Tribune/China Times	《時事新報》
Chen Bijun	陳璧君
Chen Duxiu	陳獨秀
Chen Wangdao	陳望道
Chiang Kai-shek (Jiang Jieshi)	蔣介石
Collected Letters of New People's Study Society	
	《新民學會會員通信集》
Current Affairs Newspaper	《時事新報》
Democracy Newspaper	《民治報》
Ding Ling	丁玲
Deng Chunlan	鄧春蘭
Deng Enming	鄧恩銘
Dewey, John	杜威
Duan Qirui	段祺瑞
Eastern Miscellany	《東方雜誌》
Golden Mean	《中庸》
Gong Ding'an (Zizhen)	龔定庵(自珍)

Guangdong Masses Newspaper	《廣東群報》
Hu Shi (Shizhi)	胡適(適之)
Ibsen, Henrik	易卜生
Kang Youwei	康有爲
Li Chao	李超
Li Dazhao	李大釗
Liu Bannong	劉半農
Liu Hezhen	劉和珍
Liang Qichao	梁啓超
Lu Qiuxin	陸秋心
Lu Xun (Zhou Shuren)	魯迅(周樹人)
Lu Yin	盧隱
Luo Jialun	羅家倫
Magazine for Middle School Students	《中學生雜誌》
Mao Zedong (Runzhi)	毛澤東(潤之)
Morning Post Supplement	《晨報》副刊
New Century	《新世紀》
New Education	《新教育》
New Moon	《新月》
New People's Study Society	《新民學會》
New Tide	《新潮》
New Women	《新婦女》
New Youth	《新青年》
Nora	娜拉
Promote the New	《勵新》
Public Interest (Dagong Bao)	《大公報》
Puppet's House (Ein Puppenheim)	《玩偶之家》
Qian Xuantong	錢玄同
Qiu Jin	秋瑾

Qu Qiubai	瞿秋白
Qu Duyi	瞿獨伊
Republican Daily	《民國日報》
Shao Lizi	邵力子
Shaw, Bernard	蕭伯納
Short Story Monthly	《小說月報》
Shen Yanbing	沈雁冰
Stuart, Leighten	司徒雷登
Sun Yat-sen (Zhongshan)	孫逸仙(中山)
Tang Jicang	湯濟蒼
Tang Xianzu	湯顯祖
Tao Qian (Yuanming)	陶潛 (淵明)
Tao Yi	陶毅
Wang Huiwu	王會悟
Wang Jianhong	王劍虹
Wang Jingwei	汪精衛
Weekly Review	《每週評論》
(The) Wilderness	《莽原》
Women's Bell	《女界鐘》
Women's Critic 《婦女評論》	《民國日報》副刊
Women's Improvement Society	婦女成美會
Women's Magazine	《婦女雜誌》
Women's Voice	《婦女聲》
Xi Shangzhen	席上珍
Xiang Jingyu	向警予
Yan Fu	嚴復
Yanjing (Yenching) University	燕京大學
Yang Dequn	楊德群
Yang Xiaochun	楊效春

Yang Zhihua	楊之華
Ye Shengtao(Shaojun)	葉聖陶(紹鈞)
Young China	《少年中國》
Yu Si	《語絲》
Yun Daiying	惲代英
Zhang Guotao	張國燾
Zhang Ruoming	張若名
Zhang Shenfu (Songnian)	張申府(崧年)
Zhang Weici	張慰慈
Zhang Zuolin	張作霖
Zhao Wuzhen	趙五貞
Zhou Zuoren	周作人

Index

Hua R. Lan received a B.A. and M.A. from Shanghai Shifan University and his Ed.D. and Ph.D. from the University of Massachusetts, Amherst. He is currently Assistant Professor of Chinese and Chinese Literature at Amherst College.

Vanessa Fong received her B.A. in Anthropology from Amherst College and is currently a Ph.D. candidate in Social Anthropology at Harvard University.